LIVING LANGUAGE®

COMPLETE
FRENCH
THE BASICS

REVISED & UPDATED

COMPLETE
FRENCH
THE BASICS

REVISED & UPDATED

REVISED BY LILIANE LAZAR, PH.D.

Columbia University

Adjunct Assistant Professor of French
Hofstra University

French Teacher
Great Neck Public Schools

◆

Based on the original by Ralph Weiman

LIVING LANGUAGE®

Published in the United States by Living Language, A Random House Company

www.livinglanguage.com

Editor: Chris Warnasch
Production Editor: John Whitman
Production Managers: Helen Kilcullen and Heather Lanigan

ISBN 1-4000-2133-2

Library of Congress Cataloging-in-Publication Data available upon request.

This book is available for special discounts for bulk purchases for sales promotions or premiums. Special editions, including personalized covers, excerpts of existing books, and corporate imprints, can be created in large quantities for special needs. For more information, write to Special Markets/Premium Sales, 1745 Broadway, MD 6-2, New York, New York 10019 or e-mail specialmarkets@randomhouse.com.

PRINTED IN THE UNITED STATES OF AMERICA

10 9 8 7 6 5 4 3 2 1

CONTENTS

INTRODUCTION	xvii
COURSE MATERIAL	xviii
INSTRUCTIONS	xviii

LESSON 1 — 1
A. Sounds of the French Language — 1
B. Cognates: Words Similar
in English and French — 2

LESSON 2 — 4
A. Special French Sounds — 4

LESSON 3 — 7
A. Vowel Sounds — 7

LESSON 4 — 11
A. Special Consonant Sounds — 11
B. The French Alphabet — 13

LESSON 5 — 13
A. More English-French Cognates — 13
B. General Spelling Equivalents — 16

LESSON 6 — 19
A. Days and Months — 19
B. Numbers 1–10 — 19
C. Colors — 19
D. North, South, East, West — 20

QUIZ 1   20

E. Word Study   20

LESSON 7   21

A. Greetings   21

B. How's the Weather?   24

QUIZ 2   24

SUPPLEMENTAL VOCABULARY 1:
WEATHER   25

LESSON 8   26

A. Do You Have . . . ?   26

B. In a Restaurant   26

QUIZ 3   28

SUPPLEMENTAL VOCABULARY 2:
FOOD   29

LESSON 9   30

A. To Give: *Donner*   30

B. To Speak: *Parler*   33

C. Asking a Question I   34

D. Linking Sounds: *Liaison*   36

REVIEW QUIZ 1   38

LESSON 10   40

A. Where?   40

B. Here and There   41

C. To the Right, etc.   41

D. Near and Far   42

E. There   42

QUIZ 4   43

SUPPLEMENTAL VOCABULARY 3:
PEOPLE   44

LESSON 11   45
   A. The and A; *Élision*   45
   B. Masculine and Feminine   46
   C. Position of Adjectives   47
   D. Plural   48
   E. Word Study   48

LESSON 12   49
   A. Of and To   49
   B. Word Study   51
   C. To Be or Not to Be: *Être*   51
   D. My, Your, His (Possessive Adjectives)   55
      QUIZ 5   56

LESSON 13   57
   A. It Is   57
   B. Asking a Question II   58
   C. Word Study   60

LESSON 14   61
   A. To Have and To Have Not: *Avoir*   61
   B. Idioms with *Avoir*   64

LESSON 15   64
   A. There Is   64
   B. Ago   65
   C. Also, Too   65
   D. As . . . As   66
   E. I'm Sorry   66
      QUIZ 6   67

SUPPLEMENTAL VOCABULARY 4:
AT HOME   68

LESSON 16   70
   A. Do You Speak French?   70
   B. Please Speak More Slowly   71

C. What Did You Say?   72
D. Thanks   72
     QUIZ 7   73
E. Word Study   74

LESSON 17   74
A. This and That (Demonstrative
    Adjectives and Pronouns)   74
     QUIZ 8   78
B. Not, Nothing, Never   78
C. Isn't It? Aren't You? etc.   79
     QUIZ 9   80
D. Word Study   80

LESSON 18   81
A. It's Me (I), etc. (Disjunctive Pronouns I)   81
B. Mine, etc. (Possessive Pronouns)   82
C. To/For/About Me, etc.
    (Disjunctive Pronouns II)   83
D. Me, etc./To Me, etc. (Direct
    and Indirect Object Pronouns)   83
E. Myself, etc. (Reflexive Pronouns)   85
     QUIZ 10   87
F. Word Study   88

SUPPLEMENTAL VOCABULARY 5:
THE HUMAN BODY   88

LESSON 19   90
A. Hello, How Are You?   90
B. How Are Things?   91
C. Good-bye!   92
     QUIZ 11   93

LESSON 20   94
A. Have You Two Met?   94
B. I'd Like You to Meet . . .   95

C. My Address and Telephone
Number Are . . . 96
   QUIZ 12 97
   REVIEW QUIZ 2 98
D. Word Study 101

LESSON 21 101
A. Numbers 101
B. More Numbers 104
   QUIZ 13 107

LESSON 22 108
A. It Costs . . . 108
B. The Telephone Number Is . . . 109
C. My Address Is . . . 109
D. Some Dates 110
   QUIZ 14 110
E. Word Study 111

LESSON 23 112
A. What Time Is It? 112
B. Time Past the Hour 115
C. When Will You Come, etc.? 116
   QUIZ 15 117
D. Word Study 118
E. It's Time 118

SUPPLEMENTAL VOCABULARY 6:
TRAVEL AND TOURISM 120

LESSON 24 120
A. Morning, Noon, Night, etc. 120
B. This Week, Next Month, One of
These Days 122
C. Expressions of Past, Present, and
Future 124

LESSON 25 125

    A. What Day Is Today? 125

        QUIZ 16 127

    B. Months and Dates 129

    C. The Seasons 130

        QUIZ 17 130

    D. *Devant le kiosque journaux*
       (At the Newsstand) 132

LESSON 26 133

    A. To Go: *Aller* 133

    B. A Few Action Phrases 136

    C. Word Study 138

LESSON 27 138

    A. One, They, People 138

        QUIZ 18 140

    B. Word Study 141

    C. A Little and a Lot 141

    D. Too Much 143

    E. More or Less 143

    F. Enough and Some More 145

SUPPLEMENTAL VOCABULARY 7:
IN THE OFFICE 146

LESSON 28 147

    A. Good 147

    B. Well, Good 148

        QUIZ 19 150

    C. Word Study 151

    D. Beautiful, Nice, Fine 151

LESSON 29 153

    A. Like, As 153

    B. All 154

    C. Some, Any of It 156

        QUIZ 20 158

SUPPLEMENTAL VOCABULARY 8:
AT SCHOOL   159

LESSON 30   160
   A. Of Course, I Suppose So, etc.   160
   B. It's a Pity, It Doesn't Matter, etc.   162
   C. What a Surprise!   163
   D. The Same   164
   E. Already   165
     QUIZ 21   166
   F. Word Study   166

LESSON 31   167
   A. I Like It   167
   B. I Don't Like It   169
     QUIZ 22   171
   C. I Had a Good Time   172
   D. I Didn't Have a Good Time   172
     REVIEW QUIZ 3   173

SUPPLEMENTAL VOCABULARY 9:
SPORTS AND RECREATION   175

LESSON 32   176
   A. Who? What? When? etc.   176
     QUIZ 23   185
   B. Word Study   187
   C. How Much?   187
   D. How Many?   188
     QUIZ 24   189

LESSON 33   190
   A. Some, Someone, Something   190
   B. Once, Twice   191
   C. Up To, Until   192
   D. I Need It, It's Necessary   193
   E. I Feel Like . . .   194

F. At the Home Of 194
G. Here It Is, There It Is 195
    QUIZ 25 195
    REVIEW QUIZ 4 196

LESSON 34 199
A. On the Road 199
B. Walking Around 200
C. Bus, Train, Subway 201

SUPPLEMENTAL VOCABULARY 10:
NATURE 203

LESSON 35 204
A. Writing and Mailing Letters 204
B. Faxes and E-mail 205
C. Telephones 205
D. *Une Plaisanterie* (A Joke) 207

SUPPLEMENTAL VOCABULARY 11:
COMPUTERS AND THE INTERNET 208

LESSON 36 210
A. What's Your Name? 210
B. Where Are You From? 211
C. How Old Are You? 212
D. Professions 213
E. Family Matters 215
    REVIEW QUIZ 5 216

SUPPLEMENTAL VOCABULARY 12:
FAMILY AND RELATIONSHIPS 220

SUPPLEMENTAL VOCABULARY 13:
ON THE JOB 221

LESSON 37 222
  A. Shopping 222
    QUIZ 26 225
  B. Ordering Breakfast 227
  C. To Eat: *Manger, Prendre* 230
    REVIEW QUIZ 6 232

SUPPLEMENTAL VOCABULARY 14:
CLOTHING 233

LESSON 38 234
  A. In, On, Under, etc. 234
    QUIZ 27 237
  B. Apartment Hunting 238
    QUIZ 28 243
    REVIEW QUIZ 7 245
  C. Word Study 247

SUPPLEMENTAL VOCABULARY 15:
IN THE KITCHEN 247

SUPPLEMENTAL VOCABULARY 16:
IN THE BATHROOM 249

LESSON 39 250
  A. To Come: *Venir* 250
  B. To Say: *Dire* 251
    QUIZ 29 252
  C. To Do, To Make: *Faire* 253
    QUIZ 30 254
    REVIEW QUIZ 8 255
  D. Could You Give Me Some Information? 258
    QUIZ 31 263

SUPPLEMENTAL VOCABULARY 17:
IN TOWN 264

SUPPLEMENTAL VOCABULARY 18:
ENTERTAINMENT   266

LESSON 40   267
A. The Most Common Verb Forms   267
   QUIZ 32   279
B. Discussing Vacation Plans   280
C. At the Pharmacy   282
   QUIZ 33   283
D. Other Common Verbs   285
E. Common Notices and Signs   300
   FINAL QUIZ   304

SUMMARY OF FRENCH GRAMMAR   308
1. About the Sounds   308
2. The Alphabet   310
3. The Consonants   310
4. Simple Vowels   312
5. The Nasalized Vowels   313
6. The Apostrophe   315
7. The Definite Article   316
8. The Indefinite Article   318
9. The Possessive   319
10. Contractions   319
11. Gender   320
12. Plural of Nouns   323
13. Feminine of Adjectives   324
14. Plural of Adjectives   325
15. Agreement of Adjectives   326
16. Position of Adjectives   327
17. Comparison of Adjectives   328
18. Possessive Adjectives   330
19. Possessive Pronouns   331
20. Demonstrative Adjectives   332
21. Demonstrative Pronouns   333
22. Personal Pronouns   334

23. Position of Pronouns 336
24. Relative Pronouns 338
25. Indefinite Pronouns 339
26. Nouns Used as Indirect Objects 339
27. Repetition of Prepositions 340
28. The Partitive 340
29. Negation 341
30. Word Order in Questions 342
31. Adverbs 342
32. The Infinitive 346
33. The Past Participle 346
34. The Indicative 347
35. The Imperative 351
36. Verbs Followed by the Infinitive 352
37. The Subjunctive 353

VERB CHARTS 357

I. FORMS OF THE REGULAR VERBS 357
A. Classes I, II, III 357
B. Verbs Ending in *-CER* and *-GER* 360
C. Verbs Ending in *-ER* with Changes
in the Stem 362
D. Verbs Ending in *-OIR* 366
E. Verbs Ending in *-NDRE* 367
F. Compound Tenses of Verbs Conjugated
with *ÊTRE* 369
G. Compound Tenses of Reflexive Verbs 370
H. Infrequently Used and "Literary" Tenses 371

**II. FREQUENTLY USED
IRREGULAR VERBS** 373

LETTER WRITING 387
1. Formal Invitations and Acceptances 387
2. Formal Thank-You Notes 388
3. Business Letters 389

4. Informal Letters   391
5. Forms of Salutations and
   Complimentary Closings   394
6. Form of the Envelope   397

E-MAIL AND INTERNET RESOURCES   398
1. Sample E-Mail   398
2. Important E-Mail Vocabulary and
   Expressions   399
3. Internet Resources   399

INTRODUCTION

Living Language® French makes it easy to learn how to speak, read, and write French. This course is a thoroughly revised and updated version of *Living French: The Complete Living Language Course®*. The same highly effective method of language instruction is still used, but the content has been updated to reflect modern usage and the format has been clarified. In this course, the basic elements of the language have been carefully selected and condensed into 40 short lessons. If you can study about 30 minutes a day, you can master this course and learn to speak French in a few weeks.

You'll learn French the way you learned English, starting with simple words and progressing to more complex phrases. Just listen and repeat after the native instructors on the recordings. To help you immerse yourself in the language, you'll hear only French spoken. Hear it, say it, absorb it through use and repetition.

This *Living Language® French Coursebook* provides English translations and brief explanations for each lesson. The first five lessons cover pronunciation, laying the foundation for learning the vocabulary, phrases, and grammar which are explained in the later chapters. If you already know a little French, you can use the book as a phrase book and reference. In addition to the 40 lessons, you will find a Summary of French Grammar, Verb Charts, and a section on letter and e-mail writing.

Also included in the course package is the *Living Language® French Dictionary*. It contains more than 20,000 entries, with many of the definitions illustrated by phrases and idiomatic expressions. More than 1,000 of the most essential words are capitalized to make them easy to find. You can increase your vocabulary and range of expression just by browsing through the dictionary.

Practice your French as much as possible. Even if you can't manage a trip abroad, watching French movies, reading French magazines, eating at French restaurants, and talking with French-speaking friends are enjoyable ways to help you reinforce what you have learned with *Living Language® French*. Now, let's begin. The instructions on the next page will tell you what to do. *Bonne chance!* Good luck!

Course Material

1. Two 90-minute cassettes or three 60-minute compact discs.

2. *Living Language® French Coursebook*. This book is designed for use with the recorded lessons, but it may also be used alone as a reference. It contains the following sections:

   > Basic French in 40 Lessons
   > Summary of French Grammar
   > Verb Charts
   > Letter Writing

3. *Living Language® French Dictionary*. The French/English–English/French dictionary contains more than 20,000 entries. Phrases and idiomatic expressions illustrate many of the definitions. More than 1,000 of the most essential words are capitalized.

Instructions

1. Look at page 1. The words in **boldface** type are the ones you will hear on the recording. Pauses after

each word or phrase give you time to repeat what you have just heard.

2. Now read Lesson 1 all the way through. Note the points to listen for when you play the recording; the first word you will hear is **Albert.**

3. Start the recording, listen carefully, and say the words aloud in the pauses provided. Go through the lesson once and don't worry if you can't pronounce everything correctly the first time around. Try it again and keep repeating the lesson until you are comfortable with it. The more often you listen and repeat, the longer you will remember the material.

4. Now go on to the next lesson. If you take a break between lessons, it's always good to review the previous lesson before starting a new one.

5. There are two kinds of quizzes in the manual. With matching quizzes, you must select the English translation of the French sentence. The other type requires you to fill in the blanks with the correct French word chosen from the three given directly below the sentence. If you make any mistakes, reread the section.

6. There are 18 supplemental vocabulary lists throughout the course. Each one focuses on a useful theme that is related to the content of the course. Practice the lists through repetition, flash cards, or self-quizzes to build a solid foundation in French vocabulary.

7. Even after you have finished the 40 lessons and achieved a perfect score on the Final Quiz, keep practicing your French by listening to the recordings and speaking with French-speaking friends. For further study, try *Complete French: Beyond*

the Basics, Ultimate French, Ultimate French Advanced, 2000+ Essential French Verbs, or *French Without the Fuss,* all from the experts at Living Language, or go to our website at www. livinglanguage.com for more information.

LIVING LANGUAGE®

COMPLETE
FRENCH

THE BASICS

REVISED & UPDATED

LESSON 1

A. SOUNDS OF THE FRENCH LANGUAGE

Many French sounds are like English. Listen to and repeat the following French names and notice which sounds are similar and which are different:

Albert	Jacques	Paul
André	Jean	Paulette
Charles	Jeanne	René
Claire	Jérôme	Richard
Denise	Jules	Robert
François	Louis	Roger
Françoise	Lucie	Simone
Georges	Marie-Louise	Suzanne
Hélène	Marie-Rose	Yvette
Henri	Marie-Thérèse	Yvonne

NOTES

a. Each sound is pronounced clearly and crisply—sounds are not slurred the way they often are in English.

b. Each syllable is spoken evenly, with a slight stress on the last one.

c. The cedilla (¸) is placed under the letter *c* (*ç*) to show that it has the sound of *s* before *a, o,* and *u*:

    François   Frank

d. There are three marks (called "accents") used over French vowels:

   1. acute accent (´) placed over the letter *e:*

       André

2. grave accent (`) placed over *a, e, u:*
   Hélène

3. circumflex accent (ˆ) placed on *a, e, i, o, u:*
   Jérôme

These accents usually indicate the pronunciation of the vowel but in some cases they distinguish words:

ou	or	*où*	where
la	the	*là*	there
a	has	*à*	at, to

B. Cognates: Words Similar in English and French

Now listen to and repeat the following words which are similar in English and French. These words are descended from the same root and are called "cognates." Notice how French spelling and pronunciation differ from English:

adresse	address
âge	age
ambitieux	ambitious
américain	American
banque	bank
bref	brief
bureau	bureau desk; office
café	coffee; café
chef	chief
chèque	check
cinéma	cinema, movies
civilisation	civilization
condition	condition
curieux	curious

démocratie	democracy
différence	difference
difficulté	difficulty
excellent	excellent
garage	garage
grand	big, grand, tall
guide	guide
hôtel	hotel
important	important
journal	journal, newspaper
lettre	letter
ligne	line
machine	machine
nation	nation
nécessaire	necessary
opéra	opera
ordinaire	ordinary
papier	paper
possible	possible
potentiel	potential
principal	principal
problème	problem
public	public
question	question
radio	radio
restaurant	restaurant
sérieux	serious
signal	signal
silence	silence
station	station
télégramme	telegram
téléphone	telephone
thé	tea
théâtre	theater
train	train
visite	visit

LESSON 2

A. SPECIAL FRENCH SOUNDS

1. Final consonants are not pronounced except for
c, r, f, and *l* (the consonants in CaReFuL):

NOT PRONOUNCED

moment	moment	**Richard**	Richard
sérieux	serious	**Jacques**	Jack

PRONOUNCED

public	public	**chef**	chief
cher*	dear	**hôtel**	hotel

2. *e* is silent at the end of most words:

télégraphe	telegraph	**adresse**	address
histoire	history	**paie**	pays

But it is pronounced at the end of some very
common short vowels.

le	the	**me**	me
se	oneself	**de**	of, from

3. *h* is never pronounced:

Henri	Henry	**hôtel**	hotel

H, as seen in the examples above, is never pronounced, but in some cases *h* is aspirated. *Aspirate h* is not pronounced, but it prevents both
linking (see page 36) and elision (see page 45).

---

*Note that *r* is not pronounced after *e* at the end of most words of
more than one syllable.

Some of the most frequently used words with aspirate *h* are:

huit	eight	**héros**	hero
hors d'oeuvre	appetizer	**honte**	shame

4. *ch* is pronounced like the English *sh:*

chef	chief	**machine**	machine

5. *j* is pronounced like the *s* in *pleasure, measure:*

Jean	John	**journal**	newspaper

6. *g* is like the *g* in *go* before *a, o,* and *u:*

garage	garage

—is like the *s* in *pleasure* (or French *j*) before *e* or *i:*

général	general	**Georges**	George
danger	danger		

7. *c* is pronounced like *k* before *a, o,* and *u:*

café	coffee; café	**condition**	condition
curieux	curious		

—like *s* before *e* or *i:*

certain	certain	**cinéma**	movies
police	police		

8. *gu* is like the *g* in *go:*

guide   guide

9. *qu* is pronounced *k:*

question   question

10. *gn* is pronounced like the *ni* in *onion* or the *ny* in *canyon:*

signe   sign   **signal**   signal

11. *s* between vowels is like English *z:*

civilisation civilization   **visite**   visit

12. *ss* between vowels is like English *s* in *see:*

possible   possible   **nécessaire** necessary

13. *t* is like the English *t* except in the following combinations where it is like *s* in *see: -tion, -tial, -tiel, -tieux* (that is, before *i*).⸱
   -tion is pronounced as *see-on:*

station   station   **condition**   condition
nation   nation

   -tie is like *see:*

démocratie democracy

   -tial is like *see-al:*

impartial   impartial

-*tiel* is like *see-el:*

potentiel   potential

-*tieux* is like *see-uh:*

ambitieux   ambitious

-*stion* is like *stee-on:*

question   question
suggestion   suggestion

LESSON 3

A. VOWEL SOUNDS

The following groups of words will give you some additional practice in spelling and pronunciation:

1. The sound *a* in *ah* or *father:*

madame	madam, Mrs.	**table**	table
date	date	**page**	page

2. The sound *ee* in *see* or *i* in *police* but cut off sharply (that is, not drawled):

ami	friend	**il**	he
ici	here	**facile**	easy
vie	life	**difficile**	difficult

3. The sound *o* as in *go* but not drawled:

hôtel	hotel	**aussi**	also
chose	thing	**eau**	water
mot	word	**beau**	beautiful, pretty
au	to the		

Notice the various French spellings for this sound: *o, au, eau.*

4. The sound *e* in *get* but not drawled:

elle	she	**père**	father
il est	he is	**j'ai**	I have
très	very	**raison**	reason
scène	scene		

Notice the various French spellings for this sound: *e, è, ai.*

5. The sound *ay* in *day* but not drawled:

café	coffee, café	**donner**	to give
téléphone	telephone	**Donnez!**	Give!
cinéma	cinema, movies		

Notice the various spellings for this sound: *é,* the ending *-er* in words of more than one syllable and the ending *-ez.*

6. The sound *o* in *north* but shorter and more rounded:

note	note	**ordre**	order
homme	man	**Donnez!**	Give!
force	force		

7. The sound *ou* as in *group* but not drawled:

ou	or	**jour**	day
où	where	**pour**	for
nous	we	**toujours**	always

8. The sound *u* in *burn:*

le	the	**cela**	that
de	of	**ceci**	this
je	I	**petit**	small

9. The sound spelled *u* in French. There is no similar sound in English. To make it, round the lips as though to pronounce *o* in *go* and without moving them say *ee* (that is, it is an *ee* sound pronounced with the lips rounded and slightly protruded). Listen carefully:

tu	you (*familiar*)	**minute**	minute
du	of the	**utile**	useful
rue	street	**su**	known
vue	view, sight	**lu**	read
plume	pen		

10. The sound spelled *eu*. The nearest sound in English is the vowel in *burn*. You can make the French sound by saying the *u* in *burn* with your lips rounded and slightly protruded. Listen carefully:

deux	two	**auteur**	author
peuple	people	**mieux**	better
neuf	nine	**sœur**	sister
jeune	young	**bœuf**	beef

Notice that this sound is spelled two ways: *eu* and *œu*.

11. The sound spelled *oi* (*"wah"*):

moi	me	**voilà**	there is, there are
trois	three	**avoir**	to have
trois fois	three times	**histoire**	story
voici	here is, there are		

12. The sound spelled *ui:*

lui	to him, her	**je suis**	I am
huit	eight	**aujourd'hui**	today

13. *ou* before a vowel sounds like the *w* in *west:*

oui	yes	**Louis**	Louis
ouest	west	**Edouard**	Edward

14. The nasal vowels. Certain vowels when followed by *n* (in a few cases *m*) are pronounced through the nose. The *n* or *m* is not pronounced, though. Listen to the following examples:

a. Words with *an, en, am, em:*

an	year	**en**	in
dans	in	**enveloppe**	envelope
ample	ample	**accent**	accent
France	France	**temps**	time

b. Words with *in, im, ain, aim, ien, oin:*

chemin	road	**américain**	American
simple	simple	**faim**	hunger
important	important	**bien**	well
train	train	**combien**	how much
coin	corner		

c. Words with *on, om:*

bon	good	**savon**	soap
mon	my	**long**	long
garçon	boy, waiter	**bombe**	bomb

d. Words with *un, um:*

un	one	**quelqu'un**	somebody
lundi	Monday	**humble**	humble

LESSON 4

A. SPECIAL CONSONANT SOUNDS

1. The sound *y* in *yes* (spelled *y, -i-, -ail-, -eil-, -eill, -ill-,* etc.):

les yeux	the eyes	**soleil**	sun
voyage	voyage	**meilleur**	better
papier	paper	**billet**	ticket
mieux	better	**fille**	daughter
travail	work	**famille**	family

2. The sound *sh* (spelled *ch* in French):

| cher | dear | **chose** | thing |
| **chercher** | to look for | **riche** | rich |

3. The sound of *s* in *pleasure:*

joli	pretty	**âge**	age
jour	day	**rouge**	red
déjà	already	**origine**	origin

Notice that this sound is spelled with both *j* and *g* (*g* only before *e* and *i*).

4. The *ni* in *onion* or the *ny* in *canyon* (spelled *gn* in French):

ligne	line	**signal**	signal
signe	sign	**espagnol**	Spanish
Espagne	Spain	**oignon**	onion

5. Notice that the *r* sounds something like a gargle:

| **rouge** | red | **par** | by |
| **frère** | brother | **parler** | to speak |

Notice that the final *r* is pronounced in words of one syllable but not in words of more than one syllable (there are a few exceptions, which will be treated later):

But—	*par*	by
	parler	to speak
But—	*mer*	sea
	aimer	to love

6. Notice the pronunciation of *-re* at the end of a word:

lettre	letter	**livre**	book
nombre	number	**quatre**	four

7. Notice the pronunciation *-le* at the end of a word:

table	table	**simple**	simple
peuple	people		

B. THE FRENCH ALPHABET

LETTER	NAME	LETTER	NAME	LETTER	NAME
a	*a*	j	*ji*	s	*esse*
b	*bé*	k	*ka*	t	*té*
c	*cé*	l	*elle*	u	*u*
d	*dé*	m	*emme*	v	*vé*
e	*e*	n	*enne*	w	*double*
f	*effe*	o	*o*		*vé*
g	*gé*	p	*pé*	x	*iks*
h	*ache*	q	*ku*	y	*i grec*
i	*i*	r	*erre*	z	*zède*

LESSON 5

A. MORE ENGLISH-FRENCH COGNATES

1. Building up a French vocabulary is fairly easy
because, as you already see, a great number of
words are similar in French and English. Many
words are spelled exactly the same, though they
may differ considerably in pronunciation:

art	art	*police*	police
date	date	*cause*	cause
exact	exact	*effort*	effort
place	place	*force*	force
message	message	*second*	second
passage	passage	*excuse*	excuse
village	village	*source*	source
central	central	*capable*	capable
original	original	*probable*	probable
chance	chance	*possible*	possible
distance	distance	*terrible*	terrible
intelligence	intelligence	*visible*	visible
patience	patience	*double*	double
science	science	*action*	action
certain	certain	*conversation*	conversation
point	point	*description*	description
direct	direct	*direction*	direction
respect	respect	*exception*	exception
article	article	*instruction*	instruction
automobile	automobile	*intention*	intention
fruit	fruit	*satisfaction*	satisfaction
justice	justice	*situation*	situation

2. There are many words spelled exactly the same except that the French word has an accent:

éducation	education	*différence*	difference
général	general	*expérience*	experience
spécial	special	*extrême*	extreme
grâce	grace	*privilège*	privilege
préface	preface	*sincère*	sincere
élément	element	*région*	region
évident	evident	*émotion*	emotion
présent	present	*révolution*	revolution

président	president	*zéro*	zero
récent	recent		

3. In many cases the word is similar except that the French word ends in *-e:*

acte	act	*méthode*	method
affaire	affair	*moderne*	modern
aide	aid	*origine*	origin
blonde	blond	*poste*	post
capitale	capital	*rapide*	rapid
charme	charm	*riche*	rich
classe	class	*sorte*	sort
forme	form	*soupe*	soup
groupe	group	*terme*	term
liste	list	*verbe*	verb

4. In some cases there are other slight differences:

adresse	address	*problème*	problem
immédiat	immediate	*matériel*	material
lac	lake	*ouest*	west
parc	park	*appétit*	appetite
rasoir	razor	*chapitre*	chapter
sens	sense	*médecine*	medicine
agréable	agreeable	*signe*	sign
confortable	comfortable	*ligne*	line
désagréable	disagreeable	*coton*	cotton
remar-	remarkable	*façon*	fashion
quable		*nord*	north
langage	language	*oncle*	uncle
mariage	marriage	*raison*	reason
cercle	circle	*saison*	season
idée	idea	*système*	system
rivière	river	*personne*	person
circon-	circum-	*commun*	common
stance	stance	*numéro*	number

exemple	example	*sud*	south
développe- ment	develop- ment	*peuple*	people
gouverne- ment	govern- ment	*diction- naire*	diction- ary
		manière	manner
capitaine	captain	*membre*	member
complet	complete	*nombre*	number
crème	cream	*ordre*	order
enveloppe	envelope	*est*	east

B. General Spelling Equivalents

1. French *-é* = English *-y:*

beauté	beauty	*réalité*	reality
nécessité	necessity	*société*	society
qualité	quality	*université*	university
quantité	quantity		

2. French *-ie* = English *-y:*

comédie	comedy	*industrie*	industry
copie	copy	*philosophie*	philosophy

3. French *-tie* = English *-cy:*

démocratie	democracy	*diplomatie*	diplomacy

4. French *-nce* = English *-ncy:*

tendance	tendency

5. French *-eur* = English *-or (-er):*

acteur	actor	*inférieur*	inferior
conducteur	conductor	*moteur*	motor

directeur	director	*porteur*	porter
docteur	doctor	*supérieur*	superior
erreur	error	*visiteur*	visitor
faveur	favor		

6. French *-oire* = English *-ory:*

gloire	glory	*territoire*	territory
histoire	history	*victoire*	victory
mémoire	memory		

7. French *-ique* = English *ic(al):*

comique	comic(al)	*musique*	musical
critique	critic	*politique*	political
logique	logical	*pratique*	practical

8. French *-ment* = English *-ly:*

| **absolument** | absolutely | *certainement* | certainly |
| *naturellement* | naturally | | |

9. French *-aire* = English *ary:*

| **anniversaire** | anniversary | *militaire* | military |
| *contraire* | contrary | *secrétaire* | secretary |

10. French *-é* = English *ed:*

| **arrangé** | arranged | *découragé* | discouraged |
| *sacré* | sacred | | |

11. French *-ès* = English *-ess:*

| **progrès** | progress | **succès** | success |

12. French -*eux* = English -*ous:*

curieux	curious	*merveilleux*	marvelous
dangereux	dangerous	*précieux*	precious
fameux	famous		

13. French -*iste* = English -*ist:*

artiste	artist	*journaliste*	journalist
dentiste	dentist	*pianiste*	pianist

14. French -*et* = English -*ect:*

effet	effect	*projet*	project
objet	object	*sujet*	subject

15. French (^) = English *s:*

côté	coast	*hôpital*	hospital
coûter	to cost	*hôte*	host
fête	feast	*intérêt*	interest
forêt	forest	*maître*	master

16. French *é-* = English initial *s-:*

école	school	*étudiant*	student
étrange	strange	**étudier**	to study

17. French *es-* = English initial *s-:*

espace	space	*esprit*	spirit
Espagne	Spain	*estomac*	stomach
espagnol	Spanish		

LESSON 6

A. Days and Months

lundi[1]	Monday	**mercredi**	Wednesday
mardi	Tuesday	**jeudi**	Thursday
vendredi	Friday	**août**	August
samedi	Saturday	**septembre**	September
dimanche	Sunday	**octobre**	October
janvier	January	**novembre**	November
février	February	**décembre**	December
mars	March		
avril	April		
mai	May		
juin	June		
juillet	July		

B. Numbers 1–10

un	one	**six**	six
deux	two	**sept**	seven
trois	three	**huit**	eight
quatre	four	**neuf**	nine
cinq	five	**dix**	ten

C. Colors

bleu	blue	**noir**	black
rouge	red	**brun**	brown (hair)
jaune	yellow	**marron**	brown (leather, sugar, etc.)

---

[1] Notice that when you give the days of the week in French you begin with Monday. Notice also that days and months are not capitalized.

vert	green	**gris**	gray
blanc	white		

D. NORTH, SOUTH, EAST, WEST

nord	North	**est**	East
sud	South	**ouest**	West

QUIZ 1

Try matching the following two columns:

1. *dimanche*	a. Thursday
2. *août*	b. brown
3. *mercredi*	c. ten
4. *gris*	d. Sunday
5. *jeudi*	e. red
6. *neuf*	f. August
7. *marron*	g. Monday
8. *huit*	h. July
9. *juillet*	i. five
10. *jaune*	j. white
11. *rouge*	k. gray
12. *lundi*	l. nine
13. *cinq*	m. Wednesday
14. *blanc*	n. yellow
15. *dix*	o. eight

ANSWERS

1—d; 2—f; 3—m; 4—k; 5—a; 6—l; 7—b; 8—o; 9—h; 10—n; 11—e; 12—g; 13—i; 14—j; 15—c.

E. WORD STUDY

The Word Study sections point out words that are similar in French and English.

le charme	charm
la classe	class
considérable	considerable
la différence	difference
l'élément (*m.*)	element
la gloire	glory
l'opération (*f.*)	operation
le parent	parent
royal	royal

LESSON 7

A. GREETINGS

Bonjour.	Hello! Good morning. Good afternoon. ("Good day.")[1]
Monsieur	Mr.
Monsieur Lenoir	Mr. Lenoir
Bonjour, Monsieur Lenoir.	Good morning (Good afternoon), Mr. Lenoir.
Bonsoir.	Good evening.
Madame	Madam
Madame Lenoir	Mrs. Lenoir
Bonsoir, Madame Lenoir.	Good evening, Mrs. Lenoir.
bonne	good
nuit	night
Bonne nuit, Madame Lenoir.	Good night, Mrs. Lenoir.

[1] Words in parentheses and quotation marks are literal translations.

comment	how
allez-vous	are you ("do you go"; *pol.*)[1]
Comment allez-vous?	How are you? How do you do (*pol.*)?
Mademoiselle	Miss
Mademoiselle Lenoir	Miss Lenoir
Comment allez-vous, Mademoiselle Le-noir?	How do you do, Miss Lenoir?
Salut.	Hi (*fam.*).
comment	how
vas-tu	are you ("do you go"; *fam.*)
Comment vas-tu?	How are you? How do you do (*fam.*)?
Comment ça va?	How are you? How are things? ("How does it go?"; *fam.*)
Ça va.	Fine.
très	very
bien	well
Très bien.	Very well.
Merci.	Thank you. Thanks.
Très bien, merci.	Very well, thanks.
Et vous?	And you (*pol.*)?
Et toi?	And you (*fam.*)?
Merci, très bien.	Very well, thanks.
parlez	speak
lentement	slowly
Parlez lentement.	Speak slowly.
s'il vous plaît	please

[1] Throughout this program, *pol.* stands for polite, to indicate the polite or formal form, and *fam.* indicates the familiar form.

Parlez lentement, s'il vous plaît.	Please speak slowly.
Répétez.	Repeat.
Répétez, s'il vous plaît.	Please repeat.
merci	thanks
beaucoup	much, a lot
Merci beaucoup.	Thank you very much. Thanks a lot.
Je vous remercie.	Thank you (*pol.*).
Je vous en remercie.	Thank you for it.
Je te remercie.	Thank you (*fam.*).
Je t'en remercie.	Thank you for it (*fam.*).
Je vous en prie.	You're welcome (*pol.*).
Je t'en prie.	You're welcome (*fam.*).
De rien.	You're welcome ("It's nothing"; not at all).
À demain.	Till tomorrow. See you tomorrow.
À samedi.	Till Saturday. See you Saturday.
À lundi.	Till Monday. See you Monday.
À jeudi.	Till Thursday. See you Thursday.
À ce soir.	Till this evening. See you this evening.
À demain soir.	Till tomorrow evening. See you tomorrow evening.
À la semaine prochaine.	Till next week. See you next week.
À bientôt.	See you soon.

À tout à l'heure.	See you in a little while.
À plus tard.	See you later.
Au revoir.	Good-bye.

B. HOW'S THE WEATHER?

Quel temps fait-il?	How's the weather? What's the weather like?
Il fait froid.	It's cold.
Il fait frais.	It's cool.
Il fait chaud.	It's hot.
Il fait beau.	It's nice.
Il fait du vent.	It's windy.
Il fait du soleil.	It's sunny.
Il pleut.	It's raining.
Il neige.	It's snowing.

QUIZ 2

1. *très bien*	a. speak
2. *bonsoir*	b. how
3. *parlez*	c. much, a lot
4. *merci*	d. see you tomorrow (until tomorrow)
5. *comment*	e. How are you?
6. *s'il vous plaît*	f. very well
7. *beaucoup*	g. slowly
8. *à demain*	h. thank you
9. *Comment allez-vous?*	i. please
10. *lentement*	j. good evening
11. *Quel temps fait-il?*	k. It's raining.
12. *Il fait chaud.*	l. You're welcome.
13. *Je vous en prie.*	m. How are things?

14. *Il pleut.*

15. *Comment ça va?*

n. What's the weather like?

o. It's hot.

ANSWERS
1—f; 2—j; 3—a; 4—h; 5—b; 6—i; 7—c; 8—d; 9—e;
10—g; 11—n; 12—o; 13—l; 14—k; 15—m.

SUPPLEMENTAL VOCABULARY 1: WEATHER

weather	*le temps*
It's raining.	*Il pleut.*
It's snowing.	*Il neige.*
It's hailing.	*Il grêle.*
It's windy.	*Il fait du vent.*
It's hot.	*Il fait chaud.*
It's cold.	*Il fait froid.*
It's sunny.	*Il fait du soleil.*
It's cloudy.	*Il fait nuageux.*
It's beautiful.	*Il fait beau.*
storm	*l'orage (m.)*
wind	*le vent*
sun	*le soleil*
thunder	*le tonnerre*
lightening	*l'éclair (m.)*
hurricane	*l'ouragan (m.)*
temperature	*la température*
degree	*le degré*
rain	*la pluie*
snow	*la neige*
cloud	*le nuage*
fog	*le brouillard*
umbrella	*le parapluie*

LESSON 8

A. Do You Have . . . ?

Avez-vous . . . ?	Do you have . . . (*pol.*)?
As-tu . . . ?	Do you have . . . (*fam.*)?
de l'eau	some water
un plan de la ville	a city map
une télécarte	a phone card
un téléphone portable?	a cell phone
du savon	some soap
du papier	some paper

Notice that "some" or "any" is translated by *de* "of" (other forms of *de* are *du, des, d';* see page 49) and that in many cases French uses *de* (for example, *du feu*) where we don't use "some" or "any" in English. See Lesson 14 for more on the verb *To Have*.

B. In a Restaurant

le petit déjeuner	breakfast
le déjeuner	lunch
le dîner	dinner, supper
Vous désirez . . . ?	What will you have? ("You wish . . . ?")
Bonjour, Monsieur[1]**, vous désirez . . . ?**	Good afternoon. What would you like?

[1] In French you add *Monsieur* (*Madame, Mademoiselle*) when addressing a stranger and *s'il vous plaît* when asking a question or requesting something.

Donnez-moi . . .	Give me . . .
S'il vous plaît.. . .	Please.
Donnez-moi la carte,	Give me a menu,
s'il vous plaît.	please.
Je voudrais . . .	I'd like . . .
du pain	some bread
du beurre	some butter
de la soupe	some soup
de la viande	some meat
du bœuf	some beef
des œufs	some eggs
des légumes	some vegetables
des pommes de terre	some potatoes
de la salade	some salad
du lait	some milk
du vin	some wine
du sucre	some sugar
du sel	some salt
du poivre	some pepper
Apportez-moi, s'il vous	Please bring me . . .
plaît	
une cuillère	a spoon
une cuillère à café	a teaspoon
une fourchette	a fork
un couteau	a knife
une serviette	a napkin
une assiette	a plate
un verre	a glass
Je voudrais . . .	I'd like . . .
un verre d'eau	a glass of water
une tasse de thé	a cup of tea
une tasse de café	a cup of coffee
une bouteille de vin	a bottle of red wine
rouge	
une bouteille de vin	a bottle of white
blanc	wine

encore un oeuf	another egg
une omelette nature	a plain omelette
un peu de cela	a little of that
un peu plus de cela	a little more of that
plus de pain	some more bread
un peu plus de pain	a little more bread
plus de viande	some more meat
un peu plus de viande	a little more meat
L'addition, s'il vous plaît.	The check, please.

QUIZ 3

1. *viande*	a. Bring me . . .
2. *vin rouge*	b. matches
3. *Avez-vous . . . ?*	c. Give me . . .
4. *lait*	d. meat
5. *beurre*	e. some water
6. *Donnez-moi . . .*	f. a light
7. *allumettes*	g. milk
8. *encore du pain*	h. eggs
9. *Apportez-moi . . .*	i. red wine
10. *de l' eau*	j. The check, please.
11. *du feu*	k. Do you have . . . ?
12. *du sel*	l. butter
13. *des œufs*	m. a cup of coffee
14. *une tasse de café*	n. some more bread
15. *L'addition, s'il vous plaît.*	o. some salt

ANSWERS
1—d; 2—i; 3—k; 4—g; 5—l; 6—c; 7—b; 8—n; 9—a;
10—e; 11—f; 12—o; 13—h; 14—m; 15—j.

SUPPLEMENTAL VOCABULARY 2: FOOD

food	*la nourriture*
dinner	*le dîner*
lunch	*le déjeuner*
breakfast	*le petit déjeuner*
meal	*le repas*
meat	*la viande*
chicken	*le poulet*
beef	*le boeuf*
pork	*le porc*
lamb	*l'agneau (m.)*
fish	*le poisson*
shrimp	*les crevettes*
lobster	*le homard*
bread	*le pain*
egg	*l'oeuf (m.)*
cheese	*le fromage*
rice	*le riz*
vegetable	*le légume*
lettuce	*la laitue*
tomato	*la tomate*
carrot	*la carotte*
cucumber	*le concombre*
pepper	*le poivron*
fruit	*le fruit*
apple	*la pomme*
orange	*l'orange (f.)*
banana	*la banane*
pear	*la poire*
grapes	*le raisin*
drink	*la boisson*
water	*l'eau (f.)*
milk	*le lait*
juice	*le jus*
coffee	*le café*

tea	*le thé*
wine	*le vin*
beer	*la bière*
soft drink/soda	*la boisson sans alcool/la boisson gazeuse*
salt	*le sel*
pepper	*le poivre*
sugar	*le sucre*
honey	*le miel*
hot/cold	*chaud/froid*
sweet/sour	*doux/aigre*

LESSON 9

This lesson and several of the following lessons are longer than the others. They contain the grammatical and phonetic information you need to know from the start. Don't try to memorize anything. Read each section until you understand every point. As you continue with the course try to observe examples of the points mentioned. Refer back to these grammatical sections (or the Summary of French Grammar) as often as necessary. You will find that you have a good grasp of the basic features of French grammar without any deliberate memorization of "rules."

A. To Give: *Donner*

1. I give

je donne	I give, I'm giving
tu donnes	you (*fam. sing.*) give, you are giving

il donne	he gives, he's giving; it gives
elle donne	she gives, she's giving; it gives
on donne	one gives, one is giving; they (*people*) give, they (*people*) are giving, we give,* we are giving
nous donnons	we give, we're giving
vous donnez	you give, you're giving (*pl.* or *pol. sing.* or *pl.*)
ils donnent	they give, they're giving (*masc.*)
elles donnent	they give, they're giving (*fem.*)

NOTES

a. The subject pronouns are:

je	I	*nous*	we
tu	you (*fam. sing.*)	*vous*	you (*pl.* or *pol. sing.* or *pl.*)
il	he, it	*ils*	they (*masc.*)
elle	she, it	*elles*	they (*fem.*)
on	one, we		

b. Notice the verb endings taken by each subject:

je	*-e*	*nous*	*-ons*
tu	*-es*	*vous*	*-ez*
il, elle, on	*-e*	*ils, elles*	*-ent*

c. These forms, which make up the present tense, translate into English as "I give," "I'm giving" and

On is very commonly used to mean "we" in French, and it is conjugated in the same way as *il* and *elle*.

"I do give." *Donner* is considered an *-er* verb since its infinitive ends in *-er*. Many other verbs ending in *-er* have the same forms in the present tense. They are called "regular *-er* verbs."[1]

d. *Tu* is used with people you know well (whom you call by first name in English—members of one's family and close friends) and to children, pets, etc. *Vous* is used with several people or with someone you don't know very well (whom you wouldn't call by first name in English). The *tu* form is called the "familiar" form, the *vous* form the "polite" or "formal."

e. *Il donne* means "he gives" or "it gives." "They give" is translated *ils donnent* when referring to men (or to masculine nouns) or mixed groups, and *elles donnent* when referring to women (or to feminine nouns).

f. *On donne* means "one gives." It can be translated several ways in English: "they give," "people give," "it's given," etc. It also is very commonly used to mean "we", sometimes moreso even than *nous*.

g. Notice that as far as the sound is concerned there are only three endings:

1) *je donne*
   tu donnes
   il donne   all pronounced *donn*
   on donne   whether spelled *donne,*
   ils donnent   *donnes* or *donnent*
2) *nous donn-ons*
3) *vous donn-ez*

---

[1] See Lesson 40, item A, for a comparison of all French verbs: *-er*, *-ir*, and *-re* verbs.

2. I don't give

Notice that "not" is *ne . . . pas*. The verb comes between *ne* and *pas*.

je donne	I give
je ne donne pas	I don't give
tu ne donnes pas	you don't give (*fam.*)
il ne donne pas	he doesn't give
nous ne donnons pas	we don't give
vous ne donnez pas	you don't give
ils ne donnent pas	they don't give

3. Give!

Donne!	Give! (the familiar form; compare *tu donnes* above)
Donnez!	Give! (the polite form; compare *vous donnez* above)
Ne donne pas!	Don't give! (*fam.*)
Ne donnez pas!	Don't give! (*pol.*)

This form of the verb which is used in commands and requests is called the "imperative."

B. To Speak: *PARLER*

Parler is another common regular *-er* verb.

1. I speak

je parle	I speak, I'm speaking
tu parles	you speak, you're speaking (*fam.*)

il parle[1]	he speaks, he's speaking
nous parlons	we speak, we're speaking
vous parlez	you speak, you're speaking
ils parlent[1]	they speak, they're speaking

2. Speak!

Parle!	Speak! (*fam.*)
Parlez!	Speak! (*pol.*)

C. ASKING A QUESTION I

1. To ask a question, you reverse the order of subject pronoun and verb:

Vous donnez.	You give. You're giving.
Donnez-vous?	Do you give? Are you giving?
Donnes-tu?[2]	Do you give (*fam.*)?
Donne-t-il?[3]	Does he give?
Donne-t-elle?	Does she give?
Donnons-nous?	Do we give?
Donnez-vous?	Do you give?
Donnent-ils?	Do they give?
Ne donne-t-on pas?	Doesn't one give?
Ne donnez-vous pas?	Don't you give?
Ne donnent-ils pas?	Don't they give?

[1] *Il* will represent the third-person singular forms (*il, elle, on*) and *ils* will represent the third-person plural forms (*ils, elles*).
[2] The form *Donne-je?* "Do I give?" is not used; *Est-ce que je donne?* is used instead.
[3] In the third-person singular forms, *-er* verbs take a *t* before the subject pronoun.

Oui.   Yes.
Non.   No.

2. Another way of asking a question is to put *Est-ce que*[1] before the statement:

Est-ce que je donne?	Do I give? Am I giving?
Est-ce que tu donnes?	Do you (*fam.*) give? Are you giving?
Est-ce qu'il donne?	Does he give?
Est-ce que nous don-nons?	Do we give?
Est-ce que vous don-nez?	Do you give?
Est-ce qu'ils donnent?	Do they give?
Est-ce que je ne donne pas?	Don't I give?
Est-ce que tu ne donnes pas?	Don't you (*fam.*) give?
Est-ce qu'il ne donne pas?	Doesn't he give?
Est-ce que nous ne donnons pas?	Don't we give?
Est-ce que vous ne donnez pas?	Don't you give?
Est-ce qu'ils ne donnent pas?	Don't they give?

3. Study these phrases:

Parlez-vous français?	Do you speak French?
Parles-tu français?	Do you speak French?

[1] Notice that this form of asking questions with *Est-ce que* is not used often today in spoken French, except with *je*.

Parle-t-elle anglais?	Does she speak English?
Parlent-ils anglais?	Do they speak English?
Donne-t-il de l'argent?	Does he give money?
Donnez-vous de l'argent?	Do you give money?
Donne-t-elle son adresse?	Is she giving her address?

D. Linking Sounds: *Liaison*

1. In French, when words are closely connected grammatically they are also closely connected in pronunciation. If the first word ends in a consonant and the second begins with a vowel, the consonant is carried over and begins the second word. This is called *liaison,* or "linking." In the following example, the dash shows that the *n* is carried over to the next word:

un exemple:

u—nexemple   an example

2. There are many cases in which the first word ends in a consonant which is not pronounced when the word is used by itself or before a word beginning with a consonant (*vous* pronounced *vou*) but which is pronounced when the following word begins with a vowel or *h* (*vous avez* pronounced *vou-zavez*). When this *liaison* takes place:

s is pronounced z: *vous avez* (*vou-zavez*) you
have
les amis (*lay-zamis*) the
friends

x is pronounced z: *aux Etats-Unis* (*au-zEtat-
zUnis*) to the United
States
deux amis (*deu-zamis*)
two friends

d is pronounced t: *un grand enfant* (*un gran-
tenfant*) a big child
un grand homme (*un
gran-tomme*) a great
(important) man

3. Listen for the *liaison* in these examples:

Il est . . .	He is . . .
Est-il?	Is he?
Est-elle?	Is she?
Ils sont.	They are.
Sont-ils?	Are they (*masc.*)?
Sont-elles?	Are they (*fem.*)?
C'est . . .	It is . . .
C'est à moi.	It's mine.
C'est ici.	It's here.
Nous avons.	We have.
Vous avez.	You have.
Ils ont.	They have.
Les amis.	The friends.
Deux amis.	Two friends.
Les élèves.	The pupils.
Pas encore.	Not yet.
Très intéressant.	Very interesting.
Après une heure.	After an hour.

Venez ici.	Come here.
Allez-y.	Go there.
Un petit enfant.	A small child.
Un grand enfant.	A big child.
Je suis ici.	I'm here.
Ils sont allés.	They went.
Chez eux.	At their home.
Sans intérêt.	Without interest.

Remember that words beginning with an aspirate *h* do not have *liaison:*

le hors d'oeuvre	the appetizer
deux héros	two heroes

REVIEW QUIZ 1

Choose the correct French word equivalent to the English.

1. Five =
   a. *six*
   b. *sept*
   c. *cinq*
2. Eight =
   a. *huit*
   b. *neuf*
   c. *quatre*
3. Tuesday =
   a. *mercredi*
   b. *mardi*
   c. *vendredi*
4. Sunday =
   a. *dimanche*
   b. *samedi*
   c. *lundi*
5. August =
   a. *août*
   b. *septembre*
   c. *avril*
6. June =
   a. *juillet*
   b. *juin*
   c. *mai*
7. Red =
   a. *bleu*
   b. *orange*
   c. *rouge*
8. Green =
   a. *jaune*
   b. *vert*
   c. *gris*

9. Black =
   a. *noir*
   b. *marron*
   c. *blanc*
10. Brown =
    a. *noir*
    b. *rouge*
    c. *brun*
11. Good morning =
    a. *bonjour*
    b. *bonsoir*
    c. *comment*
12. Very well =
    a. *merci*
    b. *très bien*
    c. *très*
13. Thank you =
    a. *bien*
    b. *merci*
    c. *très*
14. Please =
    a. *parlez*

    b. *merci*
    c. *s'il vous plaît*

15. Good-bye =
    a. *à demain*
    b. *au revoir*
    c. *bonjour*
16. He gives =
    a. *il donne*
    b. *elle donne*
    c. *ils donnent*
17. We are speaking =
    a. *nous parlons*
    b. *vous parlez*
    c. *nous donnons*
18. I don't give =
    a. *il ne donne pas*
    b. *je donne*
    c. *je ne donne pas*
19. Do you give? =
    a. *Donnez-vous?*
    b. *Donne-t-il?*
    c. *Donne-t-on?*
20. Do I give? =
    a. *Est-ce que vous donnez?*
    b. *Est-ce que je donne?*
    c. *Est-ce qu'il donne?*

ANSWERS

1—c; 2—a; 3—b; 4—a; 5—a; 6—b; 7—c; 8—b; 9—a; 10—c; 11—a; 12—b; 13—b; 14—c; 15—b; 16—a; 17—a; 18—c; 19—a; 20—b.

LESSON 10

A. WHERE?

Pardon, Monsieur.	Excuse me, sir.
où	where
est	is
Où est-il?	Where is it (he)?
l'hôtel	the hotel
Où est l'hôtel?	Where is the hotel?
Où est le restaurant?	Where is the restaurant?
Où est le téléphone?	Where is the telephone?
Pouvez-vous me dire . . .	Can you tell me . . .
Pouvez-vous me dire où est le téléphone?	Can you tell me where the telephone is?
Pouvez-vous me dire où est la gare?	Can you tell me where the (railroad) station is?

Où est is the simplest way of saying "Where is" but it is more idiomatic to say: *Où se trouve . . .* ("Where does it find itself . . . ?")

Où se trouve l'hôtel?	Where is the hotel? ("Where does the hotel find itself?")
Pouvez-vous me dire où se trouve la poste?	Can you tell me where the post office is?
Pouvez-vous me dire où se trouve le téléphone?	Can you tell me where the telephone is?

B. Here and There

Ici.	Here.
Là.	There.
Là-bas.	Over there.
Par où est-ce?	Which way is it?
Par ici.	This way.
Par là.	That way.
Par là-bas.	Over that way.
C'est par ici.	It's this way.
C'est par là-bas.	It's over that way.
C'est ici.	It's here.
Ce n'est pas ici.	It's not here.
C'est là.	It's there.
Ce n'est pas là.	It's not there.
C'est là-haut.	It's up there.
Il est ici.	He's here.
Venez ici.	Come here.
Restez ici.	Stay here.
Attendez là.	Wait there.
Allez par ici.	Go this way.
Allez par là.	Go that way.
Qui est là?	Who's there?
Mettez-le ici.	Put it here.
Mettez-le là.	Put it there.

C. To the Right, etc.

À droite.	To the right.
À gauche.	To the left.
À votre droite.	To your right.
À votre gauche.	To your left.
Sur votre gauche.	On your left.
C'est à droite.	It's to the right.
C'est à gauche.	It's to the left.

Tournez à droite.	Turn right.
Tournez à gauche.	Turn left.
Continuez tout droit.	Keep straight on.
C'est tout droit.	It's straight ahead.
C'est tout droit devant vous.	It's straight ahead of you.
Allez tout droit.	Go straight ahead.
C'est en face.	It's directly opposite.
C'est en haut.	It's above.
C'est en bas.	It's below.
C'est au coin.	It's on the corner.

D. NEAR AND FAR

Près.	Near.
Près d'ici.	Near here.
Tout près.	Very near. Quite close.
Près du village.	Near the village.
Près de la route.	Near the road.
Près de lui.	Near him.
C'est tout près.	It's very near.
C'est tout près d'ici.	It's very near here.
Loin.	Far.
C'est loin? ⎱ **Est-ce loin?** ⎰	Is it far?
C'est loin.	It's far.
Ce n'est pas loin.	It's not far.
C'est loin d'ici.	It's far from here.

E. THERE

y	There. To there.
Est-il à Paris?	Is he in Paris?
Oui, il y est.	Yes, he is (there).
Paul, est-il là-bas?	Is Paul there?

Oui, il est là-bas.	Yes, he's there.
Va-t-il à Paris?	Is he going to Paris?
Oui, il y va.	Yes, he's going there.
J'y vais.	I'm going there.
Je ne veux pas y aller.	I don't want to go there.
J'y habite.	I live there.

QUIZ 4

1. *Pouvez-vous me dire où est le téléphone?*	a. It's this way.
2. *Où se trouve l'hôtel?*	b. It's to the right.
3. *C'est par ici.*	c. Turn left.
4. *C'est tout droit.*	d. It's (directly) opposite.
5. *C'est à droite.*	e. It's straight ahead.
6. *J'y demeure.*	f. Can you tell me where the telephone is?
7. *Attendez là.*	g. Where is the hotel? ("Where does the hotel find itself?")
8. *Allez par ici.*	h. I live there.
9. *Tournez à gauche.*	i. It's not here.
10. *C'est en face.*	j. Stay here.
11. *Ce n'est pas loin.*	k. Wait there.
12. *Mettez-le là.*	l. Go this way.
13. *Ce n'est pas ici.*	m. Who's there?
14. *Restez ici.*	n. Put it there.
15. *Qui est là?*	o. It's not far.

ANSWERS

1—f; 2—g; 3—a; 4—e; 5—b; 6—h; 7—k; 8—l; 9—c; 10—d; 11—o; 12—n; 13—i; 14—j; 15—m.

Supplemental Vocabulary 3: People

people	*les gens*
person	*la personne*
man	*l'homme*
woman	*la femme*
adult	*l'adulte*
child	*l'enfant*
boy	*le garçon*
girl	*la fille*
teenager	*l'adolescent (m.), l'adolescente (f.)*
tall/short	*grand/petit*
old/young	*vieux (m.) (pl: vieux), vieille (f.)/jeune*
fat/thin	*gros (m.), grosse (f.)/mince*
friendly/unfriendly	*amical (m.) (pl: amicaux)/peu amical*
happy/sad	*heureux (m.) (pl: heureux), heureuse (f.)/triste*
beautiful/ugly	*beau (m.) (pl: beaux), belle (f.)/laid*
sick/healthy	*malade/en bonne santé*
strong/weak	*fort/faible*
famous	*célèbre*
intelligent	*intelligent*
talented	*talentueux (m.) (pl: talentueux), talentueuse (f.)*

LESSON 11

A. The and A; *Élision*

1. *le, la, les* "the."

Je donne le livre à un enfant.	I give (I'm giving) the book to a child.
Il donne la lettre à une femme.	He gives (he's giving) the letter to a woman.
Nous donnons les livres à un garçon.	We give (we're giving) the books to a boy.
Vous donnez les lettres à ma fille.	You give (you're giving) the letters to my daughter.

Notice that the book is *le livre,* the letter is *la lettre*. Nouns that take *le* are called "masculine," nouns that take *la* are called "feminine." In the plural, however, both take *les:*

les livres	the books
les lettres	the letters

2. *un, une* "a."
Nouns that take *le* (masculine nouns) take *un:*

un livre	a book
un garçon	a boy

Nouns that take *la* (feminine nouns) take *une:*

une lettre	a letter
une femme	a woman

3. *le, la* before vowels and *h*

Je parle à l'ami de Jean.	I'm talking to John's friend.
Il donne la lettre à l'amie de Jeanne.	He gives (he's giving) the letter to Jean's girlfriend.
Nous entrons dans l'hôtel.	We are going into the hotel.
Je marche sur l'herbe.	I'm walking on the grass.

Notice that when *le* or *la* comes before a vowel or a mute *h* it becomes *l'*. This is called elision.

l'ami	the friend
l'homme	the man
l'heure	the hour

Words beginning with an aspirate *h* do not elide:

le haricot	the bean	**le hors d'oeuvre**	the appetizer
le héros	the hero	**la haine**	the hatred

B. MASCULINE AND FEMININE

un ami de Jean	John's friend ("a friend of John")
une amie de Jean	John's (girl) friend

Notice that *e* is often added to a masculine word to make it feminine:

un ami   une amie

This rule applies to both nouns and adjectives describing females or feminine nouns (see **C.**):

MASCULINE		FEMININE	
grand	big	**grande**	big
petit	small	**petite**	small
fatigué	tired	*fatiguée*	tired
étudiant	male student	*étudiante*	female student
client	customer	*cliente*	woman customer

C. POSITION OF ADJECTIVES

1. Adjectives usually follow the noun they modify:

un livre français	a French book
un homme intéressant	an interesting man
une idée excellente	an excellent idea

2. A number of common adjectives, however, usually precede the noun:[1]

autre	other	*jeune*	young
beau	beautiful	*joli*	pretty
bon	good	*long*	long
court	short	*mauvais*	bad
gentil	nice, pleasant	*nouveau*	new
grand	great, large, tall	*petit*	small, little
gros	big	*vieux*	old

[1] See Feminine of Adjectives in the Summary of French Grammar for the feminine forms of these and other adjectives; some are irregular.

D. PLURAL

1. The plural of most nouns ends in -*s:*

le livre	the book	**les livres**	the books
la lettre	the letter	**les lettres**	the letters

Since the *s* is not pronounced there is no difference in speech between *livre* "book" and *livres* "books." The difference between singular and plural is clear, however, as soon as you add *le* or *les:*

le livre	the book	*les livres*	the books

2. The plural of most adjectives ends in -*s:*

je suis prêt	I'm ready
elle est prête	she's ready
nous sommes prêts	we're ready
elles sont prêtes	they're ready
ils sont fatigués	they're tired
elles sont fatiguées	they're tired

E. WORD STUDY

comédie	comedy	**nord**	north
constant	constant	**oncle**	uncle
contraire	contrary	**organe**	organ
désir	desire	**poste**	post
long	long	**simple**	simple

LESSON 12

A. Of and To

OF

1. *de* "of"

la lettre de mon ami	my friend's letter (the letter of my friend)
le livre de Jean	John's book
les livres de l'élève	the pupil's books

2. *de la* "of the" "some" (*fem.*)

la lettre de la jeune fille	the girl's letter
l'ordinateur de la directrice	the director's computer
Donne-moi de la confiture.	Give me some jam.
Donnez-moi de la viande.	Give me some meat.

3. *de l'* "of the" "some" (*before vowels and mute h*)

le livre de l'ami	the friend's book
l'entrée de l'hôtel	the hotel's entrance
Donnez-moi de l'argent.	Give me some money.
Donnez-moi de l'eau.	Give me some water.

Notice that *de* is used in some cases where in English we use the possessive (John's book) and in other cases where we use the word "some" (Give me some water).

4. *du* "of the" "some" (*masc.*)
   Notice that *de + le = du.*

le livre du père	the father's book
le livre du garçon	the boy's book
Tu veux du thé?	You want some tea?
Il y a du monde!	There are a lot of people! ("some world")

5. *des* "of the" "some" (*pl.*)
   Notice that *de + les = des.*

les rues des villes	the streets of the towns
les livres des élèves	the pupils' books (the books of the pupils)
Donnez-moi des pommes de terre.	Give me some potatoes.
Il y a des messages pour toi.	There are some messages for you.

TO

1. *à* "to"

Je vais à Paris.	I'm going to Paris.

2. *à la* "to the" (*fem.*)

Je donne la lettre à la mère.	I give (I'm giving) the letter to the mother.
Mon ami porte cette valise à la gare.	My friend carries this suitcase to the station.

3. *à l'* "to the" (*before, a vowel or mute h*)

Donnez-la à l'enfant.	Give it to the child.
Je donne la lettre à	I give (I'm giving) the

l'ami de Jean.	letter to John's friend.
Il va à l'hôpital.	He's going to the hospital.

4. *au* "to the" (*masc.*)
Notice that *a + le = au.*

Je donne la lettre au père.	I give (I'm giving) the letter to the father.
Je vais au théâtre.	I'm going to the theater.
Il va au cinéma.	He's going to the movies.

5. *aux* "to the" (*pl.*) Notice that *a + les = aux.*

Il donne de l'argent aux pauvres.	He gives money to the poor.
Je vais aux concerts de l'orchestre symphonique.	I'm going to the symphony concerts.

B. WORD STUDY

la chaîne	chain	**la crème**	cream
complet	complete	**le désert**	desert
éternel	eternal	**l'officier**	officer
la fontaine	fountain	(*m.*)	
la lettre	letter	**le système**	system

C. TO BE OR NOT TO BE: *ÊTRE*

About 4,000 to 4,500 verbs in common use have the forms given for *donner* and *parler* (the "regular -*er* verbs"). Among some of the verbs that do not follow this pattern (the "irregular verbs"), there are some extremely common ones, such as:

être	to be
avoir	to have
aller	to go
venir	to come
faire	to do
dire	to say

You will learn the forms for these verbs in later lessons. Let's begin with "to be, *être*."

1. I am

je suis	I am
tu es	you are (*fam.*)
il est	he is
nous sommes	we are
vous êtes	you are (*pl.*)
ils sont	they are

2. I am not

je ne suis pas	I am not
tu n'es pas	you are not
il n'est pas	he is not
nous ne sommes pas	we are not
vous n'êtes pas	you are not
ils ne sont pas	they are not

3. Be!

Soyez!	Be!
Soyez tranquille.	Don't worry.
Sois tranquille!	Don't worry. (*fam.*)
Sois à l'heure!	Be on time!

4. Study these examples:

Je suis américain.	I'm (*masc.*) American.
Je suis à l'hôtel.	I'm at the hotel.
Il est ici.	He's here.
Elle est là.	She's there.
Ils sont ici.	They're (*masc.*) here.
Elles sont là-bas.	They're (*fem.*) over there.
Je suis prêt.	I'm ready.
Elle est prête.	She's ready.
Ils sont prêts.	They're (*masc.*) ready.
Elles sont prêtes.	They're (*fem.*) ready.
La lettre est longue.	The letter is long.
La maison n'est pas grande.	The house is not big.
Le garçon est content.	The boy is happy.
Les livres ne sont pas intéressants.	The books are not interesting.
Il est fatigué.	He's tired.
Elle est fatiguée.	She's tired.
Elle est crevée.	She's tired ("dead tired") (*fam.*).
Quelle heure est-il?	What time is it?
D'où êtes-vous?	Where are you from?
Je suis de Paris.	I'm from Paris.

5. Am I? Are you?

suis-je? or **est-ce que je suis?**	Am I?

Es-tu . . . ?	Are you . . . ?
Est-il . . . ?	Is he . . . ?
Sommes-nous . . . ?	Are we . . . ?
Êtes-vous . . . ?	Are you . . . ?
Sont-ils . . . ?	Are they . . . (*masc.*)?

6. Study these examples:

Où es-tu?	Where are you?
Où est-elle?	Where is she?
Où sommes-nous?	Where are we?
Où sont-ils?	Where are they (*masc.*)?
Êtes-vous certain, Monsieur?	Are you certain, sir?
Êtes-vous certaine, Madame?	Are you certain, madam?
Êtes-vous certaine, Mademoiselle?	Are you certain, miss?
Êtes-vous certains, Messieurs?	Are you certain, gentlemen?
Êtes-vous certaines, Mesdames?	Are you certain?
Êtes-vous certaines, Mesdemoiselles?	Are you certain?
Êtes-vous anglais?	Are you English?
Oui, je suis anglais.	Yes, I'm English.
Oui, je le suis.	Yes, I am. (Note that in French you add *le* "it.")
Non, je ne suis pas anglais.	No, I'm not English.
Non, je ne le suis pas.	No, I'm not.

D. My, Your, His (Possessive Adjectives)

Où est mon livre?	Where is my book?
Où est ton livre?	Where is your (*fam.*) book?
Où est son livre?	Where is his (her) book?
Où est notre livre?	Where is our book?
Où est votre livre?	Where is your (*pol.* or *plu.*) book?
Où est leur livre?	Where is their book?
Où est ma lettre?	Where is my letter?
Où est ta lettre?	Where is your (*fam.*) letter?
Où est sa lettre?	Where is his (her) letter?
Où est notre lettre?	Where is our letter?
Où est votre lettre?	Where is your (*pol.*) letter?
Où est leur lettre?	Where is their letter?
Où sont mes livres?	Where are my books?
Où sont tes livres?	Where are your (*fam.*) books?
Où sont ses livres?	Where are his (her) books?
Où sont nos livres?	Where are our books?
Où sont vos livres?	Where are your (*pol.* or *plu.*) books?
Où sont leurs livres?	Where are their books?
Où sont mes lettres?	Where are my letters?
Où sont tes lettres?	Where are your (*fam.*) letters?
Où sont ses lettres?	Where are his (her) letters?

Où sont nos lettres?	**Where are our letters?**
Où sont vos lettres?	**Where are your (***pol.*** or** ***plu.***) letters?**
Où sont leurs lettres?	**Where are their letters?**

Notice that my, your, his, etc., is *mon, ton, son,* before masculine nouns and *ma, ta, sa* before feminine nouns, but that in the plural the same form (*mes, tes, ses*) is used before both masculine and feminine nouns. Notice also that these possessive adjectives agree in gender with the following noun rather than with the possessor: In *Où est sa lettre?* "Where is his letter?" *sa* is feminine because *lettre* is feminine (even though "his" refers to a man). Refer to pages 330–331 in the Summary of French Grammar for more information.

QUIZ 5

1. *D'où êtes-vous?*	a. What time is it?
2. *Quelle heure est-il?*	b. Where are you from?
3. *Il est ici.*	c. Where is he?
4. *Je suis prêt.*	d. Where is his letter?
5. *Êtes-vous certain?*	e. They are ready.
6. *Où est-il?*	f. I'm tired.
7. *Où est sa lettre?*	g. I'm ready.
8. *Je suis fatigué.*	h. I'm at the hotel.
9. *Elles sont prêtes.*	i. Are you certain?
10. *Soyez tranquille.*	j. He's here.
11. *Je suis à l'hôtel.*	k. I'm (an) American.
12. *Je suis américain.*	l. Don't worry.
13. *Je ne suis pas à Bordeaux.*	m. I'm from Paris.

14. *Nous sommes.*   n. I'm not in Bordeaux.
15. *Je suis de Paris.*   o. We are.

ANSWERS
1—b; 2—a; 3—j; 4—g; 5—i; 6—c; 7—d; 8—f; 9—e;
10—l; 11—h; 12—k; 13—n; 14—o; 15—m.

LESSON 13

A. IT IS

C'est bon.	It's good.
Ce n'est pas bon.	It's no good.
C'est bien.	It's (that's) all right. ("It's well.")
Ce n'est pas bien.	It's not very good (nice). It's not right (fair).
C'est mal.	It's bad.
Ce n'est pas mal.	It's not bad.
C'est petit.	It's small.
C'est grand.	It's big.
Ce n'est rien.	It's nothing.
C'est difficile.	It's hard (difficult).
C'est facile.	It's easy.
C'est très facile.	It's very easy.
C'est assez facile.	It's easy enough.
C'est plus facile.	It's easier.
C'est moins difficile.	It's less difficult.
C'est loin.	It's far.
Ce n'est pas très loin.	It's not very far.
C'est près d'ici.	It's near here.
C'est peu.	It's (a) little.

C'est trop peu.	It's too little.
C'est assez.	It's enough.
C'est beaucoup.	It's a lot.
C'est par ici.	It's this way.
C'est par là.	It's that way.
C'est pour moi.	It's for me.
C'est pour nous.	It's for us.
C'est pour vous.	It's for you.
C'est pour les enfants.	It's for the children.
C'est cela.	That's it. That's right.
C'est ça.	That's it. That's right.

B. Asking a Question II

1. As you have already seen, there are several ways of asking a question:

   a. Reverse the order of subject and verb.

   b. *Est-ce que* . . . is used before the regular word order. This is a very common way of forming a question.

   c. Use the regular word order with the question intonation (that is, with the pitch of the voice raised at the end of the sentence).

Est-ce cela?	Is it that?
C'est cela?	Is it that?
Il est ici.[1]	He's here.
Est-ce qu'il est là? Est-il là? Il est là?	Is he here?

---

[1] Note that *là* often replaces *ici* to mean "here" in modern conversational French.

C'est vrai.	It's true.
C'est vrai?	It's true?
Est-ce que c'est vrai?	Is it true?

Est-ce vrai? C'est vrai?	It is true?

Où est-il? Il est où?	Where is he?

Où est-ce? C'est où?	Where is it?

Est-ce qu'il est prêt? Est-il prêt? Il est prêt?	Is he ready?

Est-ce que vous êtes prêt? Êtes-vous prêt? Vous êtes prêt?	Are you ready?

Est-ce qu'elles sont prêtes? Sont-elles prêtes? Elles sont prêtes?	Are they (*fem.*) ready?

Est-ce que vous venez? Venez-vous? Vous venez?	Are you coming?

Est-ce que vous avez dix euros? Avez-vous dix euros? Vous avez dix euros?	Do you have ten euros?

Est-ce que vous avez du café? Avez-vous du café? Vous avez du café?	Do you have any coffee?

Est-ce que vous parlez anglais? **Parlez-vous anglais?** **Vous parlez anglais?**	Do you speak English?

Est-ce que vous parlez français? **Parlez-vous français?** **Vous parlez français?**	Do you speak French?

2. You already know the words *oui* and *non* for "yes" and "no." The word *si* is also used for "yes" when you want to contradict a negative statement or question:

Vous ne parlez pas anglais?—Si.
You don't speak English?—Yes (I do).

C. Word Study

la bande	band, strip
le chauffeur	chauffeur
commun	common
la composition	composition
la conscience	conscience
la décoration	decoration
la description	description
la mission	mission
le numéro	number
la région	region

LESSON 14

A. To Have and To Have Not: *Avoir*

1. I have

j'ai	I have
tu as	you have
il a	he has
nous avons	we have
vous avez	you have
ils ont	they have

2. I don't have

je n'ai pas	I don't have, I haven't
tu n'as pas	you don't have, *etc.*
il n'a pas	he doesn't have
nous n'avons pas	we don't have
vous n'avez pas	you don't have
ils n'ont pas	they don't have

3. Study these examples:

Je n'ai rien.	I have nothing. I don't have anything. There's nothing wrong with me.
J'ai de l'argent.	I have money.
J'ai assez d'argent.	I have enough money.
Je n'ai pas d'argent.	I don't have any money.
J'ai assez de temps.	I have enough time.
Ils n'ont pas de cigarettes.	They don't have any cigarettes.

4. Do I have?

Ai-je . . . ? (or *Est-ce que j'ai . . . ?*)	Do I have . . . ?
As-tu . . . ?	Do you have . . . ?
A-t-il . . . ?	Does he have . . . ?
Avons-nous . . . ?	Do we have . . . ?
Avez-vous . . . ?	Do you have . . . ?
Ont-ils . . . ?	Do they have . . . ?

5. Don't I have?

N'ai-je pas . . . ?	Don't I have . . . ?
N'as-tu pas . . . ?	Don't you have . . . ?
N'a-t-il pas . . . ?	Doesn't he have . . . ?
N'avons-nous pas . . . ?	Don't we have . . . ?
N'avez-vous pas . . . ?	Don't you have . . . ?
N'ont-ils pas . . . ?	Don't they have . . . ?

6. Study these examples:

A-t-il de l'argent?	Does he have any money?
A-t-elle assez d'argent?	Does she have enough money?

N'a-t-il pas d'amis à Paris?	Doesn't he have any friends in Paris?
N'avez-vous pas de crayon?	Don't you have a pencil?
Avez-vous un stylo?	Do you have a pen?
Avez-vous un timbre?	Do you have a stamp?
Avez-vous du papier?	Do you have any paper?
Est-ce que vous avez un nouvel ordinateur? **Avez-vous un nouvel ordinateur?** **Vous avez un nouvel ordinateur?**	Do you have a new computer?
N'avez-vous pas de sucre?	Don't you have any sugar?
Avez-vous un téléphone portable?	Do you have a cell phone?
Qu'avez-vous?	What's the matter with you? What hurts you?
Qu'est-ce qu'il a?	What's the matter with him?
Combien en avez-vous?	How many of them do you have?
Avez-vous le temps de me parler?	Do you have time to talk to me?
Pourquoi n'avez-vous pas le temps?	Why don't you have time?
parce que	because
Je n'ai pas le temps parce que j'ai un rendez-vous.	I don't have time because I have an appointment.

B. IDIOMS WITH *AVOIR*

Study these idiomatic expressions with *avoir:*

J'ai faim.	I'm hungry.
J'ai soif.	I'm thirsty.
Nous avons froid.	We're cold.
Il a chaud.	He's hot.
Avez-vous chaud?	Are you hot?
Il a tort.	He's wrong.
Vous avez raison.	You're right.
Elle a peur.	She's afraid.
J'ai besoin de . . .	I need . . .
J'ai besoin de cela.	I need that.
Quel âge avez-vous?	How old are you?
J'ai vingt ans.	I'm twenty (years old).
J'ai mal aux dents.	I have a toothache.
Elle a mal à la tête.	She has a headache.

LESSON 15

A. THERE IS

Il y a . . .	There is . . . There are . . .
Il y en a.	There's some (of it).
Il n'y a rien.	There's nothing.
Il n'y a plus de cela.	There's no more of that.
Il n'y en a plus.	There isn't any more (of it).
Il n'y a pas de réponse.	There's no answer.

Il n'y a pas de différence.	There's no difference.
Il n'y a aucune difficulté.	There's no difficulty.
Il n'y a personne.	There's nobody.
Y a-t-il du courrier?	Is there any mail?
Y a-t-il beaucoup de monde?	Is there a crowd? Are there a lot of people?
Y a-t-il une pharmacie près d'ici?	Is there a drugstore near here?
Y a-t-il un café près d'ici?	Is there a café near here?
Il y a quatre personnes ici.	There are four people here.

B. Ago

Il y a . . .	. . . ago
Il y a une heure.	An hour ago.
Il y a deux heures.	Two hours ago.
Il y a un jour.	A day ago.
Il y a deux jours.	Two days ago.
Il y a trois semaines.	Three weeks ago.
Il y a cinq mois.	Five months ago.
Il y a cinq ans.	Five years ago.
Il y a dix ans.	Ten years ago.
Il y a longtemps.	A long time ago.
Il y a assez longtemps.	A rather long time ago.
Il n'y a pas longtemps.	Not so long ago.
Il y a peu de temps.	A short time ago.

C. Also, Too

Aussi.	Also, too.
Moi aussi.	I/me, too.
Toi aussi.	You, too.

Lui aussi.	He/him, too.
Elle aussi.	She/her, too.
Nous aussi.	We/us, too.
Vous aussi.	You, too.
Eux aussi.	They/them (*m.*) too.
Elles aussi.	They, them (*f.*), too.
Il vient aussi.	He's also coming.
Ils viennent aussi.	They're also coming.
Il l'a fait aussi.	He also did it.
Moi aussi je viens.	I'm also coming.

D. As . . . As

Ils sont aussi grands que les autres.	They're as tall as the others.
Ils ne sont pas aussi petits que les autres.	They're not as small as the others.
Ce n'est pas aussi bon que l'autre.	That's not as good as the other.
Ce n'est pas aussi grand que l'autre.	That's not as large as the other.
Venez aussi vite que possible.	Come as quickly as you can.
Faites-le aussi vite que possible.	Do it as quickly as possible.
Faites-le aussi bien que possible.	Do it as well as possible.

E. I'm Sorry

Je m'excuse.	I'm sorry.
Excusez-moi.	Forgive me. I'm sorry.
Je suis désolé.	I'm so sorry.
Je regrette.	I'm sorry.

Pardon. Sorry. Excuse me.
Je suis navré. I'm terribly sorry.

QUIZ 6

1. *J'ai assez de temps.*
2. *Il a raison.*
3. *J'ai besoin de cela.*
4. *Il a tort.*
5. *Il a froid.*
6. *J'ai faim.*
7. *J'ai vingt ans.*
8. *J'ai soif.*
9. *Quel âge avez-vous?*
10. *Je suis désolé.*
11. *Combien en avez-vous?*
12. *A-t-il des amis à Paris?*
13. *Je n'ai rien.*
14. *Vous avez raison.*
15. *Qu'est-ce qu'il a?*
16. *Il y a trois semaines.*
17. *Il n'y a pas de différence.*

a. There isn't any more (of it).
b. There's no answer.
c. There's no difference.
d. There's no difficulty.
e. Are there any letters for me?
f. There's nobody here.
g. A day ago.
h. Three weeks ago.
i. A long time ago.
j. Come as quickly as you can.
k. I have nothing. I don't have anything. There's nothing wrong with me.
l. I have enough time.
m. I'm hungry.
n. I'm thirsty.
o. He's cold.
p. He's right.
q. He's wrong.

18. *Il n'y a aucune difficulté.*	r. You're right.
19. *Il n'y en a plus.*	s. I need that.
20. *Il y a longtemps.*	t. I'm twenty (years old).
21. *Il n'y a personne ici.*	u. I'm sorry.
22. *Venez aussi vite que possible.*	v. Does he have (any) friends in Paris?
23. *Y a-t-il des lettres pour moi?*	w. What's the matter with him?
24. *Il y a un jour.*	x. How old are you?
25. *Il n'y a pas de réponse.*	y. How many of them do you have?

ANSWERS

1—l; 2—p; 3—s; 4—q; 5—o; 6—m; 7—t; 8—n; 9—x; 10—u; 11—y; 12—v; 13—k; 14—r; 15—w; 16—h; 17—c; 18—d; 19—a; 20—i; 21—f; 22—j; 23—e; 24—g; 25—b.

SUPPLEMENTAL VOCABULARY 4: AT HOME

at home	*à la maison*
house	*la maison*
apartment	*l'appartement (m.)*
room	*la pièce*
living room	*le salon*
dining room	*la salle à manger (pl: les salles à manger)*
kitchen	*la cuisine*
bedroom	*la chambre*
bathroom	*la salle de bain (pl: les salles de bain)*
hall	*le couloir*
closet	*le placard*

window	*la fenêtre*
door	*la porte*
table	*la table*
chair	*la chaise*
sofa/couch	*le canapé*
curtain	*le rideau*
carpet	*la moquette*
rug	*le tapis*
television	*la télévision*
CD player	*le lecteur CD*
lamp	*la lampe*
DVD player	*le lecteur DVD*
sound system	*la chaîne hifi*
painting	*la peinture*
photo	*la photo*
shelf	*l'étagère (f.)*
stairs	*les escaliers*
ceiling	*le plafond*
wall	*le mur*
floor	*le sol*
big/small	*petit/grand*
new/old	*nouveau (m.) (pl: nouveaux), nouvelle (f.)/vieux (m.) (pl: vieux), vieille (f.)*
wood/wooden	*en bois*
plastic/made from plastic	*en plastique*

LESSON 16

A. Do You Speak French?

Vous parlez français?[1]	
Parlez-vous français?	Do you speak French?
Est-ce que vous parlez français?	
Non, je ne parle pas français.	No, I don't speak French.
Je ne parle pas bien français.	I don't speak French very well.
mal	poorly
très mal	very poorly
Je parle très mal.	I speak very poorly.
un peu	a little
Oui, je parle un peu.	Yes, I speak a little.
très peu	very little
Je parle très peu.	I speak very little.
Pas beaucoup.	Not much.
Quelques mots.	A few words.
Quelques mots seulement.	Only a few words.
Comprenez-vous?	Do you understand?
Non, je ne comprends pas.	No, I don't understand.
Je ne comprends pas bien.	I don't understand well.
Je ne comprends pas bien le français.	I don't understand French very well.
Oui, je comprends.	Yes, I understand.

[1] Note: after the verb *parler* the article *le* may be used or omitted before the name of a language.

Oui, je comprends un peu.	Yes, I understand a little.
Je lis mais je ne parle pas.	I read but I can't speak.
Vous comprenez? **Comprenez-vous?** **Est-ce que vous comprenez?**	Do you understand?
Pas du tout.	Not at all.
Je comprends mal.	I understand poorly.
Ecrivez-le.	Write it (down).
Comment l'écrivez-vous?	How do you write (spell) it?
Je ne connais pas ce mot.	I don't know that word.

B. PLEASE SPEAK MORE SLOWLY

Parlez lentement, s'il vous plaît.	Please speak slowly.
Si vous parlez lentement, je peux vous comprendre.	If you speak slowly, I can understand you. If you speak slowly, I'll be able to understand you.
voulez-vous . . . ?	would you . . . ?
parler	to speak
moins vite	slower ("less quickly")
Voulez-vous parler moins vite?	Would you speak slower?
s'il vous plaît	please
Voulez-vous parler moins vite, s'il vous plaît?	Would you mind speaking a little slower, please?

C. WHAT DID YOU SAY?

Vous dites . . . ?	What did you say? ("You say . . . ?") (As in English "You were saying?" "What was that?" "What did you say?" etc.)
Comment? Vous dites . . . ?	What did you say? ("How? You say . . . ?")
Pardon?	Pardon? What did you say?
Comment dites-vous cela en français?	How do you say that in French?
Comment dit-on "Thank you" en français?	How do you say "Thank you" in French?
Que voulez-vous dire?	What do you mean? ("What do you want to say?")
Voulez-vous répéter, s'il vous plaît?	Would you please say that again?

D. THANKS

Merci.	Thanks. Thank you.
Je vous remercie.	Thanks. ("I thank you.")
Je vous en remercie.	Thanks. ("I thank you for it.")
Je vous remercie beaucoup.	Thank you very much.
De rien.	You're welcome. Not at all.

Excusez-moi. ⎫ **Excuse-moi.** ⎭	Excuse me.
Vous permettez? ⎫ **Tu permets?** ⎭	May I? ("You permit me?")
Allez-y! ⎫ **Vas-y!** ⎭	Go ahead! Please do! ("Do!")
Je vous en prie.[1] ⎫ **Je t'en prie.**[1] ⎭	Please do! ("I beg you.") You're welcome.

QUIZ 7

1. *Écrivez-le.*

2. *Non, je ne parle pas français.*

3. *Je ne comprends pas bien le français.*

4. *Comprenez-vous?*

5. *Quelques mots.*

6. *Voulez-vous répéter, s'il vous plaît?*

7. *Comment dit-on "Thank you" en français?*

8. *Que voulez-vous dire?*

a. No. I don't speak French.

b. A few words.

c. Do you understand?

d. I don't understand French very well.

e. Write (it) down.

f. How do you write (spell) it?

g. I don't know that word.

h. How do you say "Thank you" in French?

[1] This expression can mean both "Please" (in the same sense of "Please do" or "Go ahead") and "You're welcome." Thus this expression is used both as a reply to "Thank you" and as reinforcement when offering something to someone.

9. *Comment l'écrivez-vous?*

i. What do you mean? ("What do you want to say?")

10. *Je ne connais pas ce mot.*

j. Would you please say that again?

ANSWERS

1—e; 2—a; 3—d; 4—c; 5—b; 6—j; 7—h; 8—i; 9—f; 10—g.

E. WORD STUDY

le développement	development
la joie	joy
liquide	liquid
l'obligation (*f.*)	obligation
l'occupation (*f.*)	occupation
pâle	pale
populaire	popular
solide	solid
le théâtre	theater
le voyage	voyage

LESSON 17

A. THIS AND THAT (DEMONSTRATIVE ADJECTIVES AND PRONOUNS)[1]

1. *ce* "this" or "that" (*masc.*)

ce matin	this (that) morning
ce soir	this evening; tonight
ce monsieur	this (that) gentleman

[1] See Demonstrative Adjectives and Demonstrative Pronouns in Summary of French Grammar (pages 332–333) for more information.

2. *cet* "this" or "that" (*before vowel or mute h*)

cet après-midi	this afternoon
cet argent	this (that) money
cet homme	this (that) man
cet hôtel	this (that) hotel

3. *cette* "this" or "that" (*fem.*)

cette femme	this (that) woman
cette histoire	this (that) story
cette année	this (that) year

4. *ces* "these" or "those" (*masc. and fem.*)

ces messieurs	these (those) gentlemen
ces dames	these (those) ladies

5. *ce . . . -ci* "this"

ce livre-ci	this book
cet homme-ci	this man
cet hôtel-ci	this hotel
cette année-ci	this year
cette histoire-ci	this story

6. *ce . . . -là* "that"

ce livre-là	that book
ce jour-là	that day
ce mot-là	that word
cet homme-là	that man
cet hôtel-là	that hotel
cette année-là	that year
cette histoire-là	that story

7. *celui, celle* "this one," "that one," "the one"

Je préfère celui-ci.	I prefer this one (*masc.*).
Je préfère celle-ci.	I prefer this one (*fem.*).
Je préfère celui-là.	I prefer that one (*masc.*).
Je préfère celle-là.	I prefer that one (*fem.*).
Montrez-moi celui que vous préférez.	Show me the one that you prefer.
Montrez-moi celle de Marc.	Show me (the one that is) Mark's.

8. *ceux, celles* "these," "those," "the ones"

Je préfère ceux-ci.	I prefer these (*masc.*).
Je préfère celles-ci.	I prefer these (*fem.*).
Je préfère ceux-là.	I prefer those (*masc.*).
Je préfère celles-là.	I prefer those (*fem.*).
J'achète celles qui ne sont pas chères.	I buy the ones (those) that aren't expensive.
J'achète ceux de Paris.	I buy the ones (those) from Paris.

9. *ceci* "this"

Que veut dire ceci?	What does this mean?
Ceci est à moi.	This is mine.

10. *cela* "that"

C'est cela.	That's it. It's that.
Ne pensez pas à cela.	Don't think about that.
Cela va sans dire.	That goes without saying.

Ceci est à moi, cela est à vous.	This one is mine; that one is yours.
Qu'est-ce que cela veut dire?	What does that mean?

11. *ça* "that"

Ça is short for *cela* and has the same meaning. Ça is the form used in ordinary conversation; *cela* is more formal.

C'est ça.	It's that. That's it.
C'est bien ça.	That's quite right. Yes, that's right. I thought so.
Où ça?	Where? Where is that?
Ce n'est pas ça.	It isn't that. That's not it.
Ça va?	How are you? How are things?
Ce n'est pas du tout ça.	It's not that at all.
Comme ça?	Like that?
Pas comme ça.	Not like that.
Donnez-moi ça.	Give me that.
Je n'aime pas ça.	I don't like that.
Ça m'est égal.	It's the same to me.
Ça me plaît.	I like this (that).
Ça dépend.	That depends.
Comment ça va?	How are things? Are things going well with you? Are you getting along all right?
Ça ne fait rien.	That doesn't matter. Never mind. Don't bother.

QUIZ 8

1. *Je préfère celui-là.*	a. What does this mean?
2. *Que veut dire ceci?*	b. This is mine.
3. *Donnez-moi ça.*	c. That goes without saying.
4. *Ça dépend.*	d. This one is mine, that one is yours.
5. *Ça m'est égal.*	e. It's not that at all.
6. *Ce n'est pas du tout ça.*	f. Give me that.
7. *Ça va?*	g. It's the same to me.
8. *Cela va sans dire.*	h. That depends.
9. *Ceci est à moi, cela est à vous.*	i. How are you? How are things?
10. *Ceci est à moi.*	j. I prefer that one (*masc.*).

ANSWERS

1—j; 2—a; 3—f; 4—h; 5—g; 6—e; 7—i; 8—c; 9—d; 10—b.

B. Not, Nothing, Never

Ce n'est pas bon.	It's not good.
Ce n'est pas mal.	It's not bad.
Ce n'est pas ça.	It's not that.
Ce n'est pas ici.	It's not here.
Pas trop.	Not too much.
Pas trop vite.	Not too fast.
Pas beaucoup.	Not much.
Pas assez.	Not enough.

Pas souvent.	Not often.
Pas encore.	Not yet.
Pas du tout.	Not at all.
Je ne sais pas comment.	I don't know how.
Je ne sais pas quand.	I don't know when.
Je ne sais pas où.	I don't know where.
Rien.	Nothing, anything.
Je ne sais rien.	I don't know anything.
Il n'a rien dit.	He didn't say (hasn't said) anything.
Rien du tout.	Nothing at all.
Je n'ai rien.	I haven't anything.
Jamais.	Never.
Je ne le vois jamais.	I never see him.
Il ne vient jamais.	He never comes.
Qui est venu? —Personne.	Who came? —Nobody.
Je ne vois personne.	I don't see anyone.
Je n'y vais plus.	I don't go there anymore.
Il ne vient plus.	He doesn't come anymore.
Je n'ai que cent francs.	I have only a hundred francs.
Vous n'avez qu'une heure.	You have only one hour.
Il n'en a que dix.	He has only ten of them.

C. ISN'T IT? AREN'T YOU? ETC.

N'est-ce pas?	Isn't it?
C'est vrai, n'est-ce pas?	It's true, isn't it?

Vous êtes d'accord, n'est-ce pas?	You agree, don't you?
Vous venez, n'est-ce pas?	You're coming, aren't you?
Vous en avez assez, n'est-ce pas?	You have enough of it, haven't you?
Vous n'en avez pas, n'est-ce pas?	You haven't any of it, have you?

QUIZ 9

1. *Ce n'est pas ça.*	a. I don't see anyone.
2. *Je ne sais pas quand.*	b. I have only eighteen euros.
3. *Rien du tout.*	c. You have only one hour.
4. *Vous venez, n'est-ce-pas?*	d. You're coming, aren't you?
5. *Vous n'avez qu'une heure.*	e. You haven't any of it, have you?
6. *Je ne vois per-sonne.*	f. It's not that.
7. *Je n'ai que dix-huit euros.*	g. I don't know when.
8. *Vous n'en avez pas, n'est-ce pas?*	h. He didn't say (hasn't said) any-thing.
9. *Il n'a rien dit.*	i. Nothing at all.

ANSWERS
1—f; 2—g; 3—i; 4—d; 5—c; 6—a; 7—b; 8—e; 9—h

D. WORD STUDY

l'armée (*f.*)	army
la barrière	barrier

le caractère	character
curieux	curious
la curiosité	curiosity
le degré	degree
le dictionnaire	dictionary
l'officiel (*m.*)	official
ordinaire	ordinary
la pitié	pity

LESSON 18

A. IT'S ME (I), ETC. (DISJUNCTIVE PRONOUNS I)

C'est moi.	It's me (I).
C'est toi.	It's you (*fam.*).
C'est lui.	It's him (he).
C'est elle.	It's her (she).
C'est nous.	It's us (we).
C'est vous.	It's you (*pl.* or *pol. sing.* or *pl.*).
Ce sont eux.	It's them (they) (*masc.*).
Ce sont elles.	It's them (they) (*fem.*).

Disjunctive (or stressed) pronouns are most often used to show emphasis. They are also used for compound subjects or objects.

Moi, je ne veux rien.	Me, I don't want anything.
Qu'est-ce que tu fais, toi?!	What on earth are you doing?!
Il vous voit, toi et lui.	He sees you, you and him.
Lui, il n'a rien!	*He* has nothing, that one!

B. MINE, ETC. (POSSESSIVE PRONOUNS)

1. Study these forms of possessive pronouns:

SINGULAR

MASCULINE	FEMININE	
le mien	la mienne	mine
le tien	la tienne	yours
le sien	la sienne	his, hers, its
le nôtre	la nôtre	ours
le vôtre	la vôtre	yours
le leur	la leur	theirs

PLURAL

les miens	les miennes	mine
les tiens	les tiennes	yours
les siens	les siennes	his, hers, its
les nôtres	les nôtres	ours
les vôtres	les vôtres	yours
les leurs	les leurs	theirs

C'est le mien.	It's mine.
C'est le nôtre.	It's ours.
C'est le leur.	It's theirs.
C'est la sienne.	It's his (hers).
Mes amis et les vôtres.	My friends and yours.
Votre livre est meilleur que le sien.	Your book is better than his (hers).
Votre place est bonne, mais la leur est meilleure.	Your seat is good but theirs is better.

2. Here's another way to say "It's mine, yours, his," etc., using *ce* + *être* + disjunctive pronoun:

C'est à moi.	It's mine ("It's to me").
C'est à toi.	It's yours (*fam.*).
C'est à lui.	It's his.
C'est à elle.	It's hers.
C'est à nous.	It's ours.
C'est à vous.	It's yours (*pl.* or *pol. sing.* or *pl.*).
C'est à eux.	It's theirs (*masc.*).
C'est à elles.	It's theirs (*fem.*).

C. To/For/About Me, etc. (Disjunctive Pronouns II)

Il parle de toi.	He's talking about you.
Il parle de moi.	He's talking about me.
Il parle de lui.	He's talking about him.
Il chante pour elle.	He's singing for her.
Il le fait pour nous.	He's doing it for us.
Il pense à vous.	He's thinking about you.
Il le fait pour eux.	He's doing it for them.

D. Me, etc./To Me, etc. (Direct and Indirect Object Pronouns)

1. Direct object pronouns represent the persons or objects receiving the action of the verb.

Il me voit.	He sees me.
Il te voit.	He sees you.
Il le voit.	He sees him/it.
Il la voit.	He sees her/it.
Il nous voit.	He sees us.

Il vous voit.	He sees you.
Il les voit.	He sees them.

2. He understands me, etc.

Il me comprend.	He understands me.
Elle la comprend.	She understands it/her.
Je vous comprends.	I understand you.
Tu nous comprends.	You understand us.

3. Indirect object pronouns receive the action of the verb indirectly and are usually represented in English as "to him, to her, to me," etc.

Il me parle.	He speaks to me.
Il te parle.	He speaks to you.
Il lui parle.	He speaks to him/her.
Il nous parle.	He speaks to us.
Il vous parle.	He speaks to you.
Il leur parle.	He speaks to them.
	(*masc.* and *fem.*).

4. When there are both direct and indirect object pronouns in a statement, remember that:[1]

me, te, se } come before   le, la } before   lui
nous, vous   les   leur

For example: He gives it to me, etc.

Il me le donne.	He gives it to me.
Il te le donne.	He gives it to you.

[1] See page 336 of the Summary of French Grammar, Position of Pronouns.

Il le lui donne.	He gives it to him, her, (it).
Il nous le donne.	He gives it to us.
Il le leur donne.	He gives it to them (*masc.* and *fem.*).

5. Both pronouns follow the verb in affirmative commands, and *moi* and *toi* are used instead of *me* and *te*. Note that in affirmative commands, the direct object pronouns precede the indirect, as indicated above. For example: Give it to me, etc.

Donnez-le-moi.	Give it to me.
Donnez-le-lui.	Give it to him/her.
Donnez-le-nous.	Give it to us.
Donnez-le-leur.	Give it to them (*masc.* and *fem.*).
Donnez ça.	Give it! Give this/that.
Montrez-moi ça.	Show it to me.
Montrez-lui ça.	Show it to him/her.
Montrez-nous ça.	Show it to us.
Montrez-leur ça.	Show it to them (*masc.* and *fem.*).

6. In negative commands, the word order from item 4, above, is preserved:

Ne me le donnez pas.	Don't give it to me.
Ne le lui montrez pas.	Don't show it to him/her.

E. MYSELF, ETC. (REFLEXIVE PRONOUNS)

1. I wash myself, etc.

Je me lave.	I wash myself. I'm washing myself. (I get washed. I'm getting washed.)

Tu te laves.	You wash yourself.
Il se lave.	He washes himself.
Elle se lave.	She washes herself.
On se lave.	One washes oneself.
Nous nous lavons.	We wash ourselves.
Vous vous lavez.	You wash yourselves.
Ils se lavent.	They wash themselves.
Elles se lavent.	They wash themselves.

Notice that "myself, yourself," etc., is *me, te,* etc. Verbs that take *me, te,* etc., are called "reflexive verbs." Many verbs that do not take "myself, yourself," etc., in English do so in French:

Je me lève.	I get up (from bed; I raise myself).
Je me rappelle.	I recall.
Je me sers . . .	I use . . .
Je m'arrête.	I stop.
Je me trompe.	I'm mistaken. I'm wrong.
Je me tourne.	I turn around.
Je m'amuse.	I'm having a good time.
Je m'ennuie.	I'm bored.

2. Get washed!

Below are the imperative (command) forms of some of the reflexive verbs above. Note that the reflexive pronoun *te* changes to *toi* in the imperative.

Lavez-vous!	Wash yourself! Get washed!

Lave-toi!   Wash yourself! Get
                                 washed!

Lavons-nous!   Let's get washed!
Amusez-vous!   Have a good time!
Lève-toi!   Get up!

3. Other examples:

Il se peigne.   He's combing his hair
                                 ("himself").

Je me suis acheté un   I bought myself a hat.
chapeau.
Où se lave-t-on les   Where can one wash
mains?   one's hands?
Je me sers de ça.   I'm using that.

QUIZ 10

1. *Donnez-leur ça.*   a. I'm using that.
2. *Il parle de lui.*   b. I bought myself a
                                    hat.
3. *Ils parlent d'eux.*   c. My friends and
                                    yours.
4. *Il le leur donne.*   d. He washes himself.
5. *Mes amis et les*   e. I recall.
   vôtres.
6. *Je m'amuse.*   f. He gives it to them
                                    (*masc.* and *fem.*).
7. *Je me rappelle.*   g. I'm having a good
                                    time.
8. *Je me suis acheté*   h. He's talking about
   un chapeau.   him.

9. *Il se lave.*   i. Give it to them
                                       (*masc.* and *fem.*).

10. *Je me sers de ça.*   j. They're talking
                                       about them.

ANSWERS
1—i; 2—h; 3—j; 4—f; 5—c; 6—g; 7—e; 8—b; 9—d;
10—a.

F. WORD STUDY

absolu	absolute
l'aspect (*m.*)	aspect
la barre	bar
certain	certain
la combinaison	combination
le danger	danger
l'échange (*m.*)	exchange
la manière	manner

SUPPLEMENTAL VOCABULARY 5:
   THE HUMAN BODY

the human body	*le corps humain*
head	*la tête*
face	*le visage*
forehead	*le front*
eye	*l'oeil (m.) (pl: les yeux)*
eyebrow	*le sourcil*
eyelashes	*le cil, les cils*
ear	*l'oreille (f.)*
nose	*le nez*
mouth	*la bouche*
tooth	*la dent*
tongue	*la langue*

cheek	*la joue*
chin	*le menton*
hair	*les cheveux*
neck	*le cou*
chest	*la poitrine*
breast	*la poitrine, les seins*
shoulders	*les épaules (m.)*
arm	*le bras*
elbow	*le coude*
wrist	*le poignet*
hand	*la main*
finger	*le doigt*
stomach/abdomen	*l' estomac*
liver	*le foie*
penis	*le pénis*
vagina	*le vagin*
backside, bottom	*les fesses*
leg	*la jambe*
knee	*le genou, les genoux*
ankle	*la cheville*
foot	*le pied*
finger	*le doigt*
toe	*l' orteil (m.), le doigt de pied*
skin	*la peau*
blood	*le sang*
brain	*le cerveau*
heart	*le coeur*
lungs	*les poumons (m.)*
bone	*l' os (m.)*
muscle	*le muscle*
tendon	*le tendon*

LESSON 19

A. HELLO, HOW ARE YOU?

Bonjour.
Hello. Good morning. Good afternoon.

Bonjour, Monsieur Dupont.
Hello, Mr. Dupont. Good morning (afternoon), Mr. Dupont.

Salut.
Hi (*fam.*).

Comment allez-vous?
How are you? How do you do?

{ **Je vais bien, merci.**
{ **Très bien, merci.**
Very well, thanks.

Keep in mind that *Comment allez-vous?* is the formal way of saying "How are you?" The more familiar way is *Comment vas-tu?*, *Comment ça va?* or *Ça va?*

Comment ça va?
How are you? How's it going?

Comme ci, comme ça.
So, so.

Et vous?
And how are you? ("And you?")

Et toi?
And you?

Pas mal.
Not too bad.

Pas mal, merci.
Not too bad, thanks.

Pas mal du tout.
Not too bad. ("Not bad at all.")

Ça va?
How are you? How are things going?

Oui, ça va.
All right. Fine. ("Yes, it goes.")

Oui, ça va bien.
All right. Fine. ("Yes, it goes well.")

B. HOW ARE THINGS?

Ça va?
How's it going?

Ça va bien, merci.
Fine, thanks.

Et vous?
How are you? ("And you?")

Comme ci, comme ça.
So, so.

Alors, quelles nouvelles?
Well, what's new?

Quoi de neuf?
What's new?

{ **Rien de neuf.**
{ **Rien de nouveau.**
Nothing much. ("Nothing new.")

Téléphonez-moi un de ces jours.
Phone me one of these days.

C. GOOD-BYE!

À la prochaine (fois).
See you soon. ("Until the next [time].")

À bientôt.
See you soon.

À tout à l'heure.
See you soon. See you in a little while.

À lundi.
Till Monday. See you Monday.

À plus tard.
See you later. ("Until later.")

À demain.
Till tomorrow. See you tomorrow.

Je vous verrai dans huit jours.
I'll see you in a week ("in eight days").

Je vous verrai dans quinze jours.
I'll see you in two weeks ("in fifteen days").

Je vous verrai jeudi prochain.
I'll see you next Thursday.

Je vous verrai jeudi prochain à huit heures du soir.
I'll see you next Thursday at eight o'clock (in the evening).

Je vous verrai ce soir.
I'll see you this evening (tonight).

QUIZ 11

1. *Ça va?*
2. *Comme ci, comme ça.*
3. *À demain.*
4. *Salut! Quoi de neuf?*
5. *Alors, quelles nouvelles?*
6. *Je vais bien, merci.*
7. *Rien de nouveau.*
8. *Bonjour.*
9. *Pas mal du tout.*
10. *Comment allez-vous?*
11. *À tout à l'heure.*
12. *Téléphonez-moi un de ces jours.*
13. *À la prochaine.*
14. *Je vous verrai jeudi prochain.*
15. *À lundi.*

a. How are you? How do you do?
b. Very well, thanks.
c. Not too bad. ("Not bad at all.")
d. How are you? How are things? ("It goes?")
e. So, so.
f. See you tomorrow.
g. Hi! What's new?

h. Well, what's new?
i. Good morning. Good afternoon. Hello.
j. Nothing much. ("Nothing new.")
k. I'll see you next Thursday.
l. Phone me one of these days.
m. See you Monday. ("Until Monday.")
n. See you soon. ("Until the next [time].")
o. See you soon. See you in a little while.

ANSWERS
1—d; 2—e; 3—f; 4—g; 5—h; 6—b; 7—j; 8—i; 9—c;
10—a; 11—o; 12—l; 13—n; 14—k; 15—m.

LESSON 20

A. HAVE YOU TWO MET?

Est-ce que vous connaissez mon ami?
Do you know my friend?

Non, je ne pense pas.
No, I don't think so.

Non, je n'ai pas eu[1] ce plaisir.
No, I haven't had the pleasure.

Vous vous connaissez déjà, je crois?
I believe you already know one another.

Oui, nous nous sommes déjà rencontrés.
Yes, we've already met.

---

[1] *eu* (pronounced as though written *u*) is a form of *avoir; j'ai eu* "I have had."

Non, je ne connais pas monsieur.
No, I don't believe we've met before. ("No, I don't
know the gentleman.")

J'ai déjà eu le plaisir de rencontrer monsieur.
I've already had the pleasure of meeting him ("of
meeting the gentleman").

Bien sûr!
Of course!

Oui, j'ai déjà fait sa connaissance.
Yes, I've already met him/her.

B. I'D LIKE YOU TO MEET . . .

Je vous présente Madame Dupont.
Let me introduce ("to you") Mrs. Dupont.

Permettez-moi de vous présenter Monsieur Dupont.
Allow me to present ("to you") Mr. Dupont.

Je suis heureux de faire votre connaissance.
Nice to meet you. ("I am happy to make your acquaintance.")

Je suis heureuse de faire votre connaissance.[1]
Nice to meet you.

Et voici Monsieur Dupont.
This is Mr. Dupont. ("And here is . . .")

Très heureux, Monsieur!
Nice to meet you.

---

[1] In this case, a female is speaking so she says *heureuse,* the feminine form of the adjective *heureux.* See Feminine of Adjectives in Summary of French Grammar (page 324) for more information.

{Enchanté d'avoir fait votre connaissance.
{Enchanté de vous avoir rencontré.
Nice to have met you (*pol.*).

Enchanté.[1]
Nice to meet you.

Marie, je te présente mon copain Paul.
Marie, let me introduce to you my friend Paul.

Enchantée, Paul!
Nice to meet you, Paul.

C. MY ADDRESS AND TELEPHONE NUMBER ARE . . .

Vous avez mon adresse et mon numéro de téléphone?
Do you have my address and telephone number?

Non, donnez-les moi, s'il vous plaît.
No, let me have them, please. ("Give them to me.")

Mon adresse est quinze (15) Avenue de la Grande Armée.
My address is 15 Grand Army Avenue.

Mon numéro de téléphone est le zéro un, quarante-sept, vingt-trois, cinquante-quatre, cinquante-deux (01-47-23-54-52).[2]
My telephone number is 01-47-23-54-52.

---

[1] *Enchanté* alone (or *Enchantée* for a female speaker) is more colloquial.
[2] Notice that telephone numbers in Paris start with 01. 01-45-28-36-42 is read zero one, forty-five, twenty-eight, thirty-six, forty-two. Cell phones start with 06, and other areas of the country have phone numbers that start with 02, 03, 04, or 05. 08 is for free numbers, similar to 1-800 in the U.S.

Donnez-moi aussi l'adresse de votre bureau.
Give me your office address also.

Je vais[1] vous l'écrire; c'est le cent deux (102) Avenue des Champs-Elysées.
I'll write it for you. It's 102 Champs-Elysées Avenue.

Vous pouvez m'appeler à la maison le matin avant neuf heures.
You can get me at home before nine in the morning.

Ensuite au bureau.
Otherwise ("afterward") at the office.

Entendu.
Good, I'll do that.

Au revoir et n'oubliez pas de me donner un coup de fil.
Good-bye and don't forget to give me a ring.

Donnez-moi un coup de fil!
Give me a ring!

Non, je n'oublierai pas. À bientôt.
No, I won't forget. See you soon.

QUIZ 12

1. *Non, je ne pense pas.*
2. *Oui, nous nous sommes déjà rencontrés.*
3. *Non, donnez-les moi.*
4. *Donne-moi un coup de fil!*

---

[1] *Je vais* "I'm going" is from *aller* "to go" (see page 133).

5. *À bientôt.*
6. *Entendu, je n'y manquerai pas.*
7. *Vous avez mon adresse et mon numéro de téléphone?*
8. *Non, je n'ai pas eu ce plaisir.*
9. *J'espère vous revoir bientôt.*
10. *Enchanté d'avoir fait votre connaissance.*

a. Yes, we've already met.
b. No, I haven't had the pleasure.
c. No, I don't think so.
d. Glad to have met you.
e. I hope to see you soon.
f. Give me a ring!
g. No, let me have them. ("Give them to me.")
h. Do you have my address and telephone number?
i. Good, I'll do that.
j. "See you soon."

ANSWERS
1—c; 2—a; 3—g; 4—f; 5—j; 6—i; 7—h; 8—b; 9—e; 10—d.

REVIEW QUIZ 2

1. *Voulez-vous* ———(speak) *moins vite, s'il vous plaît.*
   a. *dire*
   b. *parler*
   c. *répéter*
2. *Parlez plus* ———(slowly), *s'il vous plaît.*
   a. *vite*
   b. *moins*
   c. *lentement*

3. *Je donne* ——— (the) *livre à l'enfant.*
    a. *un*
    b. *le*
    c. *la*

4. *Il donne* ——— (a) *lettre à une femme.*
    a. *une*
    b. *la*
    c. *les*

5. *Ce n'est pas bien* ——— (far).
    a. *loin*
    b. *ici*
    c. *là*

6. *Il donne de l'argent* ——— (to the) *pauvres.*
    a. *à*
    b. *aux*
    c. *je*

7. *Je* ——— (am) *dans la chambre.*
    a. *a*
    b. *suis*
    c. *pas*

8. *Il n'est pas* ——— (late).
    a. *suis*
    b. *vous*
    c. *tard*

9. *Où* ——— (are) *vos livres?*
    a. *ses*
    b. *sont*
    c. *est*

10. ——— (bring)-*moi un verre.*
    a. *voudrais*
    b. *donnez*
    c. *apportez*

11. *C'est* ——— (less) *difficile.*
    a. *moins*
    b. *plus*
    c. *rien*

12. *C'est* ——— (for) *les enfants.*
    a. *vous*
    b. *pour*
    c. *par*

13. *Je n'* ——— (have) *pas d'argent.*
    a. *ai*
    b. *ont*
    c. *rien*

14. *Est-ce que vous* ——— (have) *des cigarettes?*
    a. *a*
    b. *avons*
    c. *avez*

15. *Je ne* ——— (understand) *pas bien le français.*
    a. *comprends*
    b. *parle*
    c. *plaît*

16. *Je vous en* ——— (thank) *beaucoup.*
    a. *lentement*
    b. *remercie*
    c. *comprends*

17. *Est-il* ——— (here)?
    a. *où*
    b. *que*
    c. *ici*

18. *Sont-ils* ——— (ready)?
    a. *vrai*
    b. *prêts*
    c. *ici*

19. *Est-ce que c'est* ——— (true)?
    a. *prêt*
    b. *vrai*
    c. *où*

20. *Je comprends un* ——— (little).
    a. *seulement*
    b. *très*
    c. *peu*

ANSWERS
1—b; 2—c; 3—b; 4—a; 5—a; 6—b; 7—b; 8—c;
9—b; 10—c; 11—a; 12—b; 13—a; 14—c; 15—a;
16—b; 17—c; 18—b; 19—b; 20—c.

D. WORD STUDY

la conclusion	conclusion
la condition	condition
la considération	consideration
la décision	decision
la personne	person
la saison	season
la scène	scene
le signal	signal

LESSON 21

A. NUMBERS

1. One, two, three, etc.

un (*une*)	one
deux	two
trois	three
quatre	four
cinq	five
six	six
sept	seven
huit	eight
neuf	nine
dix	ten
onze	eleven
douze	twelve

treize	thirteen
quatorze	fourteen
quinze	fifteen
seize	sixteen
dix-sept	seventeen
dix-huit	eighteen
dix-neuf	nineteen
vingt	twenty
vingt et un	twenty-one
vingt-deux	twenty-two
vingt-trois	twenty-three
trente	thirty
trente et un	thirty-one
trente-deux	thirty-two
trente-trois	thirty-three
quarante	forty
quarante et un	forty-one
quarante-deux	forty-two
quarante-trois	forty-three
cinquante	fifty
cinquante et un	fifty-one
cinquante-deux	fifty-two
cinquante-trois	fifty-three
soixante	sixty
soixante et un	sixty-one
soixante-deux	sixty-two
soixante-trois	sixty-three
soixante-dix	seventy
soixante et onze	seventy-one (sixty and eleven)

soixante-douze	seventy-two (sixty and twelve)
soixante-treize	seventy-three (sixty and thirteen)
quatre-vingts	eighty (four twenties)
quatre-vingt-un	eighty-one
quatre-vingt-deux	eighty-two
quatre-vingt-trois	eighty-three
quatre-vingt-dix	ninety
quatre-vingt-onze	ninety-one
quatre-vingt-douze	ninety-two
quatre-vingt-treize	ninety-three

2. One hundred, one thousand, etc.

cent	hundred
cent un	a hundred one
cent deux	a hundred two
cent trois	a hundred three
cent vingt	a hundred twenty
cent vingt-deux	a hundred twenty-two
cent trente	a hundred thirty
cent quarante	a hundred forty
cent cinquante	a hundred fifty
cent soixante	a hundred sixty
cent soixante-dix	a hundred seventy
cent soixante et onze	a hundred seventy-one
cent soixante-dix-huit	a hundred seventy-eight
cent quatre-vingt	a hundred eighty
cent quatre-vingt-deux	a hundred eighty-two
cent quatre-vingt-dix	a hundred ninety
cent quatre-vingt-dix-huit	a hundred ninety-eight

cent quatre-vingt-dix-neuf	a hundred ninety-nine
deux cents	two hundred
trois cent vingt-quatre	three hundred twenty-four
huit cent soixante-quinze	eight hundred seventy-five
mille[1]	thousand
mille un	a thousand one
mille deux	a thousand two
mille trois	a thousand three

B. MORE NUMBERS

1. The pronunciation of the numbers often differs before words beginning with a vowel or mute *h*. Compare the following columns—the first containing nouns beginning with a consonant; the second, nouns beginning with a vowel or mute *h*, noting especially five, six, eight, and ten.

BEGINNING WITH A CONSONANT	BEGINNING WITH A VOWEL OR H
1. **un fils**	**un homme**
a son	a man
2. **deux jeunes filles**	**deux heures**
two young girls	two hours
3. **trois jours**	**trois enfants**
three days	three children
4. **quatre garçons**	**quatre étages**
four boys	four floors

[1] *Mille* used to be written *mil* in dates; *mil neuf cent douze*—1912. It frequently appears this way on monuments.

5. **cinq mètres** **cinq ans**
   five meters five years
6. **six kilomètres** **six autres**
   six kilometers six others
7. **sept chiens** **sept hôtels**
   seven dogs seven hotels
8. **huit semaines** **huit heures**
   eight weeks eight hours
9. **neuf mois** **neuf ans**
   nine months nine years
10. **dix leçons** **dix ans**
    ten lessons ten years
11. **vingt minutes** **vingt hommes**
    twenty minutes twenty men
12. **cent livres** **cent ans**
    a hundred books a hundred years

2. First, Second, Third

premier (première)	first
deuxième	second
troisième	third
quatrième	fourth
cinquième	fifth
sixième	sixth
septième	seventh
huitième	eighth
neuvième	ninth
dixième	tenth

le premier livre	the first book
la première chose	the first thing
le deuxième acte or *le second acte*	the second act
la troisième classe	the third class

le quatrième étage	the fourth floor
la cinquième leçon	the fifth lesson
le sixième jour	the sixth day
la septième semaine	the seventh week
le huitième mois	the eighth month
la neuvième année	the ninth year
la dixième lettre	the tenth letter
la onzième personne	the eleventh person
le douzième chapitre	the twelfth chapter
le treizième invité	the thirteenth guest
le quatorzième paquet	the fourteenth package
la quinzième porte	the fifteenth door
le seizième bateau	the sixteenth boat
la dix-septième rue	the seventeenth street
la dix-huitième édition	the eighteenth edition
la dix-neuvième auto	the nineteenth car
la vingtième maison	the twentieth house

3. Two and Two

Deux et un font trois.
Two and one are ("make") three.

Or

Deux plus un font trois.
Two and ("plus") one are three.

Deux et deux font quatre.
Two and two are four.

Or

Deux plus deux font quatre.
Two and ("plus") two are four.

Quatre et trois font sept.
Four and three are seven.

Or

Quatre plus trois font sept.
Four and ("plus") three are seven.

Cinq et deux font sept.
Five and two are seven.

Or

Cinq plus deux font sept.
Five and ("plus") two are seven.

Sept et un font huit.
Seven and one are eight.

Or

Sept plus un font huit.
Seven and ("plus") one are eight.

QUIZ 13

1. *six kilomètres*	a. the third class
2. *deux jeunes filles*	b. the eighth month
3. *vingt minutes*	c. the ninth year
4. *la troisième classe*	d. six kilometers
5. *dix-neuvième*	e. two young girls
6. *la onzième per-sonne*	f. twenty minutes
7. *dix-septième*	g. the eleventh person
8. *le huitième mois*	h. thirteenth

9. *treizième*   i. seventeenth
10. *la neuvième année*   j. nineteenth

ANSWERS
1—d; 2—e; 3—f; 4—a; 5—j; 6—g; 7—i; 8—b; 9—h;
10—c.

LESSON 22

A.   IT COSTS . . .

Ceci coûte . . .
This costs . . .

Ceci coûte vingt-cinq euros.
This costs twenty-five euros.

Ce livre coûte sept euros cinquante.
This book costs seven euros fifty (cents).

Ce chapeau m'a coûté trente-neuf euros.
This hat cost me thirty-nine euros.

J'ai payé cent euros pour cette robe.
I paid a hundred euros for this dress.

J'ai acheté cette voiture pour quinze mille euros.
I bought this car for fifteen thousand euros.

C'est deux euros le litre.
It's two euros a liter.

Cela coûte six euros le mètre.
That costs six euros a meter.

Son prix est de deux cent soixante-quinze euros.
The price is two hundred seventy-five euros.
It costs two hundred seventy-five euros.

Ils coûtent vingt-cinq cents la pièce.
They cost twenty-five cents apiece.

B.   THE TELEPHONE NUMBER IS . . .

Mon numéro de téléphone est le zéro un quarante-cinq, vingt-six, trente-six, quarante-deux.
My telephone number is 01-45-26-36-42.

Essayez donc son numéro de portable—zéro six quarante-deux, quarante-six, cinquante-deux, trente-six.
Try her cell number—06-42-46-52-36.

Mon numéro de téléphone a changé: c'est maintenant le zéro quatre, quarante-sept, soixante-deux, vingt-deux, vingt-quatre.
My telephone number has changed: It's now 04-47-62-22-24.

Leur numéro de téléphone est le zéro cinq quarante-trois, vingt-neuf, trente-trois, zéro sept.
Their phone number is 05-43-29-33-07.

C.   MY ADDRESS IS . . .

J'habite vingt-deux rue Voltaire.
I live at 22 rue Voltaire.

J'habite au numéro dix-sept de la rue Balzac.[1]
I live at 17 Balzac Street.

[1] Note that *à* (*au, à l'*) may be omitted when using the verb *habiter* to live (at, in): *J'habite numéro dix-sept.*

Il habite au numéro quatre du Boulevard Haussmann.
He lives at 4 Haussmann Boulevard.

Notre adresse est onze, rue de Nice.
Our address is 11 Nice Street.

Nous habitons (au) deux cent soixante-trois Avenue de Versailles.
We live at 263 Versailles Avenue.

D. SOME DATES

La France a été libérée en mille neuf cent quarante-quatre.
France was liberated in 1944.

Je suis né(e) en mille neuf cent soixante-quinze.
I was born in 1975.

Marie a étudié à Paris en mille neuf cent quatre-vingt-quatorze.
Marie studied in Paris in 1994.

Les jeux olympiques ont eu lieu à Athènes en deux mille quatre.
The Olympic Games took place in Athens in 2004.

Nous sommes allé(e)s au Québec en deux mille cinq.
We went to Quebec in 2005.

QUIZ 14

1. *Ceci coûte quatre-vingt euros.*
2. *Leur numéro de téléphone est zéro un, quarante-trois, vingt-neuf, trente-trois, zéro sept.*

3. *J'ai acheté cette voiture pour quinze mille euros.*
4. *J'étais à Paris en dix-neuf cent quatre-vingt-dix.*
5. *Ils coûtent vingt-cinq cents la pièce.*

a. This costs eighty euros.
b. I bought this car for fifteen thousand euros.
c. Their phone number is 01-43-29-33-07.
d. They cost twenty-five cents apiece.
e. I was in Paris in 1990.

ANSWERS
1—a; 2—c; 3—b; 4—e; 5—d.

E. WORD STUDY

l'avance (*f.*)	advance
la banque	bank
le chapitre	chapter
content	content, happy
délicieux	delicious
l'ennemi (*m.*)	enemy
le fruit	fruit
le million	million
le péril	peril
riche	rich

LESSON 23

A. What Time Is It?

When you want to specify whether you mean
"seven A.M." or "P.M." you say *sept heures du matin*
("seven hours of the morning") or *sept heures du soir*
("seven hours of the evening"). Official time
(announcements of meeting or events, timetables, etc.)
on a twenty-four-hour basis, like our military time, is
very common, too. Thus you may see *dix-sept heures
trente* for 5:30 P.M. However, *cinq heures et demie de
l'après-midi* is also possible.

Quelle heure est-il?
What time is it?

Avez-vous l'heure, s'il vous plaît?
Do you have the time, please?

Il est une heure.
It's one o'clock.

Il est deux heures.
It's two o'clock.

Il est trois heures.
It's three o'clock.

Il est quatre heures.
It's four o'clock.

Il est cinq heures.
It's five o'clock.

Il est six heures.
It's six o'clock.

Il est sept heures.
It's seven o'clock.

Il est huit heures.
It's eight o'clock.

Il est neuf heures.
It's nine o'clock.

Il est dix heures.
It's ten o'clock.

Il est onze heures.
It's eleven o'clock.

Il est midi.
It's noon. It's twelve P.M.

{ **Il est une heure de l'après-midi.**
{ **Il est treize heures.**
It's one P.M. ("thirteen o'clock").

{ **Il est deux heures de l'après-midi.**
{ **Il est quatorze heures.**
It's two P.M. ("fourteen o'clock").

{ **Il est trois heures de l'après-midi.**
{ **Il est quinze heures.**
It's three P.M. ("fifteen o'clock").

{ **Il est quatre heures de l'après-midi.**
{ **Il est seize heures.**
It's four P.M. ("sixteen o'clock").

{ **Il est cinq heures de l'après-midi.**
{ **Il est dix-sept heures.**
It's five P.M. ("seventeen o'clock").

{ **Il est six heures du soir.**
{ **Il est dix-huit heures.**
It's six P.M. ("eighteen o'clock").

{ **Il est sept heures du soir.**
{ **Il est dix-neuf heures.**
It's seven P.M. ("nineteen o'clock").

{ **Il est huit heures du soir.**
{ **Il est vingt heures.**
It's eight P.M. ("twenty o'clock").

{ **Il est neuf heures du soir.**
{ **Il est vingt et une heures.**
It's nine P.M. ("twenty-one o'clock").

{ **Il est dix heures du soir.**
{ **Il est vingt-deux heures.**
It's ten P.M. ("twenty-two o'clock").

{ **Il est onze heures du soir.**
{ **Il est vingt-trois heures.**
It's eleven P.M. ("twenty-three o'clock").

Il est minuit.
It's midnight.

Il est une heure du matin.
It's one o'clock in the morning.

Il est huit heures du matin.
It's eight o'clock in the morning.

Il est neuf heures du matin.
It's nine o'clock in the morning.

B. Time Past the Hour

seconde	second
minute	minute
heure	hour

Il est deux heures quinze.
It's two-fifteen.

Il est deux heures et quart.
It's a quarter after two.

Il est quatre heures moins le quart.
It's a quarter to four. ("It's four o'clock minus a quarter.")

Il est trois heures quarante-cinq.
It's three forty-five.

Il est deux heures et demie.
It's half past two.

Il est deux heures trente.
It's two-thirty.

Il est cinq heures moins vingt.
It's twenty to five.

Il est neuf heures trente-cinq.
It's nine thirty-five.

Il est midi moins cinq.
It's five to twelve.

Il est midi cinq.
It's five past twelve.

Il est à peu près cinq heures.
It's about five.

Il est près de sept heures.
It's about seven.

Il est presque onze heures.
It's almost eleven.

Il n'est que six heures et demie.
It's only half past six.

Il est plus de cinq heures.
It's after five.

C.   WHEN WILL YOU COME, ETC.?[1]

À quelle heure viendrez-vous?
When will you come? What time will you come?

Je serai là à quinze heures.
I'll be there at three o'clock (in the afternoon).

Elle est venue à quatorze heures quarante.
She came at twenty to three.

Il viendra à deux heures de l'après-midi.
He'll come at two P.M.

Nous serons là vers neuf heures vingt-cinq.
We'll be there about nine twenty-five.

[1] Refer to Lesson 39 to check the forms of *venir*, to come.

Je vous verrai là-bas vers huit heures et quart du matin.
I'll see you there about eight-fifteen in the morning.

Nous nous verrons à dix-huit heures.
We'll meet ("see each other") at six in the evening.

Venez entre sept et huit.
Come between seven and eight.

Venez vers dix heures ce soir.
Come at around ten o'clock tonight.

Le train arrive à sept heures vingt-trois.
The train arrives at seven twenty-three.

Le train part à neuf heures quarante.
The train leaves at nine-forty.

QUIZ 15

1. *Il est deux heures et demie.*
2. *Il est deux heures quinze. Il est deux heures et quart.*
3. *Il est neuf heures trente-cinq.*
4. *Venez entre sept et huit.*
5. *Je vous verrai là vers huit heures et quart.*
6. *Le train arrive à sept heures vingt-trois.*
7. *Venez vers dix heures ce soir.*
8. *Il est une heure du matin.*
9. *Nous serons là vers neuf heures vingt-cinq.*
10. *Il viendra à quinze heures.*

a. I'll see you there about eight-fifteen.
b. The train arrives at seven twenty-three.
c. Come between seven and eight.

d. Come at around ten o'clock tonight.
e. It's one o'clock in the morning.
f. He'll come at three P.M.
g. We'll be there about nine twenty-five.
h. It's two-fifteen. It's a quarter after two.
i. It's half past two. It's two-thirty.
j. It's nine thirty-five.

ANSWERS
1—i; 2—h; 3—j; 4—c; 5—a; 6—b; 7—d; 8—e;
9—g; 10—f.

D. WORD STUDY

l'angle (*m.*)	angle
la cause	cause
la conviction	conviction
la distance	distance
l'effet (*m.*)	effect
l'instant (*m.*)	instant
obscur (*adj.*)	obscure (*adj.*)
le propriétaire	proprietor
la qualité	quality

E. IT'S TIME

Il est temps.
It's time.

Il est temps de le faire.
It's time to do it.

Il est temps de partir.
It's time to leave.

Il est temps de rentrer.
It's time to go home.

J'ai le temps.
I have time.

J'ai assez de temps.
I have enough time.

Je n'ai pas le temps.
I haven't the time.

**Combien de temps avez-vous l'intention de
rester ici?**
How long do you intend to stay here?

**{Depuis combien de temps êtes-vous ici?
{Depuis quand êtes-vous ici?**
How long have you been here?

Il perd son temps.
He's wasting his time.

Donnez-lui le temps de le faire.
Give him time to do it.

Donnez-moi le temps de m'habiller.
Just give me enough time to get dressed.

Il vient de temps en temps.
He comes from time to time.

SUPPLEMENTAL VOCABULARY 6: TRAVEL AND TOURISM

travel and tourism	le voyage et le tourisme
tourist	le touriste, la touriste
hotel	l'hôtel (m.)
youth hostel	l'auberge (f.) de jeunesse
reception desk	la réception
to check in	s'inscrire, prendre une chambre.
to check out	régler sa note
reservation	la réservation
passport	le passeport
tour bus	le circuit en bus
guided tour	la visite guidée
camera	l'appareil (m.) photo
information center	le centre d'informations
map	la carte, le plan
brochure	la brochure
monument	le monument
to go sightseeing	aller visiter
to take a picture	prendre une photo
Can you take our picture?	Pourriez-vous nous prendre en photo, s'il vous plaît?

LESSON 24

A. MORNING, NOON, NIGHT, ETC.

le matin	morning
le midi	noon
l'après-midi	afternoon
le soir	evening

la nuit	night
le jour	the day
la semaine	the week
huit jours	a week ("eight days")
quinze jours	two weeks ("fifteen days")
le mois	month
l'année	year
hier	yesterday
aujourd'hui	today
demain	tomorrow
avant-hier	the day before yesterday
le lendemain	the next day
après-demain	the day after tomorrow
il y a un moment	a moment ago
maintenant	now
dans un moment	in a moment
il y a longtemps	a long time ago
il y a peu de temps	a little while ago
ce matin	this morning
hier matin	yesterday morning
demain matin	tomorrow morning
cet après-midi	this afternoon
hier après-midi	yesterday afternoon
demain après-midi	tomorrow afternoon
ce soir	this evening
hier soir	yesterday evening
demain soir	tomorrow evening
cette nuit	tonight
la nuit passée	last night
la nuit prochaine	tomorrow night

B. This Week, Next Month, One of These Days

{ cette semaine
{ cette semaine-ci
this week

{ la semaine passée
{ la semaine dernière
last week

la semaine prochaine
next week

dans deux semaines
in two weeks, the week after next

il y a deux semaines
two weeks ago, the week before last

{ ce mois
{ ce mois-ci
this month

{ le mois passé
{ le mois dernier
last month

le mois prochain
next month

dans deux mois
in two months, the month after next

il y a deux mois
two months ago, the month before last

cette année
this year

l'année dernière
last year

{ **l'année prochaine**
{ **l'an prochain**
next year

dans deux ans
in two years, the year after next

il y a deux ans
two years ago, the year before last

dans la matinée
in the morning

dans la soirée
in the evening

vers l'heure du déjeuner
toward lunchtime

vers l'heure du dîner
toward dinnertime

après dîner
after dinner

à la fin de la semaine
at the end of the week

à la fin du mois
at the end of the month

vers la fin de la semaine
toward the end of the week

il y a une heure
an hour ago

dans un quart d'heure
in a quarter of an hour

un de ces jours
one of these days

tous les jours
every day

toute la journée
all day (long)

toute la nuit
all night (long)

Il travaille du matin au soir.
He works from morning to night.

C. EXPRESSIONS OF PAST, PRESENT, AND FUTURE

PAST

il y a un instant	a moment ago
hier matin	yesterday morning
hier après-midi	yesterday afternoon
hier soir	yesterday evening, last night

la semaine dernière	last week
le mois dernier	last month
l'année dernière	last year
le passé	the past

PRESENT

maintenant	now
ce matin	this morning
cet après-midi	this afternoon
ce soir	this evening, tonight
cette semaine	this week
ce mois-ci	this month
cette année	this year
le présent	the present

FUTURE

dans un instant	in a moment
demain matin	tomorrow morning
demain après-midi	tomorrow afternoon
demain soir	tomorrow evening, tomorrow night
la semaine prochaine	next week
le mois prochain	next month
l'année prochaine	next year
l'avenir	the future

LESSON 25

A. WHAT DAY IS TODAY?

les jours de la semaine	the days of the week
lundi	Monday
mardi	Tuesday

mercredi	Wednesday
jeudi	Thursday
vendredi	Friday
samedi	Saturday
dimanche	Sunday

The following expressions are all used for "What's the date today?"

Quel jour est-ce aujourd'hui?
What day is today?

Quel jour sommes-nous?
"What day are we?"

Quel jour sommes-nous aujourd'hui?
"What day are we today?"

Quelle est la date d'aujourd'hui?
What's today's date?

Nous sommes le combien?
What's today's date? "We are the how many?"

Le combien sommes-nous?
What's today's date? "The how many are we?"

Le combien est-ce?
What's today's date? "The how many is it?"

Samedi, ce sera le combien?
What's the date Saturday?

Nous sommes le vingt.
Today's the twentieth.

Sommes-nous mardi ou mercredi?
Is today Tuesday or Wednesday? ("Are we Tuesday or
Wednesday?")

Nous sommes aujourd'hui mercredi.
Today's Wednesday.

C'est aujourd'hui lundi.
Today's Monday.

Venez samedi prochain.
Come next Saturday.

Il partira jeudi prochain.
He'll leave next Thursday. He's leaving next Thursday.

Il est arrivé lundi dernier.
He arrived last Monday.

Il arrivera lundi prochain.
He'll arrive next Monday. He's arriving next Monday.

QUIZ 16

1. *avant-hier*
2. *aujourd' hui*
3. *l' après-midi*
4. *il y a un instant*
5. *demain après-midi*
6. *cet après-midi*
7. *après-demain*
8. *Il perd son temps.*
9. *toute la nuit*
10. *Depuis combien de temps êtes-vous ici?*
11. *la semaine prochaine*

12. *la semaine dernière*
13. *il y a deux semaines*
14. *dans deux mois*
15. *il y a deux ans*
16. *Il est temps.*
17. *J'ai le temps.*
18. *Il est temps de rentrer.*
19. *demain soir*
20. *ce soir*

a. afternoon
b. day before yesterday
c. today
d. day after tomorrow
e. a moment ago
f. tomorrow afternoon
g. all night (long)
h. He's wasting his time.
i. this afternoon
j. How long have you been here?
k. in two months, the month after next
l. two weeks ago, the week before last
m. next week
n. two years ago, the year before last
o. last week
p. It's time to go home.
q. tomorrow night
r. tonight
s. It's time.
t. I have time.

ANSWERS
1—b; 2—c; 3—a; 4—e; 5—f; 6—i; 7—d; 8—h;
9—g; 10—j; 11—m; 12—o; 13—l; 14—k; 15—n;
16—s; 17—t; 18—p; 19—q; 20—r.

B. Months and Dates

les mois de l'année	the months of the year
janvier	January
février	February
mars	March
avril	April
mai	May
juin	June
juillet	July
août	August
septembre	September
octobre	October
novembre	November
décembre	December

C'est aujourd'hui le premier juin.
Today is the first of June.

Il est né le douze avril.
He was born (on) April 12.

Ma sœur est née le cinq mai.
My sister was born (on) May 5.

Mon anniversaire est le deux février.
My birthday is February 2.

Je viendrai le quatorze juillet.
I'll come (on) the fourteenth of July.

L'école commence le vingt septembre.
School begins (on) the twentieth of September.

Je reviendrai le vingt-deux mars.
I'll be back (on) March 22.

Le onze novembre est un jour férié.
November 11 is a holiday.

Il partira le six juillet.
He's leaving (on) July 6.

La lettre est datée du six juin.
The letter is dated June 6.

Nous viendrons vous voir le onze mai.
We'll come to see you (on) May 11.

Nous sommes le deux mai mil neuf cent quatre-vingt onze (or *dix-neuf cent quatre-vingt onze*).
Today is May 2, 1991.

C. THE SEASONS

le printemps	spring
l'été	summer
l'automne	autumn
l'hiver	winter
en hiver	in winter
en été	in summer
en automne	in autumn, in the fall
au printemps	in spring

Quelle saison préférez-vous?
Which season do you prefer?

Je préfère l'été.
I prefer summer.

QUIZ 17

1. *Quel jour sommes-nous?*
2. *un de ces jours*

3. *toute la journée*
4. *en été*
5. *dans un quart d'heure*
6. *Il arrivera lundi prochain.*
7. *C'est aujourd'hui lundi.*
8. *Venez samedi prochain.*
9. *l'hiver*
10. *dimanche*
11. *Nous sommes le vingt.*
12. *Samedi est le combien?*
13. *Je viendrai le quatorze juillet.*
14. *C'est aujourd'hui le premier juin.*
15. *La lettre est datée du six juin.*

a. Sunday
b. in a quarter of an hour
c. one of these days
d. all day (long)
e. What's today?
f. in the summer
g. winter
h. What's the date Saturday?
i. Today's the twentieth.
j. Today's Monday.
k. Come next Saturday.
l. He'll arrive next Monday. He's arriving next Monday.
m. The letter is dated June 6.
n. I'll come (on) the fourteenth of July.
o. Today is the first of June.

ANSWERS
1—e; 2—c; 3—d; 4—f; 5—b; 6—l; 7—j; 8—k; 9—g; 10—a; 11—i; 12—h; 13—n; 14—o; 15—m.

DEVANT LE KIOSQUE À JOURNAUX
(AT THE NEWSSTAND)

—*Madame, donnez-moi le Figaro, s'il vous plaît.
Mais je n'ai pas de monnaie. Avez-vous de la monnaie
sur cinq euros?*[1]

"Ma'am, give me the *Figaro,* please. But I don't have
any small change. Can you give me change for five
euros?"

—*Vous me donnerez un euro demain, dit la marchande.*
"Give me a euro tomorrow," the woman says.

—*Et si je suis écrasé ce soir?*
"But suppose I get run over tonight?"

—*Bah! Ça ne serait pas une bien grande perte!*
"So what! It wouldn't be a very great loss!"

NOTES

la monnaie coins; change ("Money" is *argent: Je n'ai
pas d'argent.* I haven't any money).

Mais but; however.

Rendre la monnaie sur cinq euros ("to give back the
change from") to change five euros.

le marchand storekeeper; *la marchande* (female)
storekeeper.

Écraser to crush, run over; *si je suis écrasé* if I get run
over.

---

[1] Notice how French punctuation in dialogue differs from English:
(1) there are no quotation marks and (2) each change of speaker is
indicated by a dash.

LESSON 26

A. To Go: *ALLER*

1. I go

je vais	I go
tu vas	you go
il va	he goes
nous allons	we go
vous allez	you go
ils vont	they go

2. I don't go

je ne vais pas	I don't go; I'm not going
tu ne vas pas	you don't go
il ne va pas	he doesn't go
nous n'allons pas	we don't go
vous n'allez pas	you don't go
ils ne vont pas	they don't go

3. Where Am I Going?

{ Où est-ce que je vais?
{ Où vais-je?
Where am I going?

Où vas-tu?
Where are you (*fam.*) going?

Où va-t-il?
Where is he going?

Où va-t-elle?
Where is she going?

Où allons-nous?
Where are we going?

Où allez-vous?
Where are you (*pl.* or *pol. sing.* or *pl.*) going?

Où vont-ils?
Where are they (*masc.*) going?

Où vont-elles?
Where are they (*fem.*) going?

4. Go!

Allez!
Go!

Va!
Go! (*fam.*)

Allez lentement.
Go slowly.

Allez là-bas.
Go (over) there.

N'y allez pas.
Don't go there.

N'allez pas là-bas.
Don't go over there.

Allez-y!
Go on ahead! Keep going!
Go on! Continue!

Vas-y!
Go on!

Allez le chercher.
Go look for it! Go get it!

Allons-y!
Let's go!

5. Study these phrases:

Où allez-vous?
Where are you going?

Il faut y aller.
We have to go there. ("It's necessary to go there.")

Je vais à l'aéroport.
I'm going to the airport.

Je vais à la banque.
I'm going to the bank.

Je vais au théâtre.
I'm going to the theater.

Il ne va pas à la campagne.
He's not going to the country.

Je vais chez Jean.
I'm going to John's place (home).

Je vais le faire.
I'm going to do it. I'll do it.

Je vais le voir.
I'm going to see it (him). I'll see it (him).

Je ne vais pas le lui dire.
I'm not going to tell him. I won't tell him.

Elle va venir.
She's going to come.

Comment allez-vous?
How are you? ("How do you go?")

Je vais bien, merci.
Well, thanks. Fine, thanks.

{ **Ça va?**
{ **Comment ça va?**
How are you? How are things?

Ça va.
Fine. All right. O.K.

B. A Few Action Phrases

Attention!
Watch out! Pay attention!

Prenez garde!
Be careful! Watch out! ("Take care!")

Vite.
Fast.

Plus vite.
Faster.

Pas si vite.
Not so fast.

Pas trop vite.
Not too fast.

Moins vite.
Slower ("less fast").

Plus lentement.
Slower.

Plus tôt.
Sooner.

Plus tard.
Later.

Dépêchez-vous.
Hurry up.

Ne vous dépêchez pas.
Don't hurry.

Je suis pressé.
I'm in a hurry.

Je ne suis pas pressé.
I'm not in a hurry.

Prenez votre temps.
Take your time.

Un instant!
Just a minute!

Dans un instant.
In a minute.

Tout à l'heure.
In a little while.

Je viens.
I'm coming.

Je viens tout de suite.
I'm coming right away.

C. Word Study

l'ambition (*f.*)	ambition
brillant	brilliant
la capitale	capital
le contact	contact
le département	department
la maman	mama
le monument	monument
l'obstacle (*m.*)	obstacle
récent	recent

LESSON 27

A. One, They, People

On.
One. They. People.

On dit que . . .
They say that . . . It's said that . . . People say that . . .

On m'a dit que . . .
I've been told that . . .

On le dit.
They say it.

On dit que c'est vrai.
They say it's true.

On m'a dit.
I've been told.

On ne sait pas.
Nobody knows.

On parle français.
French spoken.

Ici on parle anglais.
English spoken here.

Parle-t-on l'anglais ici?
Do they speak English here?

Comment dit-on cela en français?
How do you say that in French?

Comment dit-on "Good morning" en français?
How do you say "Good morning" in French?

Comment écrit-on ce mot en français?
How is this word written (spelled) in French?

On sonne à la porte.
Someone's ringing (at the door).

On ferme.
We're closing.

Qu'est-ce qu'on joue ce soir au théâtre?
What's playing at the theater tonight?

Notice that *on* can often be translated by the English passive:

On dit que . . .
It's said that . . . ("One said that")

On m'a dit que . . .
I've been told that . . . ("One told me that")

Comment écrit-on ce mot?
How is this word written? ("How does one write this word?")

QUIZ 18

1. *Je suis pressé.*
2. *Je viens tout de suite.*
3. *Tout à l'heure.*
4. *Dans un instant.*
5. *Prenez votre temps.*
6. *On sonne à la porte.*
7. *On m'a dit.*
8. *On ne sait pas.*
9. *Ici on parle anglais.*
10. *Comment dit-on cela en français?*

a. In a little while.
b. In a minute.
c. I'm in a hurry.
d. I'm coming right away.
e. Someone's ringing.
f. Take your time.
g. Nobody knows.
h. I've been told.
i. How do you say that in French?
j. English spoken here.

ANSWERS
1—c; 2—d; 3—a; 4—b; 5—f; 6—e; 7—h; 8—g; 9—j;
10—i.

B. WORD STUDY

la balle	ball
le chèque	check
civil	civil
l'éducation (*f.*)	education
l'effort (*m.*)	effort
logique	logical
l'omission (*f.*)	omission
la page	page
la table	table

C. A LITTLE AND A LOT

Peu.
A little.

Beaucoup ou peu.
A lot or a little.

Un peu.
A little.

Très peu.
Very little.

Un petit peu.
A very little.

Peu à peu.
Little by little.

C'est trop peu.
It's not enough. It's too little.

Encore un peu.
A little bit more.

Il parle peu.
He doesn't talk much.

En voulez-vous peu ou beaucoup?
Do you want a little or a lot of it?

Restons ici un peu.
Let's stay here a little.

Donnez-m'en un peu.
Give me a little of it.

Donnez-moi un peu d'eau.
Give me a little water.

Un tout petit peu.
A very little bit.

Je parle très peu le français.
I speak very little French.

Beaucoup.
Much. A lot.

Je n'ai pas beaucoup d'argent.
I don't have much money.

Je n'ai pas beaucoup de temps.
I don't have much time.

Je l'aime beaucoup.
I like/love him (her, it) a lot.

D. Too Much

Trop.
Too. Too much.

C'est trop.
It's too much.

Pas trop.
Not too much.

Trop peu.
Too little.

Trop chaud.
Too hot.

Trop froid.
Too cold.

Trop d'eau.
Too much water.

E. More or Less

Plus ou moins.
More or less.

Au plus.
At the most.

Au moins.
At the least.

De plus en plus.
More and more.

De moins en moins.
Less and less.

Six fois plus.
Six times more.

Plus tôt.
Earlier.

Plus tard.
Later.

Plus chaud.
Hotter.

Plus cher.
More expensive.

Il n'y en a plus.
There's no more of it. There's no more of it left.

C'est plus que ça.
It's more than that.

C'est le livre le plus intéressant que je connaisse.[1]
This is the most interesting book I know.

Il est plus grand que son frère.
He's taller than his brother.

---

[1] See page 353 of the Summary of French Grammar for the Subjunctive.

Elle est plus grande que moi.
She's taller than I.

Elle n'est pas plus grande que moi.
She's not taller than I am.

Elle est moins grande que moi.
She's not as tall as I (am).

Elle n'est pas aussi grande que moi.
She isn't as tall as I (am).

F. ENOUGH AND SOME MORE

Assez.
Enough.

Est-ce assez?
Is it enough?

C'est assez.
It's enough.

C'est plus qu'assez.
It's more than enough.

Ce n'est pas assez.
It's not enough.

J'en ai assez.
I have enough (of it, them).

J'en ai marre! (*fam.*)
I've had enough! ("I'm fed up with it!")

C'est assez grand.
It's large enough. It's rather large.

Assez bien.
Fairly well. Rather well.

Avez-vous assez d'argent?
Do you have enough money?

Encore.
Some more.

Encore?
Some more?

Encore un peu.
A little more. Another little bit.

Je voudrais encore un verre d'eau, s'il vous plaît.
I'd like another glass of water, please.

Encore une fois.
One more time, again.

Répétez encore une fois, s'il vous plaît.
Please repeat it.

SUPPLEMENTAL VOCABULARY 7: IN THE OFFICE

in the office	*au bureau*
office	*le bureau*
desk	*le bureau*
computer	*l'ordinateur*
telephone	*le téléphone*

fax machine	*le télécopieur*
book shelf	*l'étagère*
file	*le dossier*
boss	*le patron*
colleague	*le collègue (m.), la collègue (f.)*
employee	*l'employé (m.), l'employée (f.)*
staff	*le personnel*
company	*la société*
business	*les affaires*
factory	*l'usine*
meeting room	*la salle de conférence*
meeting	*le rendez-vous*
appointment	*le rendez-vous*
salary	*le salaire*
job	*le boulot, le travail*
busy	*occupé*
to work	*travailler*
to earn	*gagner*

LESSON 28

A. GOOD

C'est bon.
It's good (said of food, etc.).

C'est très bon.
It's very good.

Ce n'est pas bon.
It's not good.

Ce vin est bon.
This wine is good.

Cette viande est bonne.
This meat is good.

C'est une bonne idée!
That's a good idea!

Quelles bonnes nouvelles!
What good news!

Ils sont bons.
They're good.

Elles sont bonnes.
They're (*fem.*) good.

Bonjour.
Hello! Good morning. Good afternoon. Good day.

Bonne nuit.
Good night.

B. WELL

Bien.
Well, good.

C'est bien.
It's good. It's fine. It's okay.

Ce n'est pas bien.
It's not good. It's not okay.

Est-ce qu'il parle bien?
Does he speak well?

Oui, il parle bien.
Yes, he speaks well.

Pas trop bien.
Not too well.

Comment allez-vous?
How are you?

Très bien, monsieur.
Very well, sir.

Est-ce que c'est bien?
Is it good?

C'est bien fait.
It's well done (well made).

Je l'aime bien.
I like him (her, it).

En êtes-vous bien sûr(e)?
Are you really sure about it?

Je suis bien content.
I'm very glad.

Tout va bien.
Everything's going well. Everything's all right.

Il va bien mieux.
He's doing much better.

Il y en a bien d'autres.
There are many others of them.

Tout est bien qui finit bien.
All's well that ends well.

Eh bien?
Well? So what?

Il mérite bien plus.
He deserves much more.

C'est bien moins réussi.
It's much less successful.

C'est bien cher.
It's very (rather) expensive.

Il est bien tard.
It's very (rather) late.

Il est bien tôt.
It's very (rather) early.

QUIZ 19

1. *Tout va bien.*
2. *C'est très bien.*
3. *Je vais bien mieux.*
4. *Je suis bien content.*
5. *En avez-vous assez?*
6. *Encore une fois!*
7. *Répétez encore une fois s'il vous plaît.*
8. *Il ne parle pas trop bien.*
9. *Je l'aime beaucoup.*
10. *Donnez-m'en un peu.*

   a. It's very good.
   b. Do you have enough of it?
   c. Again!
   d. Give me a little of it.
   e. I like it a lot.
   f. I'm very glad.
   g. Everything's going well. Everything's all right.
   h. I'm doing much better.
   i. Please repeat it.
   j. He doesn't speak too well.

ANSWERS
1—g; 2—a; 3—h; 4—f; 5—b; 6—c; 7—i; 8—j; 9—e;
10—d.

C. WORD STUDY

anxieux	anxious
le chef	chief
la difficulté	difficulty
le docteur	doctor
l'épisode (*m.*)	episode
futur	future
glorieux	glorious
nerveux	nervous
la période	period

D. BEAUTIFUL, NICE, FINE

Beau. *Belle. Bel. Beaux. Belles.*
Beautiful.

C'est très beau.
It's very beautiful (nice, fine).

Pas très beau.
Not very beautiful.

Beau temps.
Nice weather.

Il fait beau.
It's nice out. The weather's nice.

Il est beau.
He's handsome.

Un beau pays.
A beautiful country.

Une belle journée.
A nice day.

Elle est belle.
She's beautiful (pretty).

Bel et bien.
Well and good, truly.

Un bel ouvrage.
A beautiful job (piece of work).

Un bel homme.
A handsome man.

De belles femmes.
Beautiful women.

Ils ne sont pas beaux.
They're not handsome/beautiful.

Beaux-arts.
Fine arts.

Notice that the form *bel* is used before masculine singular nouns beginning with a vowel or mute *h* and that the masculine plural form before vowels and consonants is *beaux*.

LESSON 29

A. LIKE, AS

Comme.
Like, as.

Comme moi.
Like me.

Comme ça.
Like this (that).

Comme les autres.
Like the others.

Comme ci, comme ça.
So, so.

Pas comme ça.
Not like this (that).

C'est comme cela.
That's how it is. That's the way it is.

Comme vous voulez.
As you wish.

Comme il est tôt!
How early (it is)!

Comme il est tard!
How late (it is)!

Comme c'est cher!
How expensive (it is)!

B. ALL

Tout.
All, every.

Tout homme.
Every man.

Toute femme.
Every woman.

Tous les hommes.
All (the) men.

Toutes les femmes.
All (the) women.

Tout est ici.
Everything's here.

Toute la journée.
All day, the whole day (long).

Tous les jours.
Every day.

Tout est prêt.
Everything's ready.

Ils sont tous prêts.
All (*m.*) are/Everyone (*m.*) is ready.

Elles sont toutes prêtes.
All (*f.*) are/Everyone (*f.*) is ready.

Prenez-les tous.
Take all of them.

Nous sommes tous là.
We're all here.

C'est tout.
That's all. That's the whole lot. That'll do.

Est-ce que c'est tout?
Is that all? Is that everything? Is that the whole lot?

Tout le monde.
Everybody.

Tout de suite.
Right away. Just now.

Tout à l'heure.
A moment ago. In a moment.

A tout à l'heure.
See you soon. See you in a little while.

Tout à fait.
Completely.

C. SOME, ANY OF IT

En.
Some/Any of it.

En avez-vous?
Do you have any?

A-t-il de l'argent?
Does he have any money?

Oui, il en a.
Yes, he has (some).

Avez-vous de l'argent?
Do you have any money?

Non, je n'en ai pas.
No, I don't have any.

Nous n'en avons plus.
We don't have any more of it.

Voici de l'argent. Donnez-en à Jean.
Here's some money. Give some of it to John.

J'en ai assez.
I have enough of it (of them).

Donnez-m'en.
Give me some.

Donnez-nous en.
Give us some.

Donnez-lui en.
Give him some.

Donnez-leur en.
Give them some.

Je lui en ai donné.
I gave him some.

Je lui en ai parlé.
I spoke to her about it.

Avez-vous besoin de mon livre?
Do you need my book?

Oui, j'en ai besoin.
Yes, I need it.

Vient-il de Paris?
Is he coming from Paris?

Il en vient directement.
He's coming directly from there.

Il y en a.
There is (are) some.

Y en a-t-il encore?
Is (are) there any more?

Combien de livres avez-vous?
How many books do you have?

J'en ai dix.
I have ten (of them).

Ont-ils des livres?
Do they have any books?

Oui, ils en ont beaucoup.
Yes, they have lots (of them).

Non, ils n'en ont pas.
No, they haven't any.

Qu'en pensez-vous?
What do you think of (about) it?

QUIZ 20

1. *Y en a-t-il encore?*
2. *Il y en a.*
3. *Avez-vous de l'argent?*
4. *En avez-vous?*
5. *Donnez-lui en.*
6. *Donnez m'en.*
7. *Non, ils n'en ont pas.*
8. *Qu'en pensez-vous?*
9. *Cette viande est bonne.*
10. *C'est bon.*
11. *Un bel ouvrage.*
12. *Beau temps.*
13. *C'est très beau.*
14. *Il fait beau.*
15. *Une belle journée.*

a. It's very beautiful (nice, fine).
b. Nice weather.
c. A nice day.

d. It's nice out. The weather's nice.
e. A beautiful job (work).
f. This meat is good.
g. It's good.
h. Do you have any?
i. Do you have any money?
j. Give me some.
k. Give him some.
l. There is (are) some.
m. Is (are) there any more?
n. No, they haven't any.
o. What do you think of it?

ANSWERS

1—m; 2—l; 3—i; 4—h; 5—k; 6—j; 7—n; 8—o; 9—f;
10—g; 11—e; 12—b; 13—a; 14—d; 15—c.

SUPPLEMENTAL VOCABULARY 8: AT SCHOOL

at school	*à l'école*
school	*l'école (f.)*
university	*l'université (f.)*
classroom	*la salle de classe*
course	*le cours*
teacher	*l'enseignant (m.),* *l'enseignante (f.)*
professor	*le professeur*
student	*l'étudiant (m.),* *l'étudiante (f.)*
subject	*le sujet*
notebook	*le cahier*
textbook	*le livre scolaire*
math	*les mathématiques*
history	*l'histoire*
chemistry	*la chimie*

biology	*la biologie*
literature	*la littérature*
language	*la langue*
art	*l'art*
music	*la musique*
gym	*la gymnastique*
test	*l'examen*
grade	*la note*
report card	*le bulletin scolaire*
diploma	*le diplôme*
degree	*le niveau universitaire*
difficult/easy	*difficile/facile*
to study	*étudier*
to learn	*apprendre*
to pass (a test)	*réussir (son examen)*
to fail (a test)	*râter (son examen)*

LESSON 30

A. OF COURSE, I SUPPOSE SO, ETC.

Bien sûr.
Of course. Certainly.

Entendu!
Of course! Agreed ("Understood")!

C'est entendu.
That's understood. That's settled. Agreed.

Bien entendu.
Of course. Naturally. Certainly.

En effet.
Indeed. In fact. In reality.
(*As a reply to a statement:* That's so. That's true.)

Je le crois.
I think so.

Je crois que non.
I don't think so.

D'accord!
Agreed! Okay!

Je suis d'accord.
I agree.

Je le suppose.
I suppose so.

Je suppose que non.
I suppose not.

Je l'espère.
I hope so.

J'espère que non.
I hope not.

Peut-être.
Perhaps.

Naturellement.
Naturally.

Certainement.
Certainly.

Ça dépend.
That depends.

B. IT'S A PITY, IT DOESN'T MATTER, ETC.

C'est dommage!
It's a pity! It's a shame! Too bad!

Quel dommage!
What a pity! What a shame!

Ça m'est égal.
I don't care. It's all the same to me.

Bof (*fam.*)[1] . . . *ça m'est égal.*
I don't care . . . it's all the same to me.

Je m'en fiche! (*fam.*)
I don't care about it!

C'est sans importance.
It's without importance. It's unimportant.

Ça n'a aucune importance.
That has no ("not one") importance.

Tant pis.
So much the worse. Too bad.

Tant mieux.
So much the better.

---

[1] *Bof* is a familiar exclamation used to show indifference.

Ça ne fait rien.
That's nothing. That's not important. That doesn't matter.

Ça ne me fait rien.
It doesn't matter to me. I don't care.

Si ça ne vous fait rien.
If you have no objections. If it doesn't inconvenience you.

C.   What a Surprise!

Ça alors!
Well, really!

Quelle bonne surprise!
What a nice ("good") surprise!

Je suis étonné(e).
I'm stunned. I'm amazed.

Quelle chance!
What luck! How lucky!

Je n'en reviens pas!
I can't get over it!

Je n'arrive pas à le croire!
I just can't believe it!

Ah, non, ce n'est pas possible!
Oh, no! It's not possible!

Zut, alors!
Shoot!

D.   The Same

Même.
Same.

C'est la même chose.
It's (all) the same thing.

Ce ne sont pas les mêmes.
These aren't the same.

En même temps.
At the same time.

Au même moment.
At the same moment.

Dans la même ville.
In the same town.

Enchanté!
Glad to know you.

Moi de même.
The same here.

Je le fais moi-même.
I'm doing it myself.

Tu le fais toi-même.
You're (*fam.*) doing it yourself.

Il le fait lui-même.
He's doing it himself.

Elle le fait elle-même.
She's doing it herself.

Nous le faisons nous-mêmes.
We're doing it ourselves.

Vous le faites vous-mêmes.
You're doing it yourselves.

Ils le font eux-mêmes.
They're (*masc.*) doing it themselves.

Elles le font elles-mêmes.
They're (*fem.*) doing it themselves.

E. ALREADY

Déjà
Already.

Il est déjà là.
He's already here.

Il a déjà fait ça.
He's already done that.

Est-il déjà parti?
Has he left already?

Avez-vous déjà fini?
Have you finished already?

Quel nom, déjà?
What was the name again?

QUIZ 21

1. *C'est dommage.*   •
2. *Ça ne fait rien.*
3. *Je le fais moi-même.*
4. *Ça dépend.*
5. *D'accord.*
6. *Bien entendu!*
7. *Je l'espère.*
8. *Bien sûr.*
9. *Il est déjà là.*
10. *Je le suppose.*

a. Of course, certainly.
b. Of course! Agreed!
c. Agreed.
d. He's already here.
e. I suppose so.
f. I hope so.
g. It's a pity (shame). Too bad!
h. That depends.
i. That's nothing. That's not important. That doesn't matter.
j. I'm doing it myself.

ANSWERS
1—g; 2—i; 3—j; 4—h; 5—c; 6—b; 7—f; 8—a; 9—d; 10—e.

F. WORD STUDY

l'attaque (*f.*)	attack
l'avantage (*m.*)	advantage
confortable	comfortable
le courage	courage
courageux	courageous

l'indépendance (*f.*)	independence
le langage	language
le message	message
l'opinion (*f.*)	opinion
le silence	silence

LESSON 31

A. I LIKE IT

Je l'aime bien.
I like it.

Ça me plaît.
I like that.

Ça me plaît énormément.
I'm very pleased with it. I like it very much.

Ça m'intéresse.
That interests me. I'm interested in it.

Bon!
Good!

C'est bon!
It's good.

C'est beau.
It's beautiful.

C'est excellent.
It's excellent.

C'est intéressant.
It's interesting.

C'est parfait.
It's perfect.

C'est magnifique.
It's magnificent. It's wonderful.

C'est admirable.
It's admirable.

C'est charmant.
It's charming. It's very nice. It's lovely.

C'est superbe.
It's superb. It's wonderful.

C'est sympa! (*fam.*)[1]
It's great! It's cool!

C'est carrément génial.
It's really great.

C'est super.
It's super. It's great.

C'est formidable.
It's really something!

Il est très gentil.
He's very nice.

---

[1] *Sympa* is a colloquial expression derived from *sympathique*, nice.

Elle est très gentille.
She's very nice.

Il est très aimable.
He's very pleasant (likable).

Elle est adorable.
She's sweet/cute/adorable.

Vous êtes très aimable.
You're very kind. That's very kind of you.

Elle est très sympathique.
She's very nice.

Elle est sympa!
She's nice!

Il est trop sympa.
He's really cool.

B. I Don't Like It

Je ne l'aime pas.
I don't like it.

Il ne me plaît pas.
I don't like it.

Ça ne me plaît pas.
I don't like that. (That doesn't please me.)

Ça me dérange.
That bothers me.

Ça m'ennuie.
That bothers me.

Ça m'embête. (*fam.*)
That annoys/bothers me.

Ce n'est pas bon.
It's not good (said of food, etc.).

Ce n'est pas bien.
It's not good/It's not nice.

C'est mauvais.
It's bad. (Food)

C'est mal.
It's bad. (an action)

Ce n'est pas beau.
It's not beautiful.

C'est laid.
It's ugly.

C'est vraiment moche! (*fam.*)
It's really ugly! It's really rotten!

C'est dégoûtant.
It's disgusting.

Ça me rend malade.
That makes me sick.

C'est terrible.
It's terrible.

C'est ennuyeux.
It's boring.

Ça me laisse froid.
I'm indifferent to it. ("It leaves me cold.")

C'est bizarre.
It's strange/bizarre.

QUIZ 22

1. *Je n'aime pas ça.*
2. *C'est parfait.*
3. *C'est chouette!*
4. *C'est formidable.*
5. *Ça me plaît énormément.*
6. *Il est très gentil.*
7. *C'est bizarre.*
8. *C'est mauvais.*
9. *Vous êtes très aimable.*
10. *Ça me dérange.*

a. That bothers me.
b. It's really something!
c. I'm very pleased with it.
d. He's very nice.
e. You're very kind.
f. It's bad.
g. It's strange.
h. It's neat!
i. I don't like that.
j. It's perfect.

ANSWERS

1—i; 2—j; 3—h; 4—b; 5—c; 6—d; 7—g; 8—f; 9—e;
10—a.

C. I HAD A GOOD TIME

Je me suis bien amusé.
I had a good time. ("I amused myself.")

Elle s'est bien amusée.
She had a good time.

C'était vraiment agréable.
It was really pleasant/fun.

Ça m'a beaucoup plu.
I liked it a lot. ("It pleased me very much.")

C'était drôle comme tout.
It was funny as anything.

C'était très marrant. (*fam.*)
It was very funny.

D. I DIDN'T HAVE A GOOD TIME

Je ne me suis pas bien amusé.
I didn't have a good time.

Je me suis ennuyée.
I was bored. (*fem.*)

Quelle perte de temps!
What a waste of time!

REVIEW QUIZ 3

1. *Il l'a mis* ——(in) *sa poche.*
   a. *sur*
   b. *dans*
   c. *sous*
2. *C'est* ——(under) *la chaise.*
   a. *dedans*
   b. *sous*
   c. *si*
3. *Vous pouvez le faire* ——(without) *aucune dif-*
   ficulté.
   a. *sans*
   b. *par*
   c. *si*
4. *Je l'ai trouvé* ——(under) *un tas de papiers.*
   a. *sur*
   b. *sous*
   c. *dessus*
5. *On dit que c'est* ——(true).
   a. *parle*
   b. *vrai*
   c. *cela*
6. *Je me suis* ——(a good time).
   a. *ennuyé*
   b. *reveillé*
   c. *bien amusé*
7. *Il* ——(is going) *à la campagne.*
   a. *va*
   b. *faut*
   c. *allez*
8. *Donnez-moi un* ——(little) *d'eau.*
   a. *peu*
   b. *beaucoup*
   c. *ici*

9. *Je n'ai pas* ———(much) *d'argent.*
   a. *peu*
   b. *beaucoup*
   c. *trop*

10. *C'est* ———(more) *que ça.*
    a. *moins*
    b. *plus*
    c. *tôt*

11. *Ce n'est pas* ———(enough).
    a. *encore*
    b. *bon*
    c. *assez*

12. *Elle est* ———(beautiful).
    a. *bien*
    b. *belle*
    c. *bon*

13. ———(as) *vous voulez.*
    a. *Pas*
    b. *Comme*
    c. *Tôt*

14. *Nous sommes* ———(all) *là.*
    a. *comme*
    b. *assez*
    c. *tous*

15. ———(everybody) *le sait.*
    a. *Tout le monde*
    b. *Tout à l'heure*
    c. *Tout à fait*

16. *Je* ———(think) *que non.*
    a. *tenez*
    b. *crois*
    c. *suis*

17. *J'* ———(hope) *que non.*
    a. *mieux*

  b. *espère*
  c. *suppose*
18. *Ça ne fait* ——(nothing).
  a. *même*
  b. *rien*
  c. *déjà*
19. *C'est la* ——(same) *chose*.
  a. *même*
  b. *déjà*
  c. *naturellement*
20. *Avez-vous* ——(already) *fini?*
  a. *même*
  b. *rien*
  c. *déjà*

ANSWERS
1—b; 2—b; 3—a; 4—b; 5—b; 6—c; 7—a; 8—a;
9—b; 10—b; 11—c; 12—b; 13—b; 14—c; 15—a;
16—b; 17—b; 18—b; 19—a; 20—c.

SUPPLEMENTAL VOCABULARY 9: SPORTS AND RECREATION

sports and recreation	*les sports et les loisirs*
soccer/football	*le football*
basketball	*le basket-ball*
baseball	*le baseball*
American football	*le football américain*
hockey	*le hockey*
tennis	*le tennis*
rugby	*le rugby*
game	*le match, le jeu*
team	*l'équipe (f.)*
stadium	*le stade*
coach	*l'entraîneur (m.)*

player	*le joueur, la joueuse*
champion	*le champion, la championne*
ball	*le ballon, la balle*
(to go) hiking	*(aller) faire de la marche*
(to go) camping	*(aller) camper*
to play (a sport)	*faire du sport*
to play (a game)	*jouer un match*
to win	*gagner*
to lose	*perdre*
to draw/tie	*faire match nul*
cards	*les cartes*
pool/billiards	*le billard*

LESSON 32

A. Who? What? When? etc.

{Que . . . ?
{Qu'est-ce que . . . ?
What . . . ?

Quel livre?
What book? Which book?

Quelle lettre?
What letter? Which letter?

Lequel? (m.) Laquelle? (f.)
Which one?

Quand?
When?

Qui?
Who?

Qui est-ce qui . . . ?
Who . . . ? (Who is it who . . . ?)

Quoi?
What? Huh? (fam.)

Pourquoi?
Why?

Où?
Where?

Combien?
How much/many?

Comment?
How? Also: I beg your pardon?

1. *Que* "What?"

{ **Que . . . ?**
{ **Qu'est-ce que . . . ?**
What . . . ?

{ **Que dites-vous?**
{ **Qu'est-ce que vous dites?**
What are you saying?

{ **Que dites-vous de cela?**
{ **Qu'est-ce que vous dites de cela?**
What do you say about that?

{ Qu'en dites-vous?
{ Qu'est-ce que vous en dites?
What do you say about it?

{ Que faites-vous?
{ Qu'est-ce que vous faites?
What are you doing?

{ Que voulez-vous?
{ Qu'est-ce que vous voulez?
What do you want? What would you like?

{ Que voulez-vous faire maintenant?
{ Qu'est-ce que vous voulez faire maintenant?
What do you want to do now?

{ Que voulez-vous dire?
{ Qu'est-ce que vous voulez dire?
What do you mean?

{ Que cherchez-vous?
{ Qu'est-ce que vous cherchez?
What are you looking for?

{ Qu'avez-vous?
{ Qu'est-ce que vous avez?
What do you have? What's the matter with you?
What's wrong with you?

{ Qu'a-t-il?
{ Qu'est-ce qu'il a?
What does he have? What's the matter with him?

Qu'est-ce que c'est?
What is it?

Qu'est-ce que c'est que ceci?
What's this?

Qu'est-ce que c'est que ça?
What's that?

Qu'est-ce qu'il y a?
What's the matter?

Qu'est-ce qui arrive?
What's going on? What's happening?

Qu'est-ce qui est arrivé?
What happened?

Qu'est-ce qui se passe?
What's happening? What's up?

Qu'importe?
What difference does it make? What does it matter?

Quel?
What (*masc.*)? Which (*masc.*)?

Quel homme?
What man?

Quels hommes?
What men?

Quel est votre nom?
What's your name?

Quel est le nom de cette ville?
What's the name of this town?

Donnez-moi le livre.
Give me the book.

Quel livre?
What book? Which book?

Quel jour sommes-nous?
What's today? ("What day are we?")

Quelle?
What (*fem.*)? Which (*fem.*)?

Quelle femme?
What woman?

Quelles femmes?
What women?

Quelle heure est-il?
What's the time? What time is it? ("What's the hour?")

A quelle heure?
At what time? ("At what hour?")

Quelles nouvelles?
What's new?

Quelle différence!
What a difference!

Quelle est la différence entre les deux choses?
What's the difference between the two things?

  2. *Lequel* "Which one?"

Lequel?
Which one (*masc.*)?

Lequel est-ce?
Which one is it? Which one is he?

Lequel est-il?
Which is he (it)?

Lequel est le mien?
Which (one) is mine?

Lequel est meilleur?
Which (one) is better?

Lequel est le meilleur?
Which (one) is the better one? Which (one) is best?

Lequel voulez-vous?
Which (one) do you want?

Lequel a raison?
Which one (who) is right?

Laquelle?
Which one (*fem.*)?

J'adore cette voiture.
I love that car.

Laquelle?
Which one?

La voiture verte là-bas.
The green car over there.

3. *Quand* "When?"

Quand?
When?

{ **C'est quand?**
{ **Quand est-ce?**
When is it?

À quand?
Until when?

Quand venez-vous?
When are you coming?

Quand partez-vous?
When are you leaving?

Quand va-t-il venir?
When is he going to come? When will he come?

Depuis quand êtes-vous ici?
How long have you been here?

4. *Qui* "Who?" "Whom?"

Qui?
Who?

Qui est-ce?
Who is it?

Qui êtes-vous?
Who are you?

{ **Qui sait ça?**
{ **Qui est-ce qui sait ça?**
Who knows that?

{ **Qui vient avec nous?**
{ **Qui est-ce qui vient avec nous?**
Who's coming with us?

A qui est-ce?
Whose is it? ("To whom is it?")

{**C'est pour qui?**
{**Pour qui est-ce?**
Who's it for?

A qui parlez-vous?
Whom are you talking to?

De qui parlez-vous?
Whom are you speaking about?

Avec qui venez-vous?
Whom are you coming with?

Qui voulez-vous voir?
Whom do you want to see?

{**Qui cherchez-vous?**
{**Qui est-ce que vous cherchez?**
Whom are you looking for?

  5. *Quoi* "What?"

Quoi?
What?

Avec quoi?
With what?

Sur quoi?
On what?

Quoi de neuf?
What's new?

A quoi pensez-vous?
What are you thinking about?

De quoi avez-vous besoin?
What do you need?

6. *Pourquoi* "Why?"

Pourquoi?
Why?

Et pourquoi pas?
And why not?

{ **Pourquoi dites-vous ça?**
{ **Pourquoi est-ce que vous dites ça?**
Why do you say that?

Pourquoi a-t-il fait ça?
Why did he do it?

7. *Comment* "How?"

Comment?
How?

Mais comment?
But how?

Comment ça?
How's that? What do you mean?

Comment vous appelez-vous?
What's your name? ("How do you call yourself?")

Comment ça va?
How are you?

Comment dites-vous?
What did you say? What are you saying?

Comment écrit-on ce mot en français?
How do you write this word in French? How's this word written in French?

Comment dites-vous "Thanks" en français?
How do you say "Thanks" in French?

Comment est-ce arrivé?
How did it happen?

Comment y va-t-on?
How does one go about getting there?

C'est fait comment?
How's it made?

Comment l'avez-vous fait?
How did you do (make) it?

Comment y aller?
How do you go there? ("How to go there?")

Comment faire?
What's to be done? What can one do? ("How to do?")

QUIZ 23

1. *Qu'est-ce que vous faites?*
2. *Qu'est-ce que vous voulez?*
3. *Qu'est-ce qu'il y a?*
4. *Que voulez-vous dire?*
5. *Qu'est-ce que vous cherchez?*
6. *Quel est le nom de cette rue?*

7. *Qu'importe?*
8. *Quelle différence!*
9. *Lequel est le meilleur?*
10. *Quand partez-vous?*
11. *Qui êtes-vous?*
12. *Qui voulez-vous voir?*
13. *De quoi avez-vous besoin?*
14. *Pourquoi a-t-il fait ça?*
15. *Mais comment?*
16. *Comment ça va?*
17. *Pourquoi dites-vous ça?*
18. *Et pourquoi pas?*
19. *Quoi de neuf?*
20. *Comment vous appelez-vous?*

a. What's new?
b. What do you need?
c. And why not?
d. Why do you say that?
e. Why did he do it?
f. What's your name?
g. How are you?
h. But how?
i. When are you leaving?
j. Who are you?
k. Whom do you want to see?
l. What a difference!
m. Which is the best?
n. What do you mean?
o. What are you looking for?
p. What's the matter?
q. What difference does it make? What does it matter?
r. What's the name of this street?
s. What are you doing?
t. What do you want?

ANSWERS
1—s; 2—t; 3—p; 4—n; 5—o; 6—r; 7—q; 8—l;
9—m; 10—i; 11—j; 12—k; 13—b; 14—e; 15—h;
16—g; 17—d; 18—c; 19—a; 20—f.

B. WORD STUDY

comique	comic
le coton	cotton
le détail	detail
l'employé (*m.*)	employee
le jugement	judgment
le muscle	muscle
le parc	park
le restaurant	restaurant
la rose	rose
la trace	trace

C. HOW MUCH?

{ **Quel est le prix?**
{ **C'est quel prix?**
What's the price?

Combien?
How much?

{ **C'est combien?**
{ **Combien est-ce?**
How much is it?

Combien coûte ceci?
How much is this?

Combien coûtent-ils?
How much do they cost?

{ **Combien est-ce que ça coûte?**
{ **Ça coûte combien?**
How much does that cost?

C'est combien en tout?
How much for everything? How much does it all cost?

C'est combien la pièce?
How much each?

C'est combien la douzaine?
How much a dozen?

Combien en voulez-vous?
How many do you want? How much do you want for it?

C'est cher!
That's expensive!

C'est bon marché!
It's cheap/inexpensive.

D. How Many?

Combien?
How many?

Combien d'argent veux-tu?
How much money do you want?

Combien d'hommes y-a-t-il?
How many men are there?

Combien de temps te faut-il?
How much time do you need?

Combien de temps faut-il pour y aller?
How long ("how much time") does it take to get there?

Combien y en a-t-il?
How many are there ("of it, them")?

{ **Combien en reste-t-il?**
{ **Il en reste combien?**
How many are left ("of them")?

{ **Combien en avez-vous?**
{ **Vous en avez combien?**
How many of them do you have?

{ **Nous sommes le combien?**
{ **Le combien sommes-nous?**
What's the day today? ("We are the how many?")

Lundi ce sera le combien?
What's the date Monday? ("Monday will be the how many?")

QUIZ 24

1. *Combien y en a-t-il?*
2. *Combien est-ce?*
3. *Combien en voulez-vous?*
4. *Quel prix?*
5. *Combien de temps te faut-il?*
6. *Le combien sommes-nous?*
7. *Combien en reste-t-il?*
8. *Combien en avez-vous?*
9. *C'est quel prix?*
10. *Lundi ce sera le combien?*

a. How many remain (of it, them)?
b. What's the date today? ("We are the how
   many?")
c. What's the date Monday?
d. What's the price?
e. What's the price?
f. How much is it?
g. How many do you want? How much do you
   want for it?
h. How much time do you need?
i. How many of them do you have?
j. How many are there (of it, them)?

ANSWERS
1—j; 2—f; 3—g; 4—e; 5—h; 6—b; 7—a; 8—i; 9—d;
10—c.

LESSON 33

A. Some, Someone, Something

Quelque.
Some.

Quelque chose.
Something.

Quelque chose de nouveau.
Something new.

Quelques hommes.
Some men. A few men.

Quelques mots.
Some words. A few words.

Quelqu'un.
Someone.

Y a-t-il quelqu'un?
Is there anyone there?

Quelquefois.
Sometimes.

Je le vois quelquefois.
I see him sometimes.

B.   ONCE, TWICE

Fois.
A time.

Une fois.
Once. One time.

Deux fois.
Twice. Two times.

La première fois.
The first time.

La prochaine fois.
The next time.

La dernière fois.
The last time.

Encore une fois.
Another time. Again. Once more.

Toutes les fois.
Every time. Each time.

Cette fois-ci.
This time.

C. UP TO, UNTIL

Jusque.
Up to. Until.

Jusqu'ici.
Up to now.

Jusque là.
Up to there

Jusqu'au bout.
To the end. Until the end.

Jusqu'à la gare.
Up to (as far as) the station.

Jusqu'à demain.
Up to until tomorrow.

Jusqu'à lundi.
Until Monday.

D. I Need It, It's Necessary

Use the verb *avoir* plus *besoin de* when you want to say "I need," "you need," etc.

J'ai besoin de cela.
I need it (that).

Il n'a pas besoin de celui-ci.
He doesn't need this one.

Avez-vous besoin de quelque chose?
Do you need anything?

Je n'ai besoin de rien.
I don't need anything.

Je n'en ai pas du tout besoin.
I don't need it at all.

Use *Il faut* when you want to say "it's necessary."

Il faut absolument que je vous voie.
It's absolutely necessary that I see you.

Il faut le lui dire.
You have to tell him.

Il faut rentrer de bonne heure.
You/We must come home early.

Il faut admettre la vérité.
One must recognize the truth.

E. I Feel Like . . .

Use *avoir* plus *envie de* when you want to say "I feel like," "she feels like," etc.

J'ai envie de nager.
I feel like swimming.

J'en ai envie.
I'd like to have it. I feel like having it.

Je n'ai pas envie d'y aller.
I don't feel like going there.

Il a envie de manger de la glace.
He feels like having some ice cream.

Avez-vous envie de voir ce film?
Would you like to see this (that) movie?

F. At the Home Of

Chez.
At the home of.

Marie est chez Sylvie maintenant.
Marie is at Sylvie's house now.

Nous étions chez des amis.
We were at the home of some friends.

Je vous verrai chez les Durand.
I'll see you at the Durands'.

Venez chez nous.
Come over to our place.

Quand j'habitais chez mon père . . .
When I was living with my father . . .

Monsieur Durand est-il chez lui?
Is Mr. Durand at home?

Je dois aller chez le docteur.
I have to go to the doctor's.

Faites comme chez vous.
Make yourself at home.

G. HERE IT IS, THERE IT IS

Voilà!
Here/There it is.

Le voilà.
Here/There he is.

La voilà.
Here/There she is.

Les voilà.
Here/There they are.

Vous voilà.
Here/There you are.

Voilà la réponse.
That's the answer.

QUIZ 25

1. *Quelque chose.*	a. To the end.
2. *Une fois.*	b. I need that.

3. *Jusqu'au bout.*   c. Here's the book.
4. *J'ai besoin de cela.*   d. Something.
5. *Voilà le livre.*   e. Once.

ANSWERS

1—d; 2—e; 3—a; 4—b; 5—c.

REVIEW QUIZ 4

1. ———— (what) *est le nom de cette ville?*
   a. *Lequel*
   b. *Quel*
   c. *Quand*
2. ———— (who) *êtes-vous?*
   a. *Qui*
   b. *Quel*
   c. *Quoi*
3. ———— (when) *va-t-il venir?*
   a. *Qui*
   b. *Quand*
   c. *Quel*
4. ———— (why) *est-ce que vous dites ça?*
   a. *Quelque*
   b. *Quand*
   c. *Pourquoi*
5. *Le* ———— (twelfth) *chapitre.*
   a. *douzième*
   b. *dix-septième*
   c. *sixième*
6. *Ce chapeau m'a coûté* ———— (fifty-four)
   francs.
   a. *deux*
   b. *cinquante*
   c. *cinquante-quatre*

7. *J' habite au numéro* ———— (seventeen) *de la rue
   Balzac.*
      a. *trente-trois*
      b. *dix-sept*
      c. *treize*

8. *Il est* ———— (noon).
      a. *midi*
      b. *minuit*
      c. *onze heures*

9. *Nous nous verrons à* ———— (six) *heures.*
      a. *cinq*
      b. *sept*
      c. *six*

10. *Il est* ———— (time) *de le faire.*
       a. *combien*
       b. *temps*
       c. *ici*

11. *Nous sommes aujourd' hui* ———— (Wednesday).
       a. *mardi*
       b. *mercredi*
       c. *lundi*

12. *Il partira* ———— (Tuesday) *prochain.*
       a. *mardi*
       b. *jeudi*
       c. *dimanche*

13. *C' est aujourd' hui le premier* ———— (June).
       a. *juin*
       b. *juillet*
       c. *août*

14. *Il n' a pas* ———— (need) *de celui-ci.*
       a. *cela*
       b. *besoin*
       c. *tout*

15. ———— (how) *écrit-on ce mot en français?*
    a. *Pourquoi*
    b. *Comment*
    c. *Cela*
16. *Je suis né le* ———— (twelve) *avril.*
    a. *mai*
    b. *onze*
    c. *douze*
17. ———— (here's) *le livre.*
    a. *Voici*
    b. *Voilà*
    c. *Nous*
18. *J'ai perdu mon* ———— (way).
    a. *cabine*
    b. *chemin*
    c. *court*
19. *Il travaille du* ———— (morning) *au soir.*
    a. *matin*
    b. *nuit*
    c. *jour*
20. *A quelle station dois-je* ———— (get off)?
    a. *sommes*
    b. *descendre*
    c. *encore*

ANSWERS
1—b; 2—a; 3—b; 4—c; 5—a; 6—c; 7—b; 8—a;
9—c; 10—b; 11—b; 12—a; 13—a; 14—b; 15—b;
16—c; 17—a; 18—b; 19—a; 20—b.

LESSON 34

A. ON THE ROAD

Pardon.
Pardon me.

Excusez-moi.
Excuse me.

Quel est le nom de cette ville?
What is the name of this town?

Combien de kilomètres y a-t-il d'ici à Paris?
How many kilometers from here to Paris?

C'est à vingt kilomètres d'ici.
It's twenty kilometers from here.

Comment puis-je¹ aller à Paris?
How do I get to Paris?

Suivez cette route.
Follow this road.

Vous faites mauvaise route.
You're on the wrong road.

Avez-vous une carte routière?
Do you have a road map?

Où puis-je me garer?
Where can I park?

---

¹ *Puis* is normally used instead of *peux* when a sentence with *je* is inverted.

B. WALKING AROUND

Pouvez-vous m'indiquer comment je peux me rendre à cette adresse?
Can you tell me how I can get to this address?

Pouvez-vous me dire comment je peux aller à cet endroit?
Can you tell me how I can get to this place?

Quel est le nom de cette rue?
What is the name of this street?

Pouvez-vous m'indiquer où se trouve cette rue?
Can you tell me where this street is?

Où est la rue Boileau?
Where is Boileau Street?

Avez-vous un plan de la ville?
Do you have a map of the city?

Puis-je y aller à pied?
Can I get there on foot?

Est-ce loin d'ici?
Is it far from here?

Est-ce près d'ici?
Is it near here?

C'est la troisième rue à droite.
It's the third block to the right.

Traversez la rue.
Cross the street.

{ **Allez tout droit.**
{ **Allez droit devant vous.**
Go straight ahead.

Allez au bout de la rue et prenez la première à gauche.
Go to the corner and turn left.

Tournez à droite après le carrefour.
Turn right after the intersection.

C'est après le feu.
It's after the traffic light.

Où se trouve le musée?
Where is the museum?

Où se trouve le poste de police?
Where is the police station?

Où se trouve le consulat américain?
Where is the American consulate?

C. BUS, TRAIN, SUBWAY

Où se trouve l'arrêt d'autobus?
Where is the bus stop?

Où se trouve la station de métro?
Where's the metro/subway station?

Où se trouve la gare?
Where's the train station?

À quel arrêt dois-je descendre?
At what stop do (should) I get off?

Où dois-je descendre?
Where do (should) I get off?

Où se trouve la gare?
Where is the train station?

Où puis-je prendre le train pour Paris?
Where do I get the train for Paris?

Sur la voie numéro deux.
On track two.

Le train vient de partir.
The train just left.

Quelle est l'heure de départ du prochain train?
At what time does the next train leave?

Un billet aller et retour pour Paris, s'il vous plaît.
May I have a round-trip ticket for Paris?

Combien est-ce?
How much is that?

Sept euros, vingt-cinq cents.
Seven euros, twenty-five cents.

Combien de temps faut-il pour aller jusque là?
How long does it take to get there?

Où est la station de métro la plus proche?
Where is the nearest subway station?

Quelle ligne va au Musée d'Orsay?
Which line goes to the d'Orsay Museum?

Où faut-il changer?
Where must I change?

Où faut-il prendre la correspondance?
Where must I (make the) transfer?

SUPPLEMENTAL VOCABULARY 10: NATURE

nature	*la nature*
tree	*l'arbre (m.)*
flower	*la fleur*
forest	*la forêt*
mountain	*la montagne*
field	*le champ*
river	*la rivière, le fleuve*
lake	*le lac*
ocean	*l'océan (m.)*
sea	*la mer*
beach	*la plage*
desert	*le désert*
rock	*le rocher*
sand	*le sable*
sky	*le ciel (pl: les cieux)*
sun	*le soleil*
moon	*la lune*
star	*l'étoile (f.)*
water	*l'eau (f.) (pl: les eaux)*
land	*la terre*
plant	*la plante*
hill	*la colline*
pond	*la mare/l'étang (m.)*

LESSON 35

A. WRITING AND MAILING LETTERS

Je voudrais écrire une lettre.
I'd like to write a letter.

Avez-vous un stylo?
Do you have a pen?

Avez-vous une enveloppe?
Do you have an envelope?

Avez-vous un timbre?
Do you have a stamp?

Où puis-je acheter un timbre?
Where can I buy a stamp?

Est-ce que vous avez un timbre par avion?
Do you have an air-mail stamp?

Où se trouve la poste?
Where is the post office?

Je voudrais envoyer cette lettre.
I'd like to mail this letter.

Combien de timbres faut-il mettre sur cette lettre?
How many stamps do I need on this letter?

Où se trouve la boîte aux lettres?
Where is a mailbox?

B. FAXES AND E-MAIL

Je voudrais envoyer un fax.
I'd like to send a fax.

Où se trouve fax?
Where is (there) a fax machine?

Combien coûte un fax pour Paris?
How much is a fax to Paris?

J'ai besoin d'envoyer un mêl/un e-mail.
I need to send an e-mail.

Puis-je me connecter à Internet?
Can I get on the Internet?

Avez-vous un site sur Internet?
Do you have a Web site?

Où est l'ordinateur?
Where is the computer?

Avez-vous une imprimante?
Do you have a printer?

C. TELEPHONES

Y a-t-il un téléphone ici?
Is there a phone here?

Où se trouve le téléphone?
Where is the telephone?

Où sont les cabines téléphoniques?
Where are the phone booths?

Au bureau de tabac.
In the tobacco shop.

Je voudrais une télécarte, s'il vous plaît.
I'd like a prepaid phone card please.

Y a-t-il un minitel?
Is there a minitel? (telecommunications terminal)

Avez-vous un annuaire?
Do you have a phone directory?

Je voudrais téléphoner en P.C.V.
I'd like to call collect.

Puis-je me servir de votre téléphone, s'il vous plaît?
May I use your phone?

Avez-vous un téléphone portable?
Do you have a cell phone?

Combien coûte la communication pour Paris?
How much is a telephone call to Paris?

Quel est l'indicatif?
What is the area code?

Ne quittez pas.
Hold on. ("Don't leave.")

Attendez un instant.
Hold the line a minute.

La ligne est occupée.
The line's busy.

Monsieur, vous m'avez donné un mauvais numéro.
Operator, you gave me the wrong number.

On ne répond pas.
There is no answer.

Il n'y a pas de réponse.
There is no answer.

Il n'y a personne.
There's no one there.

Puis-je parler à M. Delacroix, s'il vous plaît?
May I speak to Mr. Delacroix, please?

C'est moi.
Speaking.

C'est M. Charpentier à l'appareil.
This is Mr. Charpentier speaking.

D. Une Plaisanterie

Olive et Marius vont au restaurant et chacun commande un bifteck. Quelques instants plus tard le garçon revient avec un grand et un petit morceau de viande. Olive se précipite sur le grand morceau. Marius, furieux, lui dit:

—Mal élevée, tu ne sais pas que tu aurais dû prendre le plus petit morceau puisque tu t'es servie d'abord?

Olive lui répond:

—Si tu avais été à ma place, quel morceau aurais-tu pris?

—Le plus petit, répond Marius, bien entendu!

—Alors, s'exclame Olive, de quoi te plains-tu puisque tu l'as eu.

A JOKE

Olive and Marius go to a restaurant and each orders a steak. A few minutes later the waiter comes back with a large piece of meat and a small one. Olive seizes the large piece. Marius is furious and says to her:

"What bad manners you have! Don't you know that since you were the first to help yourself you should have taken the smaller piece?"

Olive answers:

"If you were in my place, which piece would you have taken?"

"The smaller one, of course," says Marius.

"Well, then," Olive answers, "what are you complaining about? You have it, haven't you?"

NOTES

Revient comes back; from *revenir* to come back.

Mal élevé ill-bred; ill-bred person.

Tu aurais dû you should have; *tu aurais dû prendre* you should have taken.

Aurais-tu pris would you have taken.

Bien entendu of course.

Commande orders.

Se précipite hurries, hastens; seizes, grabs.

Te plains-tu do you complain . . . (*fam.*).

Puisque since.

SUPPLEMENTAL VOCABULARY 11: COMPUTERS AND THE INTERNET

computers and the   *les ordinateurs et Internet*
  Internet

computer	*l' ordinateur (m.)*
keyboard	*le clavier*
monitor/screen	*l' écran (m.)*
printer	*l' imprimante (f.)*
mouse	*la souris*
modem	*le modem*
memory	*la mémoire*
CD-ROM	*le CD Rom*
CD-ROM drive	*le lecteur CD Rom*
file	*le fichier, le dossier*
document	*le document*
cable	*le cable*
software	*le logiciel*
Internet	*Internet*
website	*le site web*
webpage	*la page web*
e-mail	*le mail, l' e-mail, le courrier électronique*
chat room	*la salle de chat/tchatche*
instant message	*le message instantané*
attachment	*les pièces jointes*
to send an e-mail	*envoyer un courrier électronique, un mail, un e-mail*
to send a file	*envoyer un dossier*
to forward	*faire suivre*
to reply	*répondre*
to delete	*supprimer*
to save a document	*sauvegarder un document*
to open a file	*ouvrir un dossier*
to close a file	*fermer un dossier*
to attach a file	*envoyer en pièces jointes*
to download	*télécharger*
search engine	*les outils de recherche*

LESSON 36

A. What's Your Name?

Comment vous appelez-vous?
What is your name?

Comment t'appelles-tu?
What is your name? (*fam.*)

Je m'appelle Jean Granier.
My name is John Granier.

Comment s'appelle-t-il?
What is his name?

Il s'appelle Charles Lenoir.
His name is Charles Lenoir.

Comment s'appelle-t-elle?
What is her name?

Elle s'appelle Claire Durand.
Her name is Claire Durand.

Comment s'appellent-ils?
What are their names?

Il s'appelle Lucien Blamont, et elle s'appelle Marie Delacourt.
His name is Lucien Blamont and hers is Marie Delacourt.

Quel est son prénom?
What's his first name?

Son prénom est Jean.
His first name is John.

Quel est son nom de famille?
What's his last name?

Son nom de famille est Granier.
His last name is Granier.

B. WHERE ARE YOU FROM?

D'où venez-vous?
Where do you come from?

Je viens de Paris.
I'm from Paris.

D'où êtes-vous?
Where are you from?

Je suis de New York.
I'm from New York.

Elle est de Londres.
She is from London.

Où êtes-vous né?
Where were you born?

Je suis né à Marseille.
I was born in Marseilles.

Elle est née à Montréal.
She was born in Montreal.

Où habitez-vous?
Where do you live?

J'habite à Paris.[1]
I live in Paris.

C. HOW OLD ARE YOU?

Quel âge avez-vous?
How old are you?

J'ai vingt-quatre ans.
I'm twenty-four.

J'aurai vingt-quatre ans en septembre.
I'll be twenty-four in September.

Je suis né le dix-neuf août mil neuf cent soixante-trois.
I was born August 19, 1963.

Quelle est la date de votre anniversaire?
When is your birthday?

Dans deux semaines, le vingt-trois janvier, ce sera mon anniversaire.
My birthday is in two weeks, January 23.

Combien de frères avez-vous?
How many brothers do you have?

---

[1] Remember: *à* may be omitted when using the verb *habiter:*
J'habite Paris.

J'ai deux frères.
I have two brothers.

L'aîné a vingt-deux ans.
The older one is twenty-two.

Il va à l'université.
He's at (goes to) the university.

Le plus jeune a dix-sept ans.
The younger one is seventeen.

Il est en première au lycée.
He's in the last year of high school.

Combien de sœurs avez-vous?
How many sisters do you have?

J'ai une sœur.
I have one sister.

Elle est moins âgée que moi.
She's younger ("less old") than I.

Elle a quinze ans.
She's fifteen.

Elle est en troisième au lycée.
She's in the ninth grade of high school.

D. Professions

Quelle est votre profession?
What is your profession?

Je suis comptable.
I'm an accountant.

Que fait votre mari?
What does your husband do?

Que fait votre femme?
What does your wife do?

Il est avocat.
He's a lawyer.

Elle est avocate.
She's a lawyer.

Il est architecte.
He's an architect.

Elle est professeur.
She's a teacher.

Il est enseignant.
He's a teacher.

Il est professeur d'université.
He's a university professor.

Il est médecin.
He's a doctor.

Elle est médecin.
She's a doctor.

Il est homme d'affaires.
He's a businessman.

Elle est femme d'affaires.
She's a businesswoman.

Il est dans les textiles.
He's in the textile business.

Il est fermier.
He's a farmer.

Elle est fonctionnaire.
She's a government employee.

Il est ouvrier.
He's a worker.

Il travaille dans une usine d'automobiles.
He works in an automobile factory.

Elle travaille dans un grand magasin.
She works in a department store.

E. FAMILY MATTERS

Est-ce que vous avez de la famille ici?
Do you have any relatives here?

Est-ce que toute votre famille habite ici?
Does all your family live here?

Toute ma famille sauf mes grands-parents.
All my family except my grandparents.

Ils habitent dans une ferme, près de Compiègne.
They live on a farm, near Compiègne.

Êtes-vous parent avec M. Blamont?
Are you related to Mr. Blamont?

C'est mon oncle.
He's my uncle.

C'est mon cousin.
He's my cousin.

Êtes-vous parent avec Mme[1] Delacourt?
Are you related to Madame Delacourt?

C'est ma tante.
She's my aunt.

C'est ma cousine.
She's my cousin.

REVIEW QUIZ 5

1. *Quel est le nom de* ——— (this) *ville?*
   a. *cet*
   b. *ce*
   c. *cette*
2. ——— (how) *puis-je aller d'ici à Paris?*
   a. *Combien*
   b. *Comment*
   c. *Quel*
3. ——— (what) *est le nom de cette rue?*
   a. *Que*
   b. *Qui*
   c. *Quel*

---

[1] *Mme* is the abbreviation for *Madame*.

4. ——— (where) *est la rue Boileau?*
   a. *Où*
   b. *Quand*
   c. *Que*

5. ——— (go) *par là.*
   a. *Allez*
   b. *Aller*
   c. *Allons*

6. *Allez au bout de la rue et prenez la première à*
   ——— (left).
   a. *loin*
   b. *droite*
   c. *gauche*

7. ——— (how much) *est-ce?*
   a. *Comment*
   b. *Combien*
   c. *Que*

8. *Je voudrais* ——— (to write) *une lettre.*
   a. *écrivez*
   b. *écrire*
   c. *écrive*

9. *Où puis-je acheter un* ——— (stamp)?
   a. *timbre*
   b. *poste*
   c. *buvard*

10. *Au coin de la* ——— (street).
    a. *avenue*
    b. *ici*
    c. *rue*

11. ——— (there) *a-t-il un téléphone ici?*
    a. *Y*
    b. *Là*
    c. *Ça*

12. *Mademoiselle, vous m'avez donné un ———— (wrong) numéro.*
    a. *pas*
    b. *faut*
    c. *mauvais*

13. *Quel est son ———— (first name)?*
    a. *prénom*
    b. *famille*
    c. *appelle*

14. *Où êtes-vous ———— (born)?*
    a. *ne*
    b. *né*
    c. *ni*

15. *Le plus jeune a dix-sept ———— (years).*
    a. *ans*
    b. *an*
    c. *année*

16. *Elle est ———— (lawyer).*
    a. *professeur*
    b. *avocate*
    c. *fonctionnaire*

17. *Il est ———— (businessman).*
    a. *homme d'affaires*
    b. *fonctionnaire*
    c. *enseignant*

18. *Ils habitent dans une ferme, ———— (near) de Compiègne.*
    a. *près*
    b. *très*
    c. *loin*

19. *———— (follow) cette route.*
    a. *Allez*
    b. *Suivez*
    c. *Prenez*

20. *Est-ce* ——— (far) *d'ici?*
    a. *loin*
    b. *coin*
    c. *près*
21. *Sur la* ——— (track) *numéro deux.*
    a. *train*
    b. *retour*
    c. *voie*
22. *C'est* ——— (I).
    a. *moi*
    b. *je*
    c. *mien*
23. *La ligne est* ——— (busy).
    a. *occupée*
    b. *livre*
    c. *faux*
24. *Êtes-vous* ——— (related) *avec M. Blamont?*
    a. *sauf*
    b. *parent*
    c. *famille*
25. *Toute ma famille* ——— (except) *mes grands-parents.*
    a. *sauf*
    b. *sera*
    c. *usine*

ANSWERS

1—c; 2—b; 3—c; 4—a; 5—a; 6—c; 7—b; 8—b;
9—a; 10—c; 11—a; 12—c; 13—a; 14—b; 15—a;
16—b; 17—a; 18—a; 19—b; 20—a; 21—c; 22—a;
23—a; 24—b; 25—a.

SUPPLEMENTAL VOCABULARY 12: FAMILY AND RELATIONSHIPS

family and relationships	*la famille et les liens de parenté*
mother	*la mère*
father	*le père*
son	*le fils*
daughter	*la fille*
sister	*la sœur*
baby	*le bébé*
brother	*le frère*
husband	*le mari*
wife	*la femme*
aunt	*la tante*
uncle	*l'oncle*
grandmother	*la grand-mère (pl: les grands-mères)*
grandfather	*le grand-père (pl: les grands-pères)*
cousin	*le cousin, la cousine*
mother-in-law	*la belle-mère (pl: les belles-mères)*
father-in-law	*le beau-père (pl: les beaux-pères)*
stepmother	*la belle-mère*
stepfather	*le beau-père*
stepson	*le beau-fils (pl: les beaux-fils)*
stepdaughter	*la belle-fille (pl: les belles-filles)*
boyfriend	*le copain*
girlfriend	*la copine*
fiancé(e)	*le fiancé (m.), la fiancée (f.)*
friend	*l'ami (m.), l'amie (f.)*

relative	*le parent*
to love	*aimer*
to know (a person)	*connaître (une personne/quelqu'un)*
to meet (a person)	*rencontrer (une personne/quelqu'un)*
to marry (someone)	*épouser (quelqu'un)*
to divorce (someone)	*divorcer de (quelqu'un)*
to get a divorce	*divorcer*
to inherit	*hériter*

SUPPLEMENTAL VOCABULARY 13:
ON THE JOB

jobs	*les professions*
police man/woman	*le policier, la femme policier*
lawyer	*l'avocat*
doctor	*le docteur, la doctoresse*
engineer	*l'ingénieur*
businessman/woman	*l'homme d'affaires, la femme d'affaires*
salesman/woman	*le vendeur, la vendeuse*
teacher	*l'enseignant, l'enseignante*
professor	*le professeur*
banker	*le banquier (m.), la banquière (f.)*
architect	*l'architecte*
veterinarian	*le vétérinaire*
dentist	*le dentiste*
stay-at-home mom/dad	*la femme au foyer, l'homme au foyer*
carpenter	*le charpentier*
construction worker	*l'ouvrier en bâtiment*

taxi driver	le chauffeur de taxi
artist	l'artiste
writer	l'écrivain
plumber	le plombier
electrician	l'électricien
journalist	le journaliste, la journaliste
actor/actress	l'acteur (m.), l'actrice (f.)
musician	le musicien, la musicienne
farmer	le fermier, la fermière
secretary/assistant	le secrétaire, la secrétaire/l'assistant, l'assistante
unemployed	sans emploi; au chômage
retired	à la retraite
full-time	à plein temps
part-time	à temps partiel
steady job	l'emploi (m.) régulier
summer job	l'emploi saisonnier

LESSON 37

A. SHOPPING

1. **C'est combien, s'il vous plaît?**
   How much is it, please?
2. **Cinquante euros.**
   Fifty euros.
3. **C'est un peu trop cher. Vous n'avez rien d'autre?**
   It's a bit too expensive. You don't have anything else?
4. **Dans le même genre?**
   Of the same kind?

5. **Oui, dans le même genre.**
   Yes, the same kind.
6. **Il y a ceci.**
   We have this.
7. **Vous n'avez rien d'autre à me montrer?**
   Don't you have anything else to show me?
8. **De moins cher?**
   Less expensive?
9. **Si possible.**
   If possible.
10. **Est-ce que ceci vous plairait?**
    Would you like this?
11. **Oui, c'est très joli. C'est combien, s'il vous plaît?**
    Yes, it's very pretty. How much is it, please?
12. **C'est trente euros.**
    This is thirty euros.
13. **Et ceci, c'est moins cher ou plus cher?**
    How about this? Is it cheaper or more expensive?
14. **Plus cher.**
    More expensive.
15. **Vous n'avez rien d'autre?**
    Don't you have anything else?
16. **Pas pour l'instant, mais j'attends des nouveautés.**
    Not at the moment, but I'm expecting some new styles soon.
17. **Quand ça?**
    When?
18. **D'un jour à l'autre. Passez vers la fin de la semaine.**
    Any day now. Drop in toward the end of the week.
19. **Certainement. Et ça c'est combien?**
    I'll do that. And this, how much is it?

20. **Trois euros la paire.**
Three euros a pair.
21. **Donnez-m'en une douzaine.**
Let me have a dozen.
22. **Voulez-vous les emporter?**
Will you take them with you?
23. **Non, faites-les-moi livrer, s'il vous plaît.**
No, please have them delivered.
24. **Toujours à la même adresse?**
Still at the same address?
25. **Oui, c'est toujours la même.**
It's still the same.
26. **Merci beaucoup. Au revoir, Madame.**
Thank you very much. Good-bye.
27. **Au revoir.**
Good-bye.

NOTES

1. *C'est combien?* "It's how much?"—*C'est quel prix?* "It's what price?"—*Ça revient à combien?* "It comes to how much?"
3. *Rien d'autre* nothing else. Notice the use of *de* (*d'* in this case because it comes before a vowel).
6. *Il y a ceci.* "There is this."
10. *Plairait* would please you; from *plaire* to please.
13. "And this, is it less expensive or more expensive?"
16. *Attendre* to expect. *Nouveautés* novelties; new styles. *Nouveauté de la saison.* Latest style.
17. "When's that?"
18. "From one day to the other."—*Passer* to pass or stop by.—*La fin de la semaine* the end of the week. *La fin de la journée* the end of the day. *La fin du mois* the end of the month. *La fin de l'année* the end of the year.

23. *Faites!* Go ahead!; from *faire* to make, do (see page 239). *Faites-les-moi livrer.* Have them delivered to me.

24. *Toujours* always. *Toujours* sometimes translates as "still": *Toujours à la même adresse?* Still the same address? *Est-il toujours à Paris?* Is he still in Paris?—Notice that *adresse* has only one *d* in French.

27. Common expressions for "good-bye" are: (*formal*) *Au revoir, Adieu* (used when one doesn't ever expect to see a person again or not for a very long time), *Au plaisir* "Till I see you again," *À la prochaine* (*fois*) "Until the next time," *À demain* "Until tomorrow," *À bientôt* "See you soon," *À tout à l'heure* "See you soon."

QUIZ 26

1. *C'est* ——— (how much)?
   a. *combien*
   b. *comment*
   c. *quand*

2. *Dans le même* ——— (kind).
   a. *genre*
   b. *chose*
   c. *cher*

3. *Vous n'avez rien d'autre* ——— (to) *me montrer?*
   a. *pour*
   b. *à*
   c. *de*

4. *Il y a* ——— (this).
   a. *ce*
   b. *ça*
   c. *ceci*

5. *De* —— (less) *cher.*
    a. *mais*
    b. *moins*
    c. *rien*

6. —— (it's) *très joli.*
    a. *C'est*
    b. *Ceci*
    c. *Ci*

7. *Pas pour l'instant,* —— (but) *j'attends des nouveautés.*
    a. *ou*
    b. *mais*
    c. *ça*

8. —— (when) *ça?*
    a. *Comment*
    b. *Combien*
    c. *Quand*

9. *Donnez-m'*—— (of them) *une douzaine.*
    a. *y*
    b. *en*
    c. *ou*

10. *Non, faites-* —— (them) *-moi livrer, s'il vous plaît.*
    a. *les*
    b. *leurs*
    c. *en*

ANSWERS
1—a; 2—a; 3—b; 4—c; 5—b; 6—a; 7—b; 8—c;
9—b; 10—a.

B. ORDERING BREAKFAST

1. *G:*[1] **Tu dois avoir faim.**
   G: You must be hungry.
2. *Mme G:* **Oui, je prendrais bien quelque chose.**
   Mrs. G: Yes, I could certainly eat something.
3. *G:* **Il y a un bon restaurant à l'hôtel.**
   G: There's a good restaurant at the hotel.
4. *Mme G:* **C'est une bonne idée, allons-y.**
   Mrs. G: That's a good idea. Let's go there.
5. *G:* **Monsieur!**
   G: Waiter!
6. *W:* **Vous désirez, Madame, Monsieur?**
   W: Yes, madam, sir?
7. *G:* **Le petit déjeuner.**
   G: We'd like breakfast.
8. *Mme G:* **Qu'est-ce que vous servez d'habi-tude?**
   Mrs. G: What do you usually offer?
9. *W:* **Café au lait, ou thé au citron, ou au lait, ou bien du chocolat au lait.**
   W: Coffee, tea with lemon or milk, or else hot chocolate.
10. *Mme G:* **Et avec cela?**
    Mrs. G: And what with that?
11. *W:* **Des petits pains ou des croissants ou des brioches.**
    W: Rolls or croissants or brioches.
12. *Mme G:* **Pas de beurre?**
    Mrs. G: No butter?
13. *W:* **Si, Madame, avec du beurre et de la confiture.**
    W: Of course, madam, with butter and jelly.

[1] *G* stands for *Monsieur Granier,* Mme G for *Madame Granier. W* stands for "Waiter."

14. *Mme G:* **Je voudrais un café au lait et des croissants.**
    Mrs. G: I'd like some coffee and some croissants.

15. *G:* **Donnez-moi la même chose et aussi un œuf au plat.**
    G: Let me have the same and a fried egg as well.

16. *W:* **Très bien, Monsieur. Monsieur désire-t-il quelque chose d'autre?**
    W: Certainly, sir. Would you like anything else?

17. *G:* **Non, c'est tout.**
    G: No, that'll be all.

18. *Mme G:* **Monsieur, une serviette, je vous prie.**
    Mrs. G: Waiter, may I have a napkin, please?

19. *G:* **Voulez-vous aussi me donner une fourchette?**
    G: Can you also give me a fork?

20. *Mme G:* **Un peu plus de sucre aussi, s'il vous plaît.**
    Mrs. G: And some more sugar, please.

21. *W:* **Voilà, Madame.**
    W: Here you are, madam.

22. *Mme G:* **Mon café est froid. Apportez-m'en un autre, s'il vous plaît.**
    Mrs. G: My coffee is cold. Please bring me another cup.

23. *W:* **Avec plaisir.**
    W: Gladly.

24. *G:* **Monsieur, l'addition, s'il vous plaît.**
    G: Waiter, may I have the check, please?

25. *W:* **Voilà, Monsieur.**
    W: Here you are, sir.

26. *G:* **Voici. Gardez la monnaie.**
    G: Here, keep the change.

27. *W:* **Merci beaucoup, Monsieur. Au revoir, Madame.**
W: Thank you very much, sir. Good-bye, madam.

28. *G:* **Au revoir.**
G: Good-bye.

NOTES

1. *Tu dois* you must, you should; from *devoir* (see page 294). *Devoir* also means to owe. *Tu me dois cent francs.* You owe me a hundred francs.

2. *Je prendrais* I would take; from *prendre* to take. *Bien* well. *Bien* can often be translated "certainly."

5. *Monsieur* waiter. The word also means "sir" or "Mister." A waitress would be addressed as *Mademoiselle* or *Madame. Monsieur* has now replaced the once common term for waiter, *garçon,* which also means "boy" or "fellow."

6. *Vous désirez?* "You desire?"

7. *Le petit déjeuner* breakfast. *Le déjeuner* lunch. *Le dîner* dinner.

8. "What do you usually offer?" means "What does your standard breakfast consist of?"

9. *Café au lait* ("coffee with milk") is served with the milk already in it. In small cafés you can also ask for a *café crème* but this too has milk rather than cream.

10. "And with that?"

11. *Des petits pains.* Rolls. For the use of *des* see page 50.

13. *Si* yes. *Si* is used for *yes* when it contradicts the previous negative statement.

15. *Un œuf* an egg. *Des œufs* eggs. *Un œuf à la coque* ("egg in a shell") a soft-boiled egg. *Un*

œuf dur a hard-boiled egg. *Un œuf au plat* ("an egg on the plate") a fried egg. *Des œufs brouillés* scrambled eggs. *Un œuf poché* a poached egg.

18. *Je vous prie* "I beg you"; please.

20. *Un peu plus de sucre* a little more sugar. Notice the use of *de. S'il vous plaît* ("if it pleases you") please. Abbreviated to *s.v.p.: Fermez la porte, s.v.p.* Please close the door. *Tournez le bouton, s.v.p.* Please turn the knob.

26. *La monnaie* small change. "Money" is *l'argent*.

C. To Eat: *Manger, Prendre*

1. I eat

je mange	I eat
tu manges	you eat (*fam.*)
il mange	he eats
nous mangeons	we eat
vous mangez	you eat (*pl.* and *pol.*)
ils mangent	they eat

Renée et Sabine mangent tôt.
Renée and Sabine eat early.

Philippe ne mange jamais de viande.
Philip never eats meat.

2. I take; "I'll have"

je prends	I take
tu prends	you take (*fam.*)
il prend	he takes
nous prenons	we take
vous prenez	you take (*pl.* and *pol.*)
ils prennent	they take

Je prends le déjeuner à deux heures.
I have lunch at two o'clock.

Ils prennent du gâteau comme dessert.
They're having cake for dessert.

Prendrez-vous une boisson?
Will you have a drink?

   3. A sample lunch menu

MENU

Potage aux légumes
Omelette aux fines herbes
Poulet rôti
Haricots verts
Pommes de terre Parisienne
Salade
Crêpes Suzette
Plateau de fromages
Café et digestifs

MENU

Vegetable Soup
Omelet "with savory herbs"
Roast Chicken
String Beans
Boiled Potatoes
Salad
Crêpes Suzette
Cheese Plate
Coffee and Liqueurs

REVIEW QUIZ 6

1. *Tu dois* ———— (have) *faim.*
   a. *être*
   b. *avoir*
   c. *bon*

2. *Pas de* ———— (butter).
   a. *bon*
   b. *beurre*
   c. *bonne*

3. ———— (there is) *un bon restaurant à l'hôtel.*
   a. *Il y a*
   b. *Il va*
   c. *C'est*

4. *Mon café est* ———— (cold).
   a. *froid*
   b. *chaud*
   c. *chose*

5. *Donnez-moi la* ———— (same) *chose.*
   a. *aussi*
   b. *même*
   c. *beurre*

6. *Monsieur, une* ———— (napkin) *s'il vous plaît.*
   a. *fourchette*
   b. *couteau*
   c. *serviette*

7. *Voulez-vous* ———— (also) *me donner une four-chette?*
   a. *bien*
   b. *pas*
   c. *aussi*

8. *Monsieur,* ———— (the check).
   a. *la fois*
   b. *le garçon*
   c. *l'addition*

9. *Un peu* ——— (more) *de sucre.*
   a. *plaît*
   b. *nous*
   c. *plus*
10. *Gardez la* ——— (change).
    a. *beaucoup*
    b. *monnaie*
    c. *laissez*

ANSWERS
1—b; 2—b; 3—a; 4—a; 5—b; 6—c; 7—c; 8—c;
9—c; 10—b.

SUPPLEMENTAL VOCABULARY 14: CLOTHING

clothing	*les vêtements*
shirt	*la chemise*
pants	*le pantalon*
jeans	*le jean*
tee shirt	*le T-shirt*
shoe(s)	*la chaussure*
sock(s)	*la chaussette*
belt	*la ceinture*
sneaker/tennis shoe	*la (chaussure de) basket*
dress	*la robe*
skirt	*la jupe*
blouse	*le chemisier*
suit	*le costume*
hat	*le chapeau*
glove(s)	*le gant*
scarf	*le foulard, l'écharpe (f.)*
jacket	*la veste*
coat	*le manteau*
jewelry	*le bijou, les bijoux*

earring	*la boucle d'oreille*
bracelet	*le bracelet*
necklace	*le collier*
eyeglasses	*les lunettes*
sunglasses	*les lunettes de soleil*
watch	*la montre*
ring	*la bague*
underpants	*les sous-vêtements/le caleçon*
bra	*le soutien-gorge*
panties	*le slip, la culotte*
thong	*le string*
undershirt	*le tricot de peau*
bathing trunks/suit	*le maillot de bain*
pajamas	*le pyjama*
cotton	*le coton*
leather	*le cuir*
silk	*la soie*
size	*la taille*
to wear	*porter*

LESSON 38

A. In, On, Under, etc.

1. *dans* "in, into"

C'est dans le dictionnaire.	It's in the dictionary.
Il l'a mis dans sa poche.	He put it into his pocket.
Vous le trouverez dans sa chambre.	You'll find it in his room.

J'ai quelque chose dans l'oeil.	I have something in my eye.
Mettez-le dans le tiroir.	Put it into the drawer.
Je serai là dans un instant.	I'll be there in a minute.

2. *dedans* "inside"

Regardez dans le dictionnaire, c'est dedans.	Look in the dictionary; you'll find it there.
Regardez là-dedans.	Look in there.

3. *en* "in"
  En means "in" in certain expressions:

En avril.	In April.
En été.	In the summer.
En ville.	In town.
En une seconde.	In a second.

4. *sur* "on"

Mettez cette lettre sur son bureau.	Put this letter on his desk.
Son nom est sur la porte.	His name is on the door.
Écrivez-le sur l'enve- loppe.	Write it on the enve- lope.
Vous pouvez compter sur moi.	You can count on me.

5. *sous* "under"

C'est sous la chaise.	It's under the chair.
Vous trouverez ce livre sous les autres.	You'll find this book under the others.

Il l'a mis sous le lit. He put it under the
          bed.

Je l'ai trouvé sous I found it under a
 un tas de papiers. pile of papers.

 6. *dessus* "on, on top of"

Mettez-le au-dessus. Put it on top.
Regardez donc dessus. Look on the top.
Mettez ce livre là-dessus. Put the book on that.

 7. *dessous* "under, underneath"

Mettez ça dessous. Put that underneath.
Voyez ci-dessous. Look under here. "See
         below."

 8. *si* "if"
  Si becomes *s'* before *il* or *ils*.

Si je peux. If I can.
Si j'ai de l'argent. If I have (enough)
         money.
S'il vient. If he comes.
Si vous voulez. If you wish.
S'il vous plaît. Please. ("If it
         pleases you.")
Si ça vous plaît. If you like that.

 9. *si* "so"
  Unlike *si* meaning "if," *si* meaning "so" never
  becomes *s'*.

C'est si bon It's so good!
C'est si commode! It's so convenient!

Il se fait si tard! It's so late.
Ce n'est pas si mau- It's not as bad as that.
  vais que ça.
Il n'est pas si igno- He's not as ignorant as
  rant que ça. that.

10. *par* "by"

Par où? Which way?
Par ici. This way.
Par là. That way.
Par lui. By him.
Par exemple. For example.
Parfois. Sometimes.

11. *sans* "without"

Sans moi. Without me.
Sans argent. Without money.
Sans rien. Without anything.
Sans personne. Without anyone.
Sans faute. Without fail.
Sans difficulté. Without difficulty.
Vous pouvez le faire You can do it without
  sans aucune diffi- any difficulty.
  culté.

QUIZ 27

1. *Mettez ça dessous.*
2. *Par où?*
3. *C'est dans le dictionnaire.*
4. *Écrivez-le sur l'enveloppe.*
5. *Son nom est sur la porte.*
6. *Regardez donc dessus.*

7. *Si ça vous plaît.*
8. *Ce n'est pas si mauvais que ça.*
9. *Parfois.*
10. *Sans faute.*
11. *Sans difficulté.*
12. *Sans argent.*
13. *Si vous voulez.*
14. *Mettez-le au-dessus.*
15. *Vous trouverez ce livre sous les autres.*

a. It's in the dictionary.
b. Put that underneath.
c. Which way?
d. His name is on the door.
e. Write it on the envelope.
f. You'll find this book under the others.
g. Put it on top.
h. Look on the top.
i. If you wish.
j. If you like that.
k. It's not as bad as that.
l. Sometimes.
m. Without money.
n. Without fail.
o. Without difficulty.

ANSWERS
1—b; 2—c; 3—a; 4—e; 5—d; 6—h; 7—j; 8—k;
9—l; 10—n; 11—o; 12—m; 13—i; 14—g; 15—f.

B. APARTMENT HUNTING

1. **Je viens pour l'appartement.**
   I've come about the apartment.
2. **Lequel?**
   Which one?

3. **Celui qui est à louer.**
   The one for rent.

4. **Mais il y en a deux.**
   But there are two.

5. **Puis-je avoir des détails?**
   Can you describe them?

6. **Celui du quatrième est non-meublé.**
   The one on the fifth floor* is unfurnished.

7. **Et l'autre?**
   And the other?

8. **L'appartement du deuxième est meublé.**
   The one on the third floor is furnished.

9. **Combien de pièces ont-ils chacun?**
   How many rooms does each one have?

10. **Celui du quatrième a quatre pièces, cuisine et salle de bain.**
    The one on the fifth floor has four rooms, a kitchen and bath.

11. **Donne-t-il sur la cour?**
    Does it face the courtyard?

12. **Non, sur la rue.**
    No, the street.

13. **Et celui du deuxième?**
    And how about the one on the third floor?

14. **Il a cinq pièces, trois chambres à coucher, une salle à manger et un salon.**
    It has five rooms, three bedrooms, a dining room and a parlor.

15. **Donne-t-il sur la cour aussi?**
    Is it on the courtyard?

16. **Non, sur la rue.**
    No, it faces the street.

---

*In France the ground floor is called the *rez-de-chaussée,* so the first floor (above it) corresponds to the American second floor, and so on.

17. **Quel est le prix du loyer?**
    What's the rent?

18. **Le grand est de quatre mille trois cents euros plus les charges.**
    The larger one is four thousand three hundred euros plus extras.

19. **Et celui qui est meublé?**
    And the furnished one?

20. **Cinq mille plus les charges.**
    That's five thousand euros plus extras.

21. **De quel style et dans quel état sont les meubles?**
    What kind of furniture does it have? Is it in good condition?

22. **C'est un mobilier ancien en excellent état.**
    It's antique furniture in excellent condition.

23. **Le linge et l'argenterie sont-ils compris?**
    Are linens and silverware included?

24. **Il y a tout ce qu'il faut, même la batterie de cuisine.**
    You'll find everything you need, even a complete set of kitchen utensils.

25. **Le propriétaire signe-t-il un bail, et de quelle durée?**
    Would the owner give me a lease, and for how long?

26. **Il faudrait voir le gérant.**
    You'd have to see the renting agent for that.

27. **Quelles sont les conditions?**
    What are the terms?

28. **Il faut payer trois mois d'avance.**
    You have to pay three months' rent in advance.

29. **Rien d'autre?**
    Nothing else?

30. **Il faut fournir des références, bien entendu!**
    You need to provide references, of course!

31. **Au fait, y a-t-il un ascenseur?**
    By the way, is there an elevator?

32. **Non, il n'y en a pas.**
    No, there isn't.

33. **Ah, c'est dommage.**
    That's too bad.

34. **À part ça, l'immeuble est très moderne, vous savez.**
    Apart from that, though, the building is quite modern.

35. **Comment ça?**
    What do you mean?

36. **Les deux appartements ont la climatisation, un lave-vaisselle, et un four à micro-ondes.**
    Both apartments have central air-conditioning, a dishwasher, and a microwave oven.

37. **Y a-t-il l'eau courante chaude et froide?**
    Is there hot and cold running water?

38. **Certainement. Les salles de bain ont été refaites récemment.**
    Of course. The bathrooms were recently remodelled.

39. **Y a-t-il des placards?**
    Are there any closets?

40. **Oui, il y en a plusieurs et ils sont très grands.**
    Yes, there are several of them, and they are large.

41. **Peut-on visiter?**
    Can one see the place?

42. **Seulement dans la matinée.**
    Only in the morning.

43. **C'est bien, je reviendrai demain matin. Merci beaucoup.**
    Very well, I'll come tomorrow morning. Thanks a lot.

44. **De rien, à votre service.**
    Not at all. Glad to be able to help you.

NOTES

1. *Je viens pour* "I come for."
3. *Celui qui est* "the one which is."
4. Notice the use of *en* ("of it, of them"). See pages 150–52.
5. "May (can) I have some details?"
9. *Chacun* each, each one. *Ont-ils chacun?* "Do they each have?"
11. *Donne-t-il.* For the *t,* see page 34—*Donner sur* to face out on.
14. *Chambre à coucher* ("room for sleeping") bedroom.—*Salle à manger* ("room for eating") dining room—*Le salon* living room, parlor.
17. *Quel est le prix du loyer? Quel est le montant* ("amount") *du loyer? Loyer* rent. *Louer* to rent.
18. *Plus les charges* plus the extras. "Extras" refer not to gas or electricity (paid by the tenant directly to the company) but to things like city taxes, garbage removal, etc. Some landlords charge a fixed percentage of the rent (ten percent, say) for these extras.
21. Also: *genre* class, kind. *De quel genre* what style. *Etat* state, condition.
22. *C'est un mobilier ancien.* It's antique furniture.
23. *Argenterie* silverware. *Argent* silver. *Sont-ils compris?* Are they included? *Compris* ("included") is from *comprendre* to include; also to understand.
24. *Tout ce qu'il faut* everything that's needed. Notice the *que* before *il* becomes *qu'il* (see pages 177–180).
25. *Propriétaire* owner; here it means "landlord." *Durée* duration, length of time.
26. *Gérant* manager (also hotel manager). The *gérant* of an apartment house is the agent who

manages a building and who receives a certain
percentage of the income.

27. It is customary for a tenant to leave a deposit for
three or six months' rent, which is applied to the
last three or six months of the lease—*Un bail,*
unlike our lease, is usually for three, six, or nine
years.

31. *Au fait* by the way. *Y a-t-il = Est-ce qu'il y a.*

32. Notice the use of *en* (see pages 156–158).

34. Notice this use of *vous savez* ("you know").

35. *Comment ça?* ("How's that?") How come? What
do you mean?

36. *L'air climatisé central* central air-conditioning.
Un lave-vaisselle a dishwasher. *Un four* an oven;
un four à micro-ondes a microwave oven.

40. *Énorme* large, enormous. *Nombreux* numerous.

41. *Peut-on visiter?* "Can one visit?"

42. *Matin* is the general word for "morning." When
you say "in the morning," etc., you use *matinée:*
dans la matinée in the morning.

43. *Je reviendrai* I'll return, I'll come back; from
revenir to return.

44. *De rien* ("Of nothing") is one reply to *merci.*
Another common reply is *Je vous en prie.* You
are welcome.—*À votre service* "at your service."

QUIZ 28

1. ——— (how many) *de pièces ont-ils?*
   a. *Autre*
   b. *Combien*
   c. *Chacun*

2. *Donne-t-il sur la* ——— (street)?
   a. *cour*
   b. *salon*
   c. *rue*

3. *Quel est le* —— (price) *du loyer?*
   a. *prix*
   b. *mille*
   c. *genre*

4. *On* —— (pay) *trois mois d'avance.*
   a. *sont*
   b. *entendu*
   c. *paie*

5. *La* —— (house) *est très moderne.*
   a. *dommage*
   b. *maison*
   c. *comment*

6. *Y a-t-il des* —— (closets)?
   a. *fours*
   b. *placards*
   c. *micro-ondes*

7. —— (only) *dans la matinée.*
   a. *Visiter*
   b. *Seulement*
   c. *Chauffées*

8. *Je reviendrai* —— (tomorrow) *matin.*
   a. *demain*
   b. *seulement*
   c. *bien*

9. —— (thank you) *beaucoup.*
   a. *Matin*
   b. *Service*
   c. *Merci*

ANSWERS
1—b; 2—c; 3—a; 4—c; 5—b; 6—b; 7—b; 8—a;
9—c.

REVIEW QUIZ 7

1. *Je préfère* ——— (that one).
   a. *ce*
   b. *celui-là*
   c. *cette*
2. *Que veut dire* ——— (this)?
   a. *ceci*
   b. *cela*
   c. *cet*
3. *Je ne sais pas* ——— (how).
   a. *encore*
   b. *souvent*
   c. *comment*
4. *Il ne vient* ——— (never).
   a. *quand*
   b. *jamais*
   c. *comment*
5. *Il n'a* ——— (nothing) *dit*.
   a. *plus*
   b. *quand*
   c. *rien*
6. *Votre livre est meilleur que le* ——— (his).
   a. *vôtres*
   b. *lui*
   c. *sien*
7. *Je suis* ——— (happy) *de faire votre connaissance*.
   a. *heureux*
   b. *présenter*
   c. *connaissance*
8. *À la* ——— (week) *prochaine*.
   a. *vrai*
   b. *semaine*
   c. *fois*

9. *À la* ——— (next) *fois.*
    a. *nouvelles*
    b. *prochaine*
    c. *jours*

10. *Ça va bien,* ——— (thanks).
    a. *neuf*
    b. *merci*
    c. *comment*

11. *Téléphonez-moi un de ces* ——— (days).
    a. *semaine*
    b. *jours*
    c. *neuf*

12. *Y a-t-il un* ——— (elevator)?
    a. *ascenseur*
    b. *placard*
    c. *cour*

13. *Non, je ne* ——— (think) *pas.*
    a. *plaisir*
    b. *pense*
    c. *connais*

14. *J'* ——— (hope) *vous revoir bientôt.*
    a. *enchanté*
    b. *fait*
    c. *espère*

15. *Je vais vous l'* ——— (write).
    a. *avez*
    b. *écrire*
    c. *retrouvons*

16. *Quel est le prix du* ——— (rent)?
    a. *cuisine*
    b. *four*
    c. *loyer*

17. *Enchanté de vous avoir* ——— (met).
    a. *enchanté*
    b. *rencontré*
    c. *fait*

18. —— (give)-*moi votre adresse personnelle.*
    a. *Vais*
    b. *Donnez*
    c. *Appeler*
19. *C'est très* —— (good).
    a. *bien*
    b. *bientôt*
    c. *aussi*
20. *À* —— (soon).
    a. *bientôt*
    b. *matin*
    c. *adresse*

ANSWERS
1—b; 2—a; 3—c; 4—b; 5—c; 6—c; 7—a; 8—b;
9—b; 10—b; 11—b; 12—a; 13—b; 14—c; 15—b;
16—c; 17—b; 18—b; 19—a; 20—a.

C. WORD STUDY

capable	capable
la chance	luck
la créature	creature
la direction	direction
la leçon	lesson
le papier	paper
sérieux	serious
sévère	severe
le terme	term
l'usage (*m.*)	usage

SUPPLEMENTAL VOCABULARY 15: IN THE KITCHEN

in the kitchen	*dans la cuisine*
refrigerator	*le réfrigérateur*

(kitchen) sink	*l' évier (m.) de la cuisine*
counter	*le comptoir/le bar*
stove	*la cuisinière*
oven	*le four*
microwave	*le micro-onde (pl: les micro-ondes)*
cupboard	*le placard*
drawer	*le tiroir*
plate	*l' assiette (f.)*
cup	*la tasse*
bowl	*le saladier*
glass	*le verre*
spoon	*la cuillère*
knife	*le couteau*
can	*la boîte de conserve*
box	*la boîte*
bottle	*la bouteille*
carton	*la boîte en carton*
coffee maker	*la cafetière*
tea kettle	*la théière*
blender	*le mixer*
iron	*le fer à repasser*
ironing board	*la planche à repasser*
broom	*le balai*
dishwasher	*le lave-vaisselle*
washing machine	*la machine à laver, le lave-linge*
dryer	*le sèche-linge*
to cook	*cuisiner*
to do the dishes	*faire la vaisselle*
to do the laundry	*faire la lessive*
dishwashing detergent	*la lessive vaisselle*
laundry detergent	*la lessive*
bleach	*l' eau (f.) de javel*
clean/dirty	*propre/sale*

SUPPLEMENTAL VOCABULARY 16:
IN THE BATHROOM

in the bathroom	*dans la salle de bain*
toilet	*le cabinet de toilette*
sink (wash basin)	*l' évier (de la salle de bain)*
bathtub	*la baignoire*
shower	*la douche*
mirror	*le miroir*
medicine cabinet	*l' armoire à pharmacie*
towel	*la serviette*
toilet paper	*le papier hygiénique*
shampoo	*le shampooing*
soap	*le savon*
bath gel	*le gel douche*
shaving cream	*la crème à raser*
razor	*le rasoir*
to wash oneself	*se laver*
to take a shower/bath	*prendre une douche/un bain*
to shave	*se raser*
cologne	*l' eau (f.) de cologne*
perfume	*le parfum*
deodorant	*le déodorant*
bandage	*le bandage/le pansement*
powder	*la poudre/le talc*

LESSON 39

A. To Come: *Venir*

je viens	I come	*nous venons*	we come
tu viens	you come (*fam.*)	*vous venez*	you come (*pl. and pol.*)
il vient	he comes	*ils viennent*	they come

Viens!	Come! (*fam.*)
Venez!	Come! (*pl.* and *pol.*)
Venez ici.	Come here.
Venez avec moi.	Come with me.
Revenez.	Come again.
Venez à la maison.	Come to the house.
Venez un soir.	Come some evening.
Ne venez pas.	Don't come.
D'où venez-vous?	Where are you coming from? Where do you come from?
Je viens de Paris.	I'm coming from Paris. I come from Paris.
Je viens du théâtre.	I'm coming from the theater.
Je viens tout de suite.	I'm coming right away.

Venir de . . . means "to have just."

Je viens de le voir.	I've just seen him.
Je viens de sortir de chez lui.	I've just left his place (his house).
Je viens de le faire.	I've just done it.

B. To Say: *Dire*

je dis	I say	*nous disons*	we say
tu dis	you say (*fam.*)	*vous dites*	you say (*pl.* and *pol.*)
il dit	he says	*ils disent*	they say

On dit que ...	It's said that ... People say that ... They say that ...
On m'a dit que ...	I've been told that ...
C'est-à-dire ...	That's to say ... That is ...
C'est difficile à dire.	It's hard to say.
Dites!	Say (it)! Tell (it)!
Dites-le.	Say it.
Dites-le encore.	Say it again.
Dites-le en français.	Say it in French.
Dites-le lentement.	Say it slowly.
Ne le dites pas.	Don't say it.
Ne dites pas ça.	Don't say that.
Dites donc.	(shows surprise or disbelief)
Dites donc, vous n'êtes pas sérieux, n'est-ce pas?	Say, you're not serious, are you?
Dites-moi.	Tell me.
Dites-le-moi.	Say it to me.
Dites-lui.	Tell him.
Dites-le-lui.	Tell it to him.
Dites-lui de venir.	Tell him to come.
Ne le lui dites pas.	Don't tell it to him. Don't tell him.
Ne lui dites rien.	Don't tell him anything.

Surtout ne le dites à personne.	Above all, don't tell it to anybody.
Qu'est-ce que vous dites?	What did you say? ("What is it that you say?")
Pouvez-vous me dire où se trouve l'hôtel?	Can you tell me where there's a hotel?
Qu'est-ce que vous voulez dire?	What do you mean? ("What do you want to say?")
Il n'a rien dit.	He hasn't said anything.

QUIZ 29

1. *Je viens du théâtre.*	a. Come with me.
2. *Je viens de le faire.*	b. Where are you coming from?
3. *Je viens tout de suite.*	c. Come some evening.
4. *D'où venez-vous?*	d. I'm coming right away.
5. *Dites-moi.*	e. I'm coming from the theater.
6. *Dites-le en français.*	f. Say it in French.
7. *C'est difficile à dire.*	g. That's to say . . .
8. *Venez un soir.*	h. It's hard to say.
9. *Venez avec moi.*	i. I've just done it.
10. *C'est-à-dire . . .*	j. Tell me.

ANSWERS

1—e; 2—i; 3—d; 4—b; 5—j; 6—f; 7—h; 8—c; 9—a; 10—g.

C. To Do, To Make: *FAIRE*

je fais	I do	*nous faisons*	we do
tu fais	you do	*vous faites*	you do
il fait	he does	*ils font*	they do

Je le fais.	I do it. I'm doing it.
Je ne le fais pas.	I don't do it. I'm not doing it.
Que faites-vous? *Qu'est-ce que vous faites?*	What are you doing?
Comment faites-vous ça?	How do you do that?
Qu'est-ce que vous avez fait?	What have you been doing?
Ne le faites pas.	Don't do it!
Ne le faites plus.	Don't do it anymore.
C'est fait.	It's done. It's over.
Deux et deux font quatre.	Two and two are four.
Ça me fait mal.	That hurts me.
Je ne fais rien.	I'm not doing anything.
Ça ne fait rien.	That doesn't matter. I don't mind.
Ça ne fait rien du tout.	It doesn't matter at all.
Ça ne me fait rien.	It doesn't matter to me.
Faites cela (ça)!	Do that.
Ne faites pas cela (ça)!	Don't do it!
Faites-le encore!	Do it again.
Faites-le encore une fois!	Do it once more.
Faites ça vite!	Do it quickly!
Ne faites pas cela (ça)!	Don't do that!

Ne faites rien.	Don't do anything.
Faites attention!	Pay attention!
Faites donc attention.	Mind what you're doing.
Faites bien attention.	Pay close attention.
Ne faites pas attention à cela (ça).	Don't mind that. Don't pay attention to that.
Il ne faut pas faire cela (ça).	You (we, etc.) mustn't do that. That mustn't be done.
Je viens de le faire.	I've just done it.
J'ai déjà fait sa connaissance.	I've already met him. ("I've already made his acquaintance.")
Il fait froid.	It's cold. The weather's cold.
Il fait chaud.	It's hot. The weather's hot.
Vous permettez?— Faites donc! Je vous en prie.	May I? Please do! Go ahead.
Que faire?	What's to be done? What shall we do? What can be done? ("What to do?").
Comment faire?	How shall we do it? What shall we do? ("How to do?")
Qui a fait cela (ça)?	Who did that?
Je ne sais que faire.	I don't know what to do.

QUIZ 30

1. *Qu'est-ce que vous avez fait?*   a. Do that!

2. *Ne le faites pas.*   b. Do it quickly.
3. *C'est fait.*   c. What are you doing?
4. *Ça ne fait rien.*   d. What have you done?
5. *Il fait froid.*   e. Don't do it.
6. *Faites donc atten-*   f. It's done. It's over.
   tion.
7. *Faites-le encore*   g. It's different.
   une fois.
8. *Qui a fait ça?*   h. Never mind. That
                                       doesn't matter.
9. *Je viens de le*   i. It doesn't matter at
   faire.   all.
10. *Fais attention!*   j. Do it once more.
                                       ("One more
                                       time.")
11. *C'est différent.*   k. But pay attention!
                                       Mind what you're
                                       doing.
12. *Faites ça!*   l. Pay attention!
                                       Watch out!
13. *Qu'est-ce que vous*   m. I've just done it.
    faites?
14. *Faites ça vite.*   n. It's cold.
15. *Ça ne fait rien du*   o. Who did that?
    tout.

ANSWERS
1—d; 2—e; 3—f; 4—h; 5—n; 6—k; 7—j; 8—o;
9—m; 10—l; 11—g; 12—a; 13—c; 14—b; 15—i.

REVIEW QUIZ 8

1. *Je* ——— (I'm coming) *tout de suite.*
   a. *venez*
   b. *viens*
   c. *vois*

2. *C'est difficile à* ——— (say).
   a. *venir*
   b. *venez*
   c. *dire*

3. *Qu'est ce que vous* ——— (do)?
   a. *dire*
   b. *faites*
   c. *dites*

4. *Je ne sais que* ——— (do).
   a. *dire*
   b. *venir*
   c. *faire*

5. *Quand j'habitais en France, j'* ——— (had)
   beaucoup d'amis français.
   a. *étais*
   b. *avais*
   c. *faisais*

6. *Ne le* ——— (take) *pas.*
   a. *prenez*
   b. *envoyez*
   c. *essayez*

7. ——— (stop) *tout de suite.*
   a. *Arrêtez*
   b. *Apportez*
   c. *Aidez*

8. *Mettez cette lettre* ——— (on) *le bureau.*
   a. *sous*
   b. *sur*
   c. *dans*

9. *Je ne* ——— (see) *pas.*
   a. *voyons*
   b. *savoir*
   c. *vois*

10. *Venez nous ——— (see) un soir.*
    a. *voir*
    b. *sais*
    c. *vu*

11. *Il n'en ——— (knows) pas davantage.*
    a. *vois*
    b. *sait*
    c. *savoir*

12. *Il a oublié tout ce qu'il ——— (knew).*
    a. *savait*
    b. *savez*
    c. *pouvez*

13. *Il ——— (holds, is holding) son chapeau à la main.*
    a. *tenez*
    b. *peut*
    c. *tient*

14. *Je ne vois pas comment il ——— (can) faire cela.*
    a. *tient*
    b. *peut*
    c. *puis*

15. *Il ne ——— (understand) pas.*
    a. *pouvez*
    b. *comprend*
    c. *mettre*

16. *——— (put) votre chapeau.*
    a. *Comprend*
    b. *Mettez*
    c. *Mis*

17. *Je ne ——— (know) personne dans cette ville.*
    a. *suivre*
    b. *voulez*
    c. *connais*

18. *Il* —— (wants) *revenir.*
    a. *voulez*
    b. *connaît*
    c. *veut*
19. *Vous ne me* —— (owe) *rien.*
    a. *devez*
    b. *demander*
    c. *attend*
20. *Il ne* —— (ask) *rien.*
    a. *attendre*
    b. *demande*
    c. *doit*

ANSWERS
1—b; 2—c; 3—b; 4—c; 5—b; 6—a; 7—a; 8—b;
9—c; 10—a; 11—b; 12—a; 13—c; 14—b; 15—b;
16—b; 17—c; 18—c; 19—a; 20—b.

D. COULD YOU GIVE ME SOME INFORMATION?

1. **Pardon, Monsieur.**
   I beg your pardon, sir.
2. **Je vous en prie.**
   Yes, what can I do for you?
3. **Pourriez-vous me donner quelques renseigne-ments?**
   Could you give me some information?
4. **Certainement, avec plaisir.**
   Certainly! I'd be glad to.
5. **Je ne connais pas la ville, je ne m'y retrouve pas.**
   I don't know the town, I can't find my way around.
6. **C'est pourtant bien simple.**
   It's quite simple.

7. **C'est que je ne suis pas d'ici.**
   The thing is, I'm not from here.

8. **Ça ne fait rien.**
   That's all right. ("It's nothing.")

9. **La boutique avec un drapeau, qu'est-ce que c'est?**
   The store with the flag—what's that?

10. **Le poste de police.**
    That's the police station.

11. **Il y a une autre maison avec un drapeau.**
    There's another building with a flag.

12. **C'est la mairie.**
    That's the City Hall.

13. **Je vois. Et quel est le nom de cette rue?**
    I see. (And) What's the name of this street?

14. **La rue de la Préfecture. Voyez-vous cette boutique?**
    Prefecture Street. Do you see that store?

15. **Laquelle? À droite?**
    Which one? The one on the right?

16. **Oui. Avec un grand globe vert dans la vitrine.**
    Yes. The one with a large green globe in the window.

17. **Et un rouge dans l'autre?**
    And a red one in the other?

18. **C'est ça. Eh bien, c'est la pharmacie.**
    That's right. Well, that's the pharmacy.

19. **Ah, très bien.**
    I see. ("Very well.")

20. **Le docteur habite tout à côté.**
    The doctor lives right next door.

21. **Est-ce un bon médecin?**
    Is he a good doctor?

22. **Excellent. Il est tous les matins à l'hôpital.**
    An excellent one. He's at the hospital every morning.

23. **Où se trouve l'hôpital?**
    Where's the hospital?

24. **Dans la deuxième rue à gauche, avant d'arriver à la Route Nationale.**
    Two blocks from here, to your left, just before you come to the main highway.

25. **Y a-t-il une papeterie ici?**
    Is there a stationery store here?

26. **Bien sûr, tout à côté, dans la Grand-rue, là où se trouve votre hôtel.**
    Of course. Right nearby, on Main Street, where your hotel is.

27. **Et j'ai plein d'e-mail à envoyer mais je n'ai pas encore acheté d'ordinateur. Y a-t-il un café dans le coin ou je pourrais me connecter à Internet?**
    And I have a lot of e-mail to send, but I haven't bought a computer yet. Is there a café in the neighborhood where I could get on the Internet?

28. **Non, je ne crois pas. Mais il y a des ordinateurs à la bibliothèque, et aussi à la poste. Sinon, vous pourriez acheter un ordinateur au magasin d'électronique qui se trouve juste en face de la papeterie.**
    I don't think so. But there are computers at the library, and also at the post office. Otherwise you could buy a computer at the electronics store right across from the stationery store.

29. **Maintenant j'y suis.**
    Now I get it.

30. **Pourquoi n'achèteriez-vous pas un plan ou un guide?**
    Why don't you buy a map or a guide book?

31. **C'est une bonne idée! Où puis-je en trouver?**
    That's a good idea! Where can I find one?

32. **À la gare, ou bien au kiosque à journaux.**
Either at the station or at the newspaper stand.

33. **Où se trouve la gare?**
Where's the station?

34. **La gare est à l'autre extrémité de la rue de la Préfecture.**
The station is at the other end of Prefecture Street.

35. **Où se trouve le kiosque à journaux?**
And where's there a newspaper stand?

36. **Au coin de la rue.**
On the corner.

37. **Merci beaucoup.**
Thank you very much.

38. **Ne me remerciez pas, c'est la moindre des choses.**
Don't thank me, it's the least I can do.

39. **J'ai eu de la chance de vous rencontrer. Vous paraissez bien connaître la ville.**
I was lucky to meet you. You seem to know the town very well.

40. **Naturellement. Je suis le maire de la ville.**
Naturally. I'm the mayor ("of the town").

NOTES

1. *Pardon* (or *Je vous demande pardon*) is used when you ask for something, when you pass in front of someone, etc. The reply is *Je vous en prie*.

3. *Pourriez-vous* could you; from *pouvoir* to be able (see page 288). *Renseignements* information. (Notice the plural form in French.) *Bureau de renseignements* ("Office of Information") Information (Bureau).

4. *Avec plaisir.* "With pleasure."

5. *Connaître* to be acquainted with (see page 274)—*Retrouver* to find again.

7. *C'est que . . .* "It's that . . ." Here it means: "The reason is . . ." "It's because . . ." *Je ne suis pas d'ici* "I'm not from here."

8. *Ça ne fait rien.* "It doesn't matter." = *Ça n'a pas d'importance.* "That has no importance." Both expressions can often be translated "Never mind," "Not at all," "That's nothing," "That's all right."

12. *La mairie* City Hall. There is a *mairie* in every French *commune* and one in each *arrondissement* of Paris. The mayor is *le maire,* his assistant is *l'adjoint au maire.* He is addressed as *Monsieur le Maire.*

13. *Je vois.* I see; from *voir* to see.

14. "The street of the Préfecture."

18. *Eh bien* is very common. It can often be translated "Well," "Well now," "So," etc.

19. Notice this use of *très bien*.

20. Physicians are called *docteurs* or *médecins* and are addressed as *docteur.*

22. *Tous les matins* ("all the mornings") every morning.

23. "Where does it find itself?" *Trouver* to find.

24. *Avant d'arriver* before coming to.

29. *Maintenant j'y suis.* ("Now I'm there.") Now I understand. Now I get it. Oh, now I see!

30. *Achèteriez.* Conditional form of *acheter* to buy.

32. *Kiosque à journaux* newsstand.

34. *L'autre extrémité* the other end.

36. "At the corner of the street."

38. *Ne me remerciez pas.* "Don't thank me."—*C'est la moindre des choses.* ("It's the least of things.") It's nothing. *De rien.*

QUIZ 31

1. ——— (it's nothing).
    a. *Je vous en prie*
    b. *C'est la moindre des choses.*
    c. *De rien.*
2. *Pourriez-vous me* ——— (give) *quelques renseignements?*
    a. *plaisir*
    b. *mais*
    c. *donner*
3. *Il faut tout m'* ——— (explain).
    a. *écouter*
    b. *expliquer*
    c. *commençons*
4. *Voyez-vous la* ——— (house) *au coin de la rue?*
    a. *maison*
    b. *poste*
    c. *lanterne*
5. *Quel est le nom de cette* ——— (street)?
    a. *bien*
    b. *rue*
    c. *coin*
6. *Le docteur* ——— (lives) *tout à côté.*
    a. *habite*
    b. *tombe*
    c. *fait*
7. *Avec un grand globe* ——— (green).
    a. *rouge*
    b. *vert*
    c. *vitrine*

8. *Il est tous les* ——— (mornings) *à l'hôpital.*
   a. *médecin*
   b. *matins*
   c. *trouve*
9. *J'ai eu de la* ——— (luck) *de vous rencontrer.*
   a. *merci*
   b. *coin*
   c. *chance*
10. *Où se trouve* ——— (the train station)?
    a. *la poste*
    b. *la gare*
    c. *la maison*

ANSWERS
1—c; 2—c; 3—b; 4—a; 5—b; 6—a; 7—b; 8—b;
9—c; 10—b.

SUPPLEMENTAL VOCABULARY 17: IN TOWN

in town	*en ville*
town, city	*la ville*
village	*le village*
car	*la voiture*
bus	*le bus, l'autocar (m.)*
train	*le train*
taxi	*le taxi*
subway/metro	*le métro*
traffic	*la circulation*
building	*le bâtiment*
apartment building	*l'immeuble (m.)*
library	*la bibliothèque*
restaurant	*le restaurant*
store	*le magasin*
street	*la rue*
park	*le parc*
train station	*la gare*

airport	*l'aéroport (m.)*
airplane	*l'avion (m.)*
intersection	*l'intersection (f.)*
lamp post	*le réverbère*
street light	*le lampadaire*
bank	*la banque*
church	*l'église (f.)*
temple	*le temple*
mosque	*la mosquée*
synagogue	*la synagogue*
sidewalk	*le trottoir*
bakery	*la boulangerie*
pastry shop	*la pâtisserie*
butcher shop	*la boucherie*
butcher shop for pork products	*la charcuterie*
shop for high-end/ cooked foods	*le traiteur*
café/coffee shop	*le café/le salon de thé*
drugstore/pharmacy	*la pharmacie*
supermarket	*le supermarché*
market	*le marché*
shoe store	*le magasin de chaussures*
clothing store	*le magasin de vêtements*
electronics store	*le magasin d'électronique*
bookstore	*la librairie*
department store	*le grand magasin*
mayor	*le maire*
city hall/municipal building	*la mairie*
to buy	*acheter*
to go shopping	*aller faire des courses*
near/far	*près de/loin de*
urban	*urbain*
suburban	*de banlieue*
rural	*rural*

Supplemental Vocabulary 18: Entertainment

entertainment	*le spectacle*
movie/film	*le film*
to go to the movies	*aller au cinéma*
to see a movie	*voir un film*
theater	*le théâtre*
to see a play	*voir une pièce*
opera	*l' opéra (m.)*
concert	*le concert*
club	*le club*
circus	*le cirque*
ticket (for a concert)	*la place (de concert)*
museum	*le musée*
gallery	*la galerie*
painting	*la peinture*
sculpture	*la sculpture*
television program	*l' émission*
to watch television	*regarder la télévision*
comedy	*la comédie*
documentary	*le documentaire*
drama	*le drame*
book	*le livre*
magazine	*le magazine*
to read a book	*lire un livre*
to read a magazine	*lire un magazine*
to listen to music	*écouter de la musique*
song	*la chanson*
band	*le groupe de musique*
the news	*les nouvelles*
to change channels	*changer de chaînes*
to have fun	*s' amuser*
to be bored	*s' ennuyer*
funny	*amusant*
interesting	*intéressant*

exciting	*excitant, passionnant*
scary	*effrayant*
party	*la partie, la soirée*
to go to the restaurant	*aller au restaurant*
to go to a party	*aller à une partie*
to have a party	*organiser une partie*
to dance	*danser*

LESSON 40

A. The Most Common Verb Forms

1. Regular *-er, -ir,* and *-re* verbs in the present tense: I give, I finish, I give back

Compare these forms:

DONNER TO GIVE	FINIR TO FINISH	RENDRE TO GIVE BACK
je donne	*je finis*	*je rends*
tu donnes	*tu finis*	*tu rends*
il donne	*il finit*	*il rend*
nous donnons	*nous finissons*	*nous rendons*
vous donnez	*vous finissez*	*vous rendez*
ils donnent	*ils finissent*	*ils rendent*

Verbs ending in *-er* (the vast majority) are like *donner* in the present.

Other examples:

parler	to speak
travailler	to work
regarder	to look at, to watch

Verbs ending in -*ir* are like *finir* in the present.[1]

Other examples:

obéir	to obey
choisir	to choose
réussir	to succeed
fournir	to furnish

Verbs ending in -*re* are like *rendre* in the present.

Other examples:

vendre	to sell
répondre	to answer
perdre	to lose
prendre[2]	to take

Verbs ending in -*oir* have the following forms in the present:

RECEVOIR TO RECEIVE

je reçois	*nous recevons*
tu reçois	*vous recevez*
il reçoit	*ils reçoivent*

2. Regular -*er*, -*ir*, and -*re* verbs in the future: I will give, I will finish, I will give back

DONNER TO GIVE	FINIR TO FINISH	RENDRE TO GIVE BACK
je donnerai	*je finirai*	*je rendrai*
tu donneras	*tu finiras*	*tu rendras*

[1] A few commonly used -*ir* verbs conjugate like *partir*, to leave; see Verb Chart II on page 382. Other examples are *dormir* to sleep, *sentir* to feel, and *servir* to serve.

[2] Note that the plural forms of prendre are slightly irregular: *prenons, prenez, prennent.*

il donnera	*il finira*	*il rendra*
nous donnerons	*nous finirons*	*nous rendrons*
vous donnerez	*vous finirez*	*vous rendrez*
ils donneront	*ils finiront*	*ils rendront*

a. Notice that to form the future you add the following endings to the future stem (*donner-, finir-, rendr-*). The future stem is the same as the full infinitive for regular verbs, except for *-re* verbs, which drop the final *-e*.

je—ai	*nous—ons*
tu—as	*vous—ez*
il—a	*ils—ont*

b. Some irregular futures:

I WILL BE

je serai	*nous serons*
tu seras	*vous serez*
il sera	*ils seront*

I WILL HAVE

j'aurai	*nous aurons*
tu auras	*vous aurez*
il aura	*ils auront*

I WILL MAKE OR DO

je ferai	*nous ferons*
tu feras	*vous ferez*
il fera	*ils feront*

I WILL SAY

je dirai	*nous dirons*
tu diras	*vous direz*
il dira	*ils diront*

I WILL GO

j'irai	nous irons
tu iras	vous irez
il ira	ils iront

j'écrirai	I will write
je viendrai	I will come
je verrai	I will see
je tiendrai	I will have *or* hold
je voudrai	I will want *or* wish
je recevrai	I will receive
je mettrai	I will put
je pourrai	I will be able
je saurai	I will know
je devrai	I will owe *or* have to
Il faudra que . . .	It will be necessary to . . .

3. The imperfect tense: I was, I had, I did; I used to be, I used to have, I used to do

I WAS, I USED TO BE

j'étais	nous étions
tu étais	vous étiez
il était	ils étaient

I HAD, I USED TO HAVE

j'avais	nous avions
tu avais	vous aviez
il avait	ils avaient

I DID, I USED TO DO

je faisais	nous faisions
tu faisais	vous faisiez
il faisait	ils faisaient

a. The imperfect tense is formed by taking the
nous form of a present tense verb, dropping
the *-ons* ending, and adding the following
imperfect endings (see above; *être* is the only
exception):

IMPERFECT TENSE

je—ais	*nous—ions*
tu—ais	*vous—iez*
il—ait	*ils—aient*

b. These forms make up the "imperfect tense,"
which expresses continuous or repeated
action in the past.

Quand j'habitais en France, j'avais beaucoup d'amis français.	When I lived (was living) in France, I had (used to have) many French friends.

4. The past tense (passé composé): I have given,
spoken, etc., or I gave, spoke, etc.

I HAVE GIVEN/I GAVE

j'ai donné	*nous avons donné*
tu as donné	*vous avez donné*
il a donné	*ils ont donné*

I HAVE SPOKEN/I SPOKE

j'ai parlé	*nous avons parlé*
tu as parlé	*vous avez parlé*
il a parlé	*ils ont parlé*

Other examples:

j'ai apporté	I have brought; I brought
j'ai envoyé	I have sent; I sent
j'ai acheté	I have bought; I bought

a. The forms *donner* "to give," *parler* "to speak," *demander* "to ask," etc., are called "the infinitive." The forms *donné, parlé, demandé,* etc., are called "the past participle."

b. The past (*passé composé*) is a compound tense. This means that it is comprised of two verbs: the auxiliary (*avoir* or, as you'll see below, *être*) and the past participle of the main verb.

donner	to give	*donné*	given
parler	to speak	*parlé*	spoken
demander	to ask	*demandé*	asked

The past is used when you refer to some single event that took place in the past.

Nous avons acheté une voiture.
We bought a car.

Je regardais la télévision quand il m'a téléphoné.
I was watching television (imperfect) when he called me (past indefinite).

Je lui ai donné de l'argent.
I gave him some money.

c. This tense can usually be translated by the English past ("I gave"). Sometimes, however, it is used when we could use the present perfect ("I have given").

Here are some examples of past participles formed from other types of verbs.

Verbs ending in *-ir:*

| *finir* | to finish | *fini* | finished |

Verbs ending in *-re:*

répondre	to answer	*répondu*	answered
descendre	to go down	*descendu*	gone down
vendre	to sell	*vendu*	sold

Verbs ending in *-oir:*

recevoir	to receive	*reçu*	received
voir	to see	*vu*	seen
pouvoir	to be able	*pu*	been able
savoir	to know	*su*	known

5. Common verbs in the past: I have been, have had, etc.

I HAVE BEEN/I WAS

j'ai été	*nous avons été*
tu as été	*vous avez été*
il a été	*ils ont été*

I HAVE HAD/I HAD

j'ai eu	*nous avons eu*
tu as eu	*vous avez eu*
il a eu	*ils ont eu*

I HAVE DONE OR MADE/I DID OR MADE

j'ai fait	*nous avons fait*
tu as fait	*vous avez fait*
il a fait	*ils ont fait*

I HAVE SAID/I SAID

j' ai dit	*nous avons dit*
tu as dit	*vous avez dit*
il a dit	*ils ont dit*

Notice the form or past participle of these verbs:

être	to be	*été*	been
faire	to do	*fait*	done
dire	to say	*dit*	said
avoir	to have	*eu*	had
voir	to see	*vu*	seen
savoir	to know	*su*	known

6. Verbs that take *être* in the past: I have gone/I went, etc.

I HAVE GONE/I WENT

je suis allé	*nous sommes allés*
tu es allé	*vous êtes allés*
il est allé	*ils sont allés*
elle est allée	*elles sont allées*

Compare: *j' ai donné* "I have given" and *je suis allé* "I have gone."

Notice that most verbs take *avoir* (*j' ai, tu, as, il a*, etc.) but that a few (chiefly verbs of motion) take *être* (*je suis, tu es, il est*, etc.). Also notice that the past participles of these verbs take the same endings as adjectives to agree with their subjects.

d. The most common verbs which have the latter form are:

je suis allé	I have gone, I went
je suis entré	I have entered, I entered
je suis sorti	I have gone out, I went out
je suis arrivé	I have arrived, I arrived

je suis venu	I have come, I came
je suis parti	I have left, I left
je suis monté	I have gone up, I went up
je suis descendu	I have gone down, I went down
je suis resté	I have remained, I remained
je suis tombé	I have fallen, I fell
je suis né	I was born
je suis mort	I have died, I died
je suis rentré	I have returned home

7. The pluperfect tense: I had given, gone, etc.

I HAD GIVEN

j'avais donné	*nous avions donné*
tu avais donné	*vous aviez donné*
il avait donné	*ils avaient donné*

Other examples with *avoir:*

j'avais parlé	I had spoken
j'avais demandé	I had asked
j'avais apporté	I had brought

I HAD GONE

j'étais allé	*nous étions allés*
tu étais allé	*vous étiez allés*
il était allé	*ils étaient allés*

Other examples with *être:*

j'étais arrivé	I had arrived
j'étais venu	I had come
j'étais entré	I had entered
j'étais sorti	I had gone out
j'étais parti	I had left

j'étais monté   I had gone up
j'étais tombé   I had fallen

   8. The polite imperative (command form): Help!
      Bring!

Aidez-moi!	Help me!
Apportez-moi encore du . . .	Bring me some more . . .
Apportez-le-moi.	Bring it to me.
Arrêtez!	Stop!
Arrêtez tout de suite!	Stop right away!
Arrêtez-vous là!	Stop there!
Arrêtez-le!	Stop him!
Asseyez-vous.	Sit down. Have a seat.
Croyez-moi.	Believe me.
Écoutez!	Listen!
Écoutez-moi.	Listen to me.
Écoutez-bien.	Listen carefully.
Écoutez-le.	Listen to him.
Ne l'écoutez pas.	Don't listen (to him).
Écoutez donc!	Listen! Listen, won't you?
Enlevez ça!	Take that away!
Entrez!	Enter! Come in! Go in!
Envoyez-le-lui!	Send it to him!
Envoyez-les-moi!	Send them to me.
Envoyez-lui-en!	Send him some!
Envoyez-m'en!	Send me some!
Essayez!	Try!
N'essayez pas!	Don't try!
N'essayez pas de faire cela!	Don't try to do that!
Levez-vous!	Stand up! Get up!
Montrez-moi!	Show me!

Montrez-lui.	Show him.
Ne le lui montrez pas!	Don't show it to him!
N'oubliez pas!	Don't forget!
Partez!	Leave!
Partez vite!	Leave quickly! Go right away!
Ne partez pas!	Don't leave! Don't go!
Passez!	Go!
Pensez-y!	Think about it!
Permettez-moi de vous présenter . . .	Allow me to introduce . . .
Vous permettez?	May I?
—Bien sûr!	—Of course!
—Allez-y!	—Go ahead!
Portez ça là-bas.	Carry this over there.
Prenez!	Take!
Prenez-le!	Take it!
Ne le prenez pas.	Don't take it.
Prenez le train.	Take the train.
Prenez un taxi.	Take a taxi.
Regardez!	Look!
Regardez-moi!	Look at me!
Regardez ça	Look at this (that).
Ne regardez pas.	Don't look.
Rendez-le-moi.	Return it to me.
Rentrez chez vous!	Go home!
Rentrez tôt!	Go home early!
Répétez!	Repeat! Say it again!
Répétez ça.	Repeat it (this, that). Say it (this, that) again.
Restez!	Stay!
Restez ici.	Stay here.
Restez tranquille.	Be still.
Sortez!	Go out!
Suivez-moi.	Follow me.

Suivez-le.	Follow him.
Ne touchez pas!	Don't touch!
Versez-moi du café.	Pour me some coffee.

The *-ez* form corresponds to *vous —ez*, that is, it is the formal or plural form. The familiar or singular form, the one that corresponds to the *tu* form, is as follows:

DONNER TO GIVE

tu donnes	you give
Donne!	Give!

FINIR TO FINISH

tu finis	you finish
Finis!	Finish!

PRENDRE TO TAKE

tu prends	you take
Prends!	Take!

9. The present participle: giving, speaking, being

donnant	giving
parlant	speaking
étant	being
ayant	having
faisant	doing
disant	saying
voyant	seeing
venant	coming

Suivant l'usage . . .	Following the custom . . .
Revenant au sujet principal . . .	Coming back to the main subject . . .

Quelqu' un habitant Paris.	Someone living in Paris.
Je termine en espérant recevoir bientôt de vos nouvelles.	I close hoping to hear from you soon.

Notice that the *-ant* form corresponds to our "*-ing*" form in English. It can also be used as an adjective:

Eau courante.	Running water.

10. The imperative: Let's

Allons-y!	Let's go there!
Allons là-bas!	Let's go over there!
Voyons!	Let's see!
Partons!	Let's leave!
Essayons!	Let's try!
Attendons!	Let's wait!
Prenons-en!	Let's take some!

QUIZ 32

1. *Montrez-moi*	a. Look at this (that).
2. *Passez!*	b. Look here.
3. *Vous permettez?— Allez-y!*	c. Take a taxi.
4. *Pensez-y.*	d. Get up!
5. *Permettez-moi de vous présenter . . .*	e. Take it.
6. *Prenez-le.*	f. Allow me to introduce . . .
7. *Prenez un taxi.*	g. May I?—Go ahead!
8. *Levez-vous!*	h. Think about it.

9. *Regardez ici.*   i. Go!
10. *Regardez ça.*   j. Show me.

ANSWERS
1—j; 2—i; 3—g; 4—h; 5—f; 6—e; 7—c; 8—d; 9—b;
10—a.

B. DISCUSSING VACATION PLANS

1. *J:* **Vous partez en vacances?**
   J: Are you going on vacation?
2. *A:* **Non, je vais chez mon cousin pour le week-end.**
   A: No, I'm going to my cousin's for the weekend.
3. *J:* **Vous avez de la chance! Il fait si chaud à Paris cet été. Où habite votre cousin?**
   J: How lucky you are! It's so hot in Paris this summer. Where does your cousin live?
4. *A:* **Il habite dans une vieille maison normande. Et vous, vous allez partir cet été?**
   A: He lives in an old Norman-style house. And you, are you going away this summer?
5. *J:* **Non, je vais prendre mes vacances dans les Hautes-Alpes en octobre.**
   J: No, I'll take my vacation in the Hautes-Alpes in October.
6. *A:* **Il fait froid dans les Alpes à cette saison!**
   A: It's cold in the Alps during that season!
7. *J:* **Parfois il pleut! Mais j'adore la montagne à toutes les saisons. Et vous, quand partez-vous?**
   J: Sometimes it rains! But I love the mountains during any season. And you? When are you going away?
8. *A:* **Nous allons voyager en Tunisie en novembre et à Tahiti en mars.**
   A: We're going to travel to Tunisia in November and to Tahiti in March.

9. *J:* **Vous n'avez pas peur de la chaleur?**
   J: You're not afraid of the heat?

10. *A:* **Personnellement, je préfère la neige, les sports d'hiver ... Mais ma femme déteste le froid et adore le soleil.**
    A: Personally, I prefer the snow, winter sports ... But my wife hates the cold and loves the sun.

11. *J:* **Bon, j'espère que vous allez passer un bon week-end!**
    J: Well, I hope you have a great weekend.

12. *A:* **Merci. À la semaine prochaine.**
    A: Thank you. See you next week.

NOTES

1. Note that *vacances* is always plural in French. *Partir en vacances* is "to leave on vacation" or "to go away for vacation," and *être en vacances* is "to be on vacation."

3. "To be lucky" is translated as *avoir de la chance. Vous avez de la chance!* means "you are lucky!" or "how lucky you are!"

4. Just as in English, the near future can be expressed in French with the verb *aller* plus an infinitive. *Vous allez partir cet été?* Are you going to go away this summer?

7. *Et vous?* can mean "And you?," "How about you?," or "What about you?"

9. *Avoir peur de* means "to be afraid of." Don't forget the many important French expressions that use *avoir: avoir froid* "to be cold," *avoir chaud* "to be hot," *avoir sommeil* "to be tired," *avoir envie de* "to feel like" or "to want," *avoir faim* "to be hungry," *avoir soif* "to be thirsty," *avoir raison* "to be right," and *avoir tort* "to be wrong."

C. AT THE PHARMACY

1. *A:* **À vos souhaits!**
   A: Bless you!
2. *M:* **Merci,**
   M: Thanks.
3. *A:* **À vos souhaits! Vous avez l'air d'avoir un bon rhume! Qu'est-ce que je peux faire pour vous?**
   A: Bless you! You seem to have a serious cold. What can I do for you?
4. *M:* **Je voudrais des médicaments contre les allergies. J'ai mal à la tête et je ne peux pas respirer.**
   M: I would like some medicine for allergies. I have a headache, and I cannot breathe.
5. *A:* **À quoi êtes-vous allergique, Monsieur?**
   A: What are you allergic to, sir?
6. *M:* **Je ne sais pas . . . Je suis un peu allergique aux chats, c'est tout. Qu'est-ce que vous me conseillez de prendre?**
   M: I don't know . . . I am a bit allergic to cats, that's all. What do you advise me to take?
7. *A:* **Veuillez attendre un instant, je vais vous montrer les différents remèdes. Voilà.**
   A: Wait just a moment, I'll show you different remedies. Here we are.
8. *M:* **Ah, ce sont des antihistamines?**
   M: Are these antihistamines?
9. *A:* **C'est exact. Vous pourriez aussi prendre du sirop ou ces médicaments.**
   A: That's right. You can also take some syrup or this medicine.
10. *M:* **Je vais prendre des antihistamines pour commencer. Et est-ce que vous vendez du dentifrice et de la mousse à raser?**

M: I'll take some antihistamines to start. Do you sell toothpaste and shaving cream?

11. *A:* **Bien sûr. C'est à votre gauche, sur la deuxième étagère.**
A: Of course. It's on your left, on the second shelf.

12. *M:* **Ah, merci. Ça fait combien?**
M: Thanks. How much does this come to?

13. *A:* **Dix-huit euros. Au revoir Monsieur et meilleure santé!**
A: Eighteen euros. Good-bye, and feel better!

NOTES

3. *Avoir l'air de* means to seem to, and is followed by an infinitive.

4. Notice that in English medication is taken for something, while in French, perhaps more logically, it is taken against (*contre*) something.

6. Remember that *aux* is the contraction of *à* + *les*. The other contraction used with the preposition *à* is au, *à* + *le*.

7. *Veuillez* is often heard in polite requests. *Veuillez attendre, s'il vous plaît,* "please wait," *Veuillez signer en bas* "please sign at the bottom."

QUIZ 33

1. *Je vais prendre ———— dans les Hautes-Alpes en octobre.*
    a. *ma vacance*
    b. *la vacance*
    c. *mes vacances*

2. *Vous ——— chance!*
    a. *êtes dans la*
    b. *avez de la*
    c. *avez une*

3. ———— êtes-vous allergique, Monsieur?
   a. *A quoi*
   b. *Pourquoi*
   c. *De quoi*
4. *Il* ———— *dans les Alpes à cette saison!*
   a. *fait froid*
   b. *est froid*
   c. *se fait froid*
5. *Vous* ———— *de la chaleur?*
   a. *n'êtes pas peur*
   b. *n'avez pas peur*
   c. *ne pourrez pas*
6. ———— *attendre un instant.*
   a. *Voudriez*
   b. *Veuillez*
   c. *Voulez*
7. *Vous partez* ————?
   a. *en vacances*
   b. *aux vacances*
   c. *pour vacances*
8. *Qu'est-ce que* ———— *de prendre?*
   a. *vous conseillez moi*
   b. *me vous conseillez*
   c. *vous me conseillez*
9. ————, *sur la deuxième étagère.*
   a. *C'est à votre gauche*
   b. *C'est votre gauche*
   c. *C'est dans votre gauche*
10. *Vous avez l'air* ———— *un bon rhume!*
    a. *à avoir*
    b. *d'avoir*
    c. *avoir*

ANSWERS
1—c; 2—b; 3—a; 4—a; 5—b; 6—b; 7—a; 8—c;
9—a; 10—b.

D. OTHER COMMON VERBS

1. To see: *Voir*

je vois	*nous voyons*
tu vois	*vous voyez*
il voit	*ils voient*

Voyons.
Let's see.

Je ne vois pas.
I don't see.

Il voit tout.
He sees everything.

L'avez-vous jamais vu(e)?
Have you ever seen him (her)?

Je viens de la voir.
I've just seen her.

Je ne vois pas ce que vous voulez dire.
I don't see what you mean.

Je vois ce que vous voulez dire.
I see what you mean.

Qui est-ce que vous voyez?
Qui voyez-vous?
Whom do you see?

Pouvez-vous me voir maintenant?
Can you see me now?

Venez nous voir un soir.
Come to see us some evening.

2. To know: *Savoir*

je sais	*nous savons*
tu sais	*vous savez*
il sait	*ils savent*

Je le sais.
I know it.

Je ne sais pas.
I don't know.

Je le sais bien.
I know it very well.

Il ne sait rien.
He doesn't know anything.

Je n'en sais rien.
I don't know anything about it.

Je sais qu'il est ici.
I know that he's here.

Savez-vous ça?
Do you know that?

Savez-vous où il est?
Do you know where he is?

Qui sait?
Who knows?

Il n'en sait pas davantage.
He doesn't know anything more about it.

Il n'en sait pas plus que vous.
He doesn't know any more about it than you do.

3. To hold: *Tenir*

je tiens	*nous tenons*
tu tiens	*vous tenez*
il tient	*ils tiennent*

Tenez-moi ça un instant.
Hold this for me a minute.

Il tient son chapeau à la main.
He's holding his hat in his hand.

Je le tiens maintenant.
I have it now.

Tenez bon!
Hold firm!

Il faut tenir.
We must hold on.

Tenez-vous tranquille!
Keep quiet! Keep still!

Tenez!—Pas plus tard qu'hier . . .
Look, only yesterday . . . ("Not later than yesterday . . .")

Tenez, voilà votre argent.
Look! Here's your money.

Tiens! Voilà pour toi.
Look! Here's something for you.

Tiens, le voilà.
Look, there he is.

Il tient à elle.
He likes her very much.

Il tient à le faire.
He's anxious to do it. He's set on doing it.

Tenez cela pour fait.
Consider it done.

Je le tiens de bonne source.
I have it from a good source. I have it on good authority.

Tenez votre droite.
Keep to your right.

Tiens ta promesse.
Keep your (*fam.*) promise.

4. To be able: *Pouvoir*

je peux or *puis*	*nous pouvons*
tu peux	*vous pouvez*
il peut	*ils peuvent*

Je ne peux pas.
I can't.

Je peux le faire.
I can do it.

Pouvez-vous me dire si . . .
Can you tell me if . . .

Pouvez-vous venir?
Can you come?

Je ne vois pas comment il peut faire cela.
I don't see how he can do that.

Je ne peux pas répondre à la question.
I can't answer the question.

Vous pouvez le faire sans difficulté.
You can do it without any difficulty.

Je ne peux pas y aller.
I can't go there.

Quand puis-je partir?
When can I leave?

Nous pouvons y aller.
We can go there.

Pouvez-vous m'aider?
Can you help me?

5. To understand: *Comprendre*

je comprends	*nous comprenons*
tu comprends	*vous comprenez*
il comprend	*ils comprennent*

Il ne comprend pas.
He doesn't understand.

Je comprends très bien.
I understand very well.

Je ne vous comprends pas.
I don't understand you.

Vous ne me comprenez pas?
Don't you understand me?

Comprenez-vous?
Do you understand?

Comprenez-vous le français?
Do you understand French?

Comprenez-vous tout ce qu'il vous dit?
Do you understand everything he's saying to you?

Je n'ai pas compris.
I don't understand. ("I haven't understood." "I didn't understand.")

Avez-vous compris?
Did you understand? ("Have you understood?")

Je ne peux pas me faire comprendre.
I can't make myself understood.

Il ne comprend rien aux affaires.
He doesn't understand anything about business.

Compris?
Did you understand? Do you understand?

Je n'y comprends rien.
I don't understand it at all. I don't understand anything about it.

6. To put or place: *Mettre*

je mets	*nous mettons*
tu mets	*vous mettez*
il met	*ils mettent*

Mettez-le là.
Put it there.

Où l'avez-vous mis?
Where did you put it?

Mettez votre chapeau.
Put your hat on.

Mettez-le.
Put it on.

Elle a mis la table.
She set the table.

Il a mis son nouveau costume.
He put on his new suit.

Il ne sait jamais où il met ses affaires.
He never knows where he puts (his) things.

Mettons-nous à table.
Let's sit down to eat. ("Let's sit down to the table.")

7. To know; to be familiar with: *Connaître*

je connais	*nous connaissons*
tu connais	*vous connaissez*
il connaît	*ils connaissent*

Je connais ça.
I know that.

Je ne connais pas ça.
I don't know that.

Je ne connais personne dans cette ville.
I don't know anyone in this city.

Je connais sa famille.
I know his family.

Tout le monde le connaît.
Everybody knows it.

Je le connais de vue.
I know him by sight.

Je le connais de nom.
I know him by name.

C'est très connu.
It's very well known.

Ce n'est pas bien connu en France.
That's not very well known in France.

C'est un auteur inconnu.
He's an unknown author.

8. To want: *Vouloir*

je veux	*nous voulons*
tu veux	*vous voulez*
il veut	*ils veulent*

Je le veux.
I want it.

Je ne le veux pas.
I don't want it.

Je ne veux rien.
I don't want anything.

J'en veux.
I want some.

Il n'en veut pas.
He doesn't want any of it.

Il le peut mais il ne le veut pas.
He can do it but he doesn't want to.

Que voulez-vous?
What do you want (wish)? What would you like?

Il veut revenir?
Does he want to return?

Voulez-vous venir avec nous?
Do you want to come with us?

Voulez-vous venir déjeuner avec nous?
Will you have lunch with us?

Voulez-vous venir samedi?
Will you come Saturday?

Qui est-ce qui veut cela (ça)?
Who wants that?

Qu'est-ce que vous voulez dire?
What do you mean? ("What do you want to say?")

Voulez-vous me suivre?
Will you please follow me?

Comme vous voulez.
As you wish.

C'est comme vous voulez.
As you wish. Whatever you say.

Si vous voulez.
If you wish. If you want to.

9. To owe or to have to: *Devoir*

je dois	*nous devons*
tu dois	*vous devez*
il doit	*ils doivent*

Je dois partir maintenant.
I have to go now.

Il doit venir.
He has to come.

Ils doivent être là.
They have to (should, ought to) be there.

Devez-vous y aller?
Do you have to go (there)?

Qu'est-ce que je dois faire?
What do I have to do?

Combien est-ce que je vous dois?
Combien vous dois-je?
How much do I owe you?

Vous me devez quinze euros.
You owe me fifteen euros.

Il me doit quatre euros.
He owes me four euros.

10. To wait: *Attendre*

Attendez ici.
Wait here.

Attendez là.
Wait there.

Attends-le.
Wait for it (him).

Attendez-moi.
Wait for me.

Attendez un peu.
Wait a little.

N'attendez pas.
Don't wait.

Je l'attends.
I'm waiting for him.

Elle attend les autres.
She's waiting for the others.

Qui attendez-vous?
Whom are you waiting for?

Pourquoi est-ce que vous attendez?
Why are you waiting?

Je m'excuse de vous avoir fait attendre.
I'm sorry I kept you waiting. ("I apologize for making you wait.")

11. To ask: *Demander*

Demandez là-bas.
Ask over there.

Demandez-le là-bas.
Ask about (for) it (him) over there.

Qu'est-ce qu'il demande?
What's he asking? What's he want?

Il ne demande rien.
He's not asking for anything. He doesn't want anything.

Demandez votre chemin si vous vous perdez.
Ask your way if you get lost.

Demandez-lui de vous faire de la monnaie.
Ask him to give you change.

Demandez-lui l'heure.
Ask him the time.

Demandez-lui du feu.
Ask him for a light.

Allez le lui demander.
Go and ask him ("it").

Si on me demande, je reviens dans un instant.
If someone asks for me, I'll be back in a moment.

Il a demandé où c'est.
He asked where it is.

Combien coûte ce livre?
How much is this book?

Il en demande vingt euros.
He's asking twenty euros for it.

Demandez-le au téléphone.
Call him on the phone.

On vous demande.
Someone is asking for you. You're wanted.

On vous demande au téléphone.
You're wanted on the telephone.

Je vous demande pardon.
I beg your pardon.

Je me demande si c'est vrai.
I wonder if it's true. ("I ask myself if . . .")

Je me demande pourquoi il ne vient pas.
I wonder why he doesn't come.

C'est ce que je me demande.
That's what I'd like to know.

Je vous demande un peu!
I ask you! How do you like that!

Je ne demande pas mieux.
I ask nothing better. I'll do it gladly. It's all right with me.

12. To love or to like: *Aimer*

Il l'aime.
He loves her.

Est-ce que vous l'aimez?
Do you like/love him (her, it)?

Je n'aime pas cela.
I don't like it (that).

J'aime mieux l'autre.
I like the other better.

J'aime mieux y aller ce soir.
I'd rather go there this evening. I'd prefer to go there this evening.

13. To be necessary: *Falloir*

Il le faut.
It's necessary. You must. You have to. One must. One has to.

Faut-il y aller?
Is it necessary to go there? Do I (you, we, etc.) have to go?

Faut-il venir?
Should I (you, we, etc.) come?

Il faut venir.
You (I, we, etc.) have to come.

Combien de temps faut-il pour aller de Paris à Londres?
How long does it take to go from Paris to London?

Qu'est-ce qu'il faut faire?
What's to be done? What am I to do?

Comme il faut.
As is proper. As it should be.

Un homme comme il faut.
A respectable man.

Des gens comme il faut.
Well-bred people ("people as they should be").

Faites cela comme il faut.
Do it properly. Do it the way it should be done.

14. To be worth: *Valoir*

Ça vaut combien?
How much is it worth?

Qu'est-ce que ça vaut?
What's that worth?

Ça vaut vingt euros.
It's worth twenty euros.

Ça vaut le coup.
It's worth the effort.

Ça ne vaut pas un clou.
It's not worth a hang ("a nail").

Ça ne vaut pas grand'chose.
It's no good. It's not worth much.

Ça ne vaut rien.
It's not worth anything. It's worthless.

Ça vaut son prix.
It's worth the money. ("It's worth its price.")

Ça vaut très cher.
It's worth a lot of money.

Ça ne vaut pas ça.
It's not worth that.

Ça ne vaut pas la peine.
It isn't worthwhile. It isn't worth the trouble.

E. COMMON NOTICES AND SIGNS

Avis au public	Public Notice
Messieurs ⎫ *Hommes* ⎭	Men, Gentlemen
Dames	Women, Ladies
Toilettes pour hommes	Men's Room
Toilettes pour dames	Ladies' Room
W.C.	Toilet
Fumeurs	Smokers
Non fumeurs	Nonsmokers
Défense de fumer	No Smoking
Ouvert	Open

Fermé	Closed
Clôture	Closing
Entrée	Entrance
Sortie	Exit
Sortie de secours	Emergency Exit
Ascenseur	Elevator
Rez-de-chaussée	Ground Floor
Tirez	Pull
Poussez	Push
Tournez	Turn
Sonnez S.V.P.	Please Ring
Défense d'entrer	Keep Out
Entrez	Come In
Entrez sans frapper	Come in Without Knocking
Frappez	Knock
Frappez avant d'entrer	Knock Before Entering
Sonnez avant d'entrer	Ring Before Entering
Prière de . . .	You Are Requested to . . .
Fermé pour cause de réparations	Closed for Repair
Changement de propriétaire	Under New Management
Interdit au public *Entrée interdite* }	No Admittance
Ouverture Prochaine *Sera ouvert prochainement* }	Will Be Opened Shortly
Ouvert toute la nuit	Open All Night
Défense de cracher	No Spitting
Essuyez-vous les pieds	Wipe Your Feet
Tenez les chiens en laisse	Keep Your Dog on Leash
Interdit aux piétons	Pedestrians Keep Out
Propriété Privée: *Défense d'entrer*	Private Property. No Trespassing

Bureau des réclama- tions } Réclamations	Complaint Department
Adressez-vous au guichet } S'adresser au guichet	Apply at the Window
Bureau de change	Money Exchange
À vendre	For Sale
À louer	For Rent
Appartement à louer	Unfurnished Apartment to Let
Appartement meublé à louer	Furnished Apartment to Let
Soldes	Bargains
Rabais	Reductions
En vente ici	On Sale Here
Vestiaire	Checkroom (in a hotel, restaurant, or café)
Billard	Billiard Room
Concierge	Janitor
Circulation détournée	Detour
Travaux } Route en rechargement	Road Repair
Tournant dangereux	Dangerous Curve
Défense de stationner	No Parking
Sens unique	One-Way Street
Défense de traverser les voies	Do Not Cross the Tracks
Passage à niveau	Railroad Crossing, Grade Crossing
Voie ferrée	Railroad
Passage souterrain	Underpass
Halte	Stop
Attention	Caution
Passage clouté	Pedestrian Crossing
Carrefour/Croisement	Crossroads/Intersection

Défense d'afficher	Post No Bills
Vitesse maximum 20 km	Maximum Speed 20 Kilometers Per Hour
Allure modérée	Go Slow
Attention sortie d'écoles	School Exit—Go Slow
Danger	Danger
Sens interdit	No Thoroughfare
Prenez garde à la peinture	Fresh Paint
Arrêt facultatif	Stop on Signal
Arrêt obligatoire	Stop Here
Ne pas se pencher au dehors	Don't Lean Out of the Window
Signal d'alarme	Alarm Signal
Haute tension	High Voltage
Métro ⎫ *Métropolitain* ⎬	Subway
Consigne	Baggage Room. Checkroom (in a railroad station).
Salle d'attente	Waiting Room
1ère classe[1] ⎫ *2e classe* ⎬	First Class Second Class
Arrivée	Arrival
Départ	Departure
Quai	Platform
Bureau des renseignements	Information
Bureau de poste	Post Office
Boîte aux lettres	Mailbox
Avertisseur d'incendie	Firebox
Bibliothèque municipale	Public Library
La Poste	Post Office

[1] Different kinds of railway coaches.

Commissariat de police	Police Station
Station d'essence	Gas Station
Librairie	Bookstore
Mairie, Hôtel de Ville	City Hall
Coiffeur	Barbershop. Hairdresser
Docteur, médecin	Physician
Chirurgien-dentiste	Dentist
Cordonnerie	Shoe Repairing
Tenue de soirée obliga-toire } *Tenue de soirée de rigueur*	Formal Dress
Relâche	Closed (used for theaters only). No Performance
Changement de programme	Change of Program
Apéritifs	Cocktails (Served Here)
Service compris	Tip Included in the Price

FINAL QUIZ

1. ———— (how) *allez-vous?*
    a. *Comme*
    b. *Comment*
    c. *Quand*
2. ———— (speak) *lentement.*
    a. *Parlez*
    b. *Parler*
    c. *Parles*
3. ———— (have) *-vous des cigarettes?*
    a. *J'ai*
    b. *Avoir*
    c. *Avez*

4. *Donnez* ——— (me) *la carte.*
   a. *moi*
   b. *me*
   c. *le*

5. ——— (I'd like) *une tasse de café.*
   a. *Je veux*
   b. *Je voudrais*
   c. *Je vais*

6. *Nous voudrions un* ——— (breakfast) *pour trois personnes.*
   a. *déjeuner*
   b. *petit déjeuner*
   c. *dîner*

7. ——— (bring)-*moi une cuillère à café.*
   a. *Donnez*
   b. *Apportez*
   c. *Pouvez*

8. *Où se trouve* ——— (the train station)?
   a. *la route*
   b. *la gare*
   c. *le bureau*

9. ——— (are you) *certain?*
   a. *Faites-vous*
   b. *Dites-vous*
   c. *Êtes-vous*

10. ——— (I have) *assez de temps.*
    a. *Je suis*
    b. *J'ai*
    c. *Je vais*

11. ——— (does he have) *de l'argent?*
    a. *Il y a*
    b. *Est-il*
    c. *A-t-il*

12. ——— (is there) *du courrier pour moi?*
   a. *Il y a*
   b. *Y a-t-il*
   c. *A-t-il*

13. *Est-ce que vous* ——— (understand)?
   a. *comprends*
   b. *comprenez*
   c. *étendez*

14. *Je suis* ——— (happy) *de faire votre connaissance.*
   a. *heureux*
   b. *enchanté*
   c. *honoré*

15. *En voulez-vous un peu ou* ——— (a lot)?
   a. *encore*
   b. *beaucoup*
   c. *assez*

16. *Qu'est-ce que vous* ——— (say)?
   a. *faites*
   b. *dites*
   c. *dire*

17. *Comment* ——— (does one say) *cela en français?*
   a. *dites-vous*
   b. *dit-on*
   c. *écrit-on*

18. *Leur numéro de téléphone est le 01-42-82-* ——— (33-07)
   a. *vingt-six, seize*
   b. *trente-trois, zéro sept*
   c. *trente-six, quarante-deux*

19. ——— (I need) *de cela.*
   a. *J'ai envie*
   b. *J'en ai*
   c. *J'ai besoin*

20. *Je reviendrai* ——— (tomorrow morning).
   a. *après-midi*
   b. *demain matin*
   c. *hier soir*
21. ——— (it's necessary) *voir le gérant pour cela.*
   a. *Il y a*
   b. *Il faut*
   c. *Y a-t-il*
22. *Je vous* ——— (ask) *pardon.*
   a. *demande*
   b. *prie*
   c. *dit*
23. *Comment vous* ——— (call)-*vous?*
   a. *appelez*
   b. *demandez*
   c. *écrivez*
24. ——— (the check) *s'il vous plaît.*
   a. *Le beurre*
   b. *L'argent*
   c. *L'addition*
25. *Voulez-vous me* ——— (give) *une serviette?*
   a. *apporter*
   b. *donner*
   c. *passer*

ANSWERS
1—b; 2—a; 3—c; 4—a; 5—b; 6—b; 7—b; 8—b;
9—c; 10—b; 11—c; 12—b; 13—b; 14—a; 15—b;
16—b; 17—b; 18—b; 19—c; 20—b; 21—b; 22—a;
23—a; 24—c; 25—b.

SUMMARY OF FRENCH GRAMMAR

1. ABOUT THE SOUNDS

Very few sounds are exactly alike in both English and French. The pronunciation equivalents given below can therefore be only approximate. Although exceptions exist for almost every pronunciation rule, the guidelines in this section should prove useful to the student.

The Consonants. French consonant sounds are generally softer than those of English. A number of them are produced by bringing the tongue in contact with different parts of the mouth cavity from those used for the equivalent English consonant, or by changing the pressure of the airstream. For example, the English speaker produces the sound of *d, t,* or *n* by placing the tip of the tongue against the gum ridge behind the upper teeth. The French speaker produces these sounds by placing the tip of the tongue against the back of the upper teeth.

In pronouncing a *p* at the beginning of a word such as "pat" or "pen," the English speaker produces a puff of air, whereas the French speaker does not. Try holding your hand in front of your mouth and saying the words "pit," "pack," and "punch." You will feel the puff of air each time you say the *p* at the beginning of each of these words. The French speaker, on the other hand, produces the *p* at the beginning of words *without* the puff of air. The French *p* is close in sound to the English *p* in words like "speak" or "spot."

The pronunciation of the sound *l* also varies in the two languages. American English has two *l* sounds— one which is used at the beginning of a word (the "light" *l*), and another which is used in the middle or

at the end of a word (the "dark" *l*). Contrast the *l* sound
in the words "like" and "beautiful." The *l* in "like" is a
"light" *l*, and this is the *l* sound pronounced in French.

The Vowels. Some of the vowel sounds of French
resemble the vowels in English. Many vowel sounds,
however, are quite different, and some do not exist in
English at all. For example, the sound represented by *é*
resembles the English *ay* in the word "day," but the two
sounds are not the same. When an English speaker says
"day," he is actually pronouncing two sounds: an *a* and
a *y,* which glide together to form a diphthong. Try
holding your hand on your jaw and saying the words
listed below. As you do so, notice how your jaw closes
up a bit toward the end of the *ay* sound:

day   say   may   ray   nay   tray   jay

In French, however, the jaw does not move as you
say the *é* sound; it remains steady. Pronounce the following French words, while holding the jaw still.

des   bébé   fâché   mes   réalité

A similar phenomenon occurs with the sound *o.*
Say the following words in English:

bow   tow   know   so

Note that the jaw rises at the end of the sound as
though to close on the sound *w.* Hold your hand on
your jaw and say the above words "in slow motion."
Now, leaving off the *w* sound at the end by holding the
jaw steady, say the following words in French:

beau   tôt   nos   sot
(the final consonants are silent)

Space does not permit us to compare every English sound with its French counterpart, but the charts below will help to clarify the sounds. Repeated imitation of the speakers on the recordings is the best way to learn how to pronounce French correctly.

2. THE ALPHABET

LETTER	NAME	LETTER	NAME	LETTER	NAME
a	a	j	ji	s	esse
b	bé	k	ka	t	té
c	cé	l	elle	u	u
d	dé	m	emme	v	vé
e	e	n	enne	w	double vé
f	effe	o	o	x	iks
g	gé	p	pé	y	i grec
h	ache	q	ku	z	zède
i	i	r	erre		

3. THE CONSONANTS

The letters b, d, f, k, l, m, n, p, s, t, v, and z are pronounced approximately as in English when they are not in final position, but with the differences indicated above. Note however:

c   before a, o, u, l and r is like the c in "cut." Ex., carte, cœur, cuisine, clarté, croire
before e and i is like s in "see." Ex., centre, cinéma

ç   (c with cedilla) is like s in "see." Ex., français, garçon

ch   is like sh in "ship." Ex., chéri, cheval. But: chr is pronounced like English kr. Ex., chrétien

g   before a, o, u, l, r is like g in "go." Ex., gare, goût, guerre, glace, grand;

before *e* and *i*, is like the *s* sound in "measure."
Ex., *genre, voyageur, Gigi*

gn is like *ni* in "onion" or *ny* in "canyon." Ex.,
oignon, soigner

h is not pronounced. Ex., *heure*

j is like the *s* sound in "measure." Ex., *bonjour, joie*

l is always "light" (as explained above) when it is
pronounced as *l*. However, in the following
combinations it is pronounced like the *y* in
"yes": *-ail, -eil, -eille, -aille, -ille, -ill.* Ex.,
chandail, vermeil, oreille, grisaille, vieillard.
But: in *mille, ville* the *l*'s are pronounced as *l*.

qu before *a, e, i, o, u* is like *k*. Ex., *qui, quotidien;*
with *oi* is like *kwa*. Ex., *quoi*

r is made farther back in the throat than the
English *r;* almost like a gargle. Ex., *rouge, rue*

s is generally like the *s* in "see." Ex., *soir, estimer;*
between vowels is like the *s* in "rose." Ex., *rose,
vase*

w (occurring only in foreign words) is generally
pronounced *v*. Ex., *wagon;* the first letter in
whisky, however, is pronounced *w*.

FINAL CONSONANTS

As a general rule, final consonants are silent.
However, words ending in *c, f, l,* and *r* often
do pronounce the final consonant. Ex.:

-c: parc, sac, trafic

-f: bref, chef, œuf

-l: moral, Noël, journal

-r: sur, erreur, manoir

There are several cases in which the final *r* is
generally silent:

1) The infinite ending of *-er* verbs. Ex., *parler,
aller, jouer*

2) Names of certain tradespeople. Ex., *le boucher, le boulanger, le plombier*
3) Nouns ending in *-er*. Ex., *verger, soulier, tablier*

There are many common words ending in *c, l* and *f* in which the final consonant is silent. Ex., *estomac, banc, blanc, gentil, pareil, clef*

4. SIMPLE VOWELS

a   as in "ah!" or "father." Ex., *pâté, mâle, Jacques*

        as in "marry." Ex., *ami, mal*

e   as in "let." Ex., *belle, cher, cette*

        as in "day," without the *y* sound at the end (as explained above). This occurs in monosyllables or words ending in *-er, -et* or *-ez*, and is the same sound as *é*. Ex., *les, des, laver, filet, allez*

        as in "the" (the "mute" *e* between two single consonants or in monosyllabic words). Ex., *depuis, le, petit, tenir, besoin*

        The unaccented *e* is silent ("mute") at the end of a word. Ex., *parle, femme, limonade*

é   (*accent aigu*) as in "day," without the *y* sound at the end. Ex., *église, école, fâché, réalité*

è   (*accent grave*) as in "let." Ex., *père, mètre, Agnès*

ê   (*accent circonflexe*) as in "let." Ex., *tête, être*

i   as in "machine." The letter *y*, when it acts as a vowel, is pronounced the same way. Ex., *machine, lycée, qui, bicyclette*

o   (closed *o*) as in "go" (without the *w* sound at the end, as explained above). Ex., *tôt, mot, dos*

        (open *o*) as in "north." Ex., *robe, alors, bonne, gosse*

u   has no equivalent in English. To approximate the sound, say *ee,* keep the tongue in the position of *ee* (with the tip of the tongue against the bottom teeth), and then round the lips. Ex., *lune, nuit, assure*

ai   as in "let." Ex., *mais, caisson, lait*

ei   as in "let." Ex., *reine, peine*

au   as in "go" (without the *w* sound at the end). Ex., *auprès, pauvre, eau, eau(x)*

eu   has no equivalent in English. To approximate the sound, place the tongue as if for *é,* but round the lips as for *o.* Ex., *deux, feu, peu, ceux*

œ   has no equivalent in English. It is more "open" than *eu.* To form the sound, place the tongue as if for the *e* of "let," but round the lips. This sound is usually followed by a consonant, as in *sœur, cœur*

oi   pronounced *wa.* Ex., *moi, voilà*

ou   as in "too." Ex., *nous, vous, cousin, rouge, amour*

5.   THE NASALIZED VOWELS

When the consonants *n* and *m* are preceded by a vowel, the sound is generally nasalized; that is, the airstream escapes partly through the nose. The four categories of nasalized vowels are as follows:

1. *an, am, en,* and *em* are like the *au* in the British *aunt* pronounced through the nose:

an	year
ample	ample
en	in

| *enveloppe* | envelope |
| *temps* | time |

2. *on* and *om* are like the vowel in *north* pronounced through the nose:

| *bon* | good |
| *tomber* | to fall |

3. *in, im, ein, eim, ain,* and *aim* are like the vowel in *at* pronounced through the nose:

fin	end
simple	simple
faim	hunger
plein	full

4. *un* and *um* are like the vowel in *burn* pronounced through the nose:

un	one
chacun	each one
humble	humble

Vowels are nasalized in the following cases:

1. When the *n* or *m* is the final consonant or one of the final consonants:

| *fin* | end |
| *pont* | bridge |

champ	field
temps	time

2. In the middle of a word, when the *n* or *m* is not followed by a vowel:

NASALIZED

chambre	room	*impossible*	impossible

NOT NASALIZED

inutile	useless	*inoccupé*	unoccupied
initial	initial	*imitation*	imitation

Note: *mm* and *nn* do not cause the nasalization of the preceding vowel:

flamme	flame	*innocent*	innocent
donner	to give	*immense*	immense

6. THE APOSTROPHE

Certain one-syllable words ending in a vowel drop ("elide") the vowel when they come before words beginning with a vowel sound.

This dropping of the vowel or "elision" is marked by an apostrophe. Common cases are:

1. The *a* of *la:*

je l'aime	I like her (or it)	*l'heure*	the hour
l'amande	the almond		

2. The vowel *e* in one-syllable words (*le*, *je*, *se*, *me*, *que*, etc.):

l'argent	the money	*j'habite*	I live
j'ai	I have		

3. the vowel *i* in *si* "if," when it comes before *il* "he" or *ils* "they":

s'il vous plaît   please ("if it pleases you")

4. *moi* and *toi* when they come before *en* are written *m'* and *t'*:

Donnez-m'en   Give me some of it (of them).

5. A few words like *aujourd'hui* today, *entr'acte* interlude, etc.

7.   THE DEFINITE ARTICLE

	SINGULAR	PLURAL
Masculine	*le*	*les*
Feminine	*la*	*les*

SINGULAR

le garçon   the boy
la fille   the girl

PLURAL

les garçons	the boys
les filles	the girls

1. *Le* and *la* become *l'* before words beginning with a vowel sound:
   This contraction takes place before most words beginning with *h* (this *h* is called "mute" *h*). There are a few words where this contraction does not occur (this *h* is called "aspirate" *h*):

l'ami	the friend	*l'heure*	the hour
le héros	the hero	*la hache*	the ax

2. Unlike English, the definite article is used in French before a noun used in a general sense, before titles, days of the week, parts of the body, etc.:

l'avion	the airplane
le dimanche	Sunday (or Sundays)
le Comte . . .	Count . . .
J'aime les livres.	I like books.
Le fer est utile.	Iron is useful.
L'avarice est un vice.	Avarice is a vice.
Je vais me laver les mains.	I'm going to wash my hands.

3. The definite article is used with names of languages, unless preceded by *en:*

Le français est difficile.	French is difficult.

But—

Elle raconte l'histoire en français.	She tells the story in French.

> Note: The article is usually omitted with the name of a language used immediately after the verb *parler:*

Elle parle français.	She speaks French.

4. Unlike English, the definite articles must be repeated before each noun they modify.

les portes et les fenêtres	the doors and windows

8. THE INDEFINITE ARTICLE

	SINGULAR	PLURAL
Masculine	*un*	*des*
Feminine	*une*	*des*

SINGULAR

un homme	a man
une femme	a woman

PLURAL

des hommes	men; some men; a few men
des femmes	women; some women; a few women

1. The indefinite article is omitted before an unmodified statement of profession, nationality, rank, etc.:

Je suis médecin.	I am a doctor.
Elle est américaine.	She is an American.
Il est capitaine.	He is a captain.

But, with an adjective:

C'est un bon médecin.   He is a good doctor.

  2. The indefinite articles are repeated before each
noun:

un homme et une femme   a man and a woman

9.   THE POSSESSIVE

The possessive is expressed in the following way:
State the thing possessed + *de* ("of ") + the possessor:

le livre de Marie   Mary's book ("the
                        book of Mary")
le stylo de l'élève   the pupil's pen ("the
                        pen of the pupil")

10.   CONTRACTIONS

  1. The preposition *de* "of " combines with the definite articles *le* and *les* as follows:

de + le = du: *le livre du*   the teacher's
                   professeur   book
de + les =   *les stylos des*   the pupils'
des: *élèves*   pens

There is no contraction with *la* or *l'*.

  2. The preposition *à* "to" combines with the articles *le* and *les* as follows:

à + le = au: *Il parle au*   He's talking
                   garçon.   to the boy.

a + les =   *Il parle aux*   He's talking
aux: *garçons.*   to the boys.

There is no contraction with *la* or *l'*.

11. GENDER

All English nouns take the articles *the* or *a(n)*. Adjectives modifying English nouns do not change their form. In French, however, all nouns show gender (*masculine* or *feminine*), and adjectives agree with nouns in gender and number (*singular* or *plural*).

Masculine nouns: Take the definite article *le* in the singular and *les* in the plural, and the indefinite article *un*. They are modified by the masculine form of an adjective.

le costume bleu   the blue suit
les costumes bleus   the blue suits

Feminine nouns: Take the definite article *la* in the singular and *les* in the plural, and the indefinite article *une*. They are modified by the feminine form of an adjective.

la robe bleue   the blue dress
les robes bleues   the blue dresses

The gender of each noun must be learned with the noun. The following tables describing which noun classes are masculine and which are feminine provide a general rule of thumb. There are a number of exceptions to each statement.

The following classes of nouns are generally masculine:

1. Nouns naming a male person. Ex., *le père* father, *le roi* king.
   But: *la sentinelle,* sentinel
2. Nouns ending in a consonant. Ex., *le parc* park, *le pont* bridge, *le tarif* rate, tariff.
   But: Nouns ending in *-ion* and *-son* are generally feminine. Ex., *l'action* action, *la conversation* conversation, *la raison* reason
3. Nouns ending in any vowel except "mute" *e*. Ex., *le pari* bet, wager, *le vélo* bicycle, *le menu* menu
4. Nouns ending in *-ment, -age, -ege* (note that *-age* and *-ege* end in "mute" *e*). Ex., *le ménage* household, *le manège* riding school, *le document* document, *l'usage* usage
5. Names of days, months, seasons, metals, colors, trees, shrubs. Ex.:

le jeudi	Thursday	*le bleu*	blue
(le) septembre	September	*le chêne*	oak
le printemps	spring	*l'olivier*	olive tree
l'or	gold	*le genêt*	broom (a
le plomb	lead		shrub)

6. The names of parts of speech when used as nouns. Ex., *le nom* noun, *le verbe* verb, *le participe* participle.
7. Decimal weights and measures. Ex., *le mètre* meter, *le litre* liter, *le kilogramme* kilogram. Note the contrast with a nondecimal measure: *la livre* pound
8. The names of the cardinal points. Ex., *le nord* north, *l'est* east, *le sud* south, *l'ouest* west.

The following classes of nouns are generally feminine.

1. Nouns naming a female person. Ex., *la mère* mother, *la reine* queen.

   But: *le professeur* teacher (*m.* or *f.*)

2. Nouns ending in *-te, -son, -ion*. Ex., *la détente* détente, *la raison* reason, *la conversation* conversation.

   But: *le camion* truck, *l'avion* airplane, *le million* million

3. Names of qualities or states of being ending in: *-nce, -esse, -eur, -ude*.

la distance	distance
la gentillesse	niceness
la largeur	width
la douceur	sweetness

   (But: *le bonheur* happiness, *le malheur* unhappiness, misfortune.)

la gratitude	gratitude

4. Most nouns ending in mute *e*. Ex., *la blague* joke, *la voiture* car.

   But: See exceptions mentioned in item 4, page 308, under nouns of masculine gender.

5. Names of moral qualities, sciences, and arts. Ex., moral qualities: *la bonté* kindness, *l'avarice* greed

   science: *l'algèbre* algebra, *la chimie* chemistry.

   art: *la peinture* painting, *la musique* music.

   But: *l'art* (*m.*), art.

6. Most names of fruits. Ex., *la pomme* apple, *la cerise* cherry.

   But: *le pamplemousse* grapefruit, *le raisin* grapes.

7. Nouns ending in -té (very few exceptions, if any). Ex., *l'activité* activity, *la générosité* gen-

erosity, *la proximité* proximity, *la priorité* priority.

12. PLURAL OF NOUNS

1. Most nouns add *-s* to form the plural:

la ville	the city	*les villes*	the cities
l'île	the island	*les îles*	the islands

2. Nouns ending in *-s, -x, -z* do not change:

le fils	the son	*les fils*	the sons
la voix	the voice	*les voix*	the voices
le nez	the nose	*les nez*	the noses

3. Nouns ending in *-au* or *-eu* add *-x:*

le chapeau	the hat	*les cha-peaux*	the hats
l'eau	water	*les eaux*	waters
le jeu	the game	*les jeux*	the games

4. Nouns ending in *-al* and *-ail* form the plural with *-aux*.

l'hôpital	the hospital	*les hôpi-taux*	the hospitals
le travail	work	*les travaux*	works

SOME IRREGULAR PLURALS:

le ciel	the sky	*les cieux*	the heavens
l'œil	the eye	*les yeux*	the eyes
Madame	Madam, Mrs.	*Mesdames*	Madams

Mademoi- selle	Miss	*Mesdemoi- selles*	Misses
Monsieur	Sir, Mr.	*Messieurs*	Sirs
le bon- homme	the fellow	*les bons- hommes*	the fellows

13. FEMININE OF ADJECTIVES

1. The feminine of adjectives is normally formed
   by adding -*e* to the masculine singular, but if the
   masculine singular already ends in -*e*, the adjective has the same form in the feminine:

MASCULINE

| *un petit garçon* | a little boy |
| *un jeune homme* | a young man |

FEMININE

| *une petite fille* | a little girl |
| *une jeune femme* | a young woman |

2. Adjectives ending in -*er* change the *e* to *è* and
   then add -*e:*

| *étranger* (*m.*) | *étrangère* (*f.*) | foreign |

3. Most adjectives ending in -*eux* change this ending to -*euse:*

| *heureux* (*m.*) | *heureuse* (*f.*) | happy |
| *sérieux* (*m.*) | *sérieuse* (*f.*) | serious |

4. Some adjectives double the final consonant and add *-e:*

bon (*m.*)	*bonne* (*f.*)	good
ancien (*m.*)	*ancienne* (*f.*)	former, ancient
gentil (*m.*)	*gentille* (*f.*)	nice
gros (*m.*)	*grosse* (*f.*)	fat

5. Adjectives ending in *-eau* change the *-au* to *-lle:*

beau (*m.*)	*belle* (*f.*)	beautiful
nouveau (*m.*)	*nouvelle* (*f.*)	new

6. There are a number of irregular feminines:

actif (*m.*)	*active* (*f.*)	active
blanc (*m.*)	*blanche* (*f.*)	white
doux (*m.*)	*douce* (*f.*)	sweet, gentle, soft
faux (*m.*)	*fausse* (*f.*)	false
long (*m.*)	*longue* (*f.*)	long
vieux (*m.*)	*vieille* (*f.*)	old

14. PLURAL OF ADJECTIVES

1. The plural of adjectives is regularly formed by adding *-s* to the singular, but if the masculine singular ends in *-s* or *-x*, the masculine plural has the same form:

SINGULAR		PLURAL	
un petit garçon	a little boy	*deux petits garçons*	two little boys

| *une petite fille* | a little girl | *deux petites filles* | two little girls |
| *un mauvais garçon* | a bad boy | *deux mauvais garçons* | two bad boys |

2. Adjectives ending in *-au* add *-x:*

| *un nouveau livre* | a new book | *des nouveaux livres* | new books |

3. Adjectives ending in *-al* change to *-aux:*

| *un homme loyal* | a loyal man | *des hommes loyaux* | loyal men |

15. AGREEMENT OF ADJECTIVES

1. Adjectives agree with the nouns they modify in gender and number; that is, they are masculine if the noun is masculine, plural if the noun is plural, etc.:

| *Marie et sa sœur sont petites.* | Mary and her sister are little. |

2. An adjective that modifies nouns of different gender is in the masculine plural:

| *Marie et Jean sont petits.* | Mary and John are little. |

16. Position of Adjectives

1. Adjectives usually follow the noun:

un livre français	a French book
un homme intéressant	an interesting man
une idée excellente	an excellent idea

2. When they describe an inherent quality or when they form a set phrase, etc., they precede the noun:

une jeune fille	a young girl
le savant auteur	the learned author
une grande amitié	a close friendship
une éclatante victoire	a striking victory

3. The following common adjectives usually precede the nouns they modify:

autre	other	*jeune*	young
beau	beautiful	*joli*	pretty
bon	good	*long*	long
court	short	*mauvais*	bad
gentil	nice, pleasant	*nouveau*	new
grand	great, large, tall	*petit*	small, little
gros	big, fat	*vieux*	old

4. The following common adjectives differ in meaning depending on whether they come before or after the noun.

	BEFORE THE NOUN	AFTER THE NOUN
ancien	former	ancient
grand	great	tall
brave	worthy	brave
cher	dear (beloved)	dear (expensive)
pauvre	poor (wretched)	poor (indigent)
propre	own	clean
même	same	himself, herself, itself, very

5. The following adjectives have two forms for the masculine singular:

MASCULINE SINGULAR		FEMININE SINGULAR	
BEFORE A CONSONANT	BEFORE A VOWEL OR "MUTE" H		
beau	*bel*	*belle*	beautiful, fine, handsome
nouveau	*nouvel*	*nouvelle*	new
vieux	*vieil*	*vieille*	old

Examples:

un beau livre	· a beautiful book
un bel arbre	a beautiful tree
une belle femme	a beautiful woman

17. COMPARISON OF ADJECTIVES

Most adjectives form the comparative and superlative by placing *plus* and *le plus* (*la plus*) before the adjective and using *que* where English uses "than":

POSITIVE

petit	small
grand	large

COMPARATIVE

plus petit que	smaller than
plus grand que	larger than

SUPERLATIVE

le plus petit	the smallest
le plus grand	the largest

Common exceptions:

POSITIVE

bon	good
mauvais	bad

COMPARATIVE

meilleur	better
plus mauvais ⎫ *pire* ⎭	worse

SUPERLATIVE

le meilleur	the best
le plus mauvais ⎫ *le pire* ⎭	the worst

18. Possessive Adjectives

1. Possessive adjectives agree in gender and number with the thing possessed:

BEFORE SINGULAR NOUNS:		BEFORE PLURAL NOUNS:	
MASCULINE	FEMININE	MASCULINE AND FEMININE	
mon	ma	mes	my
ton	ta	tes	your (*fam.*)
son	sa	ses	his, her, its
notre	notre	nos	our
votre	votre	vos	your
leur	leur	leurs	their

Examples:

mon chien	my dog
sa mère	his (or her) mother
ma robe	my dress
votre livre	your book
leurs crayons	their pencils

2. Notice that these adjectives agree in gender not with the possessor as in English, but with the noun they modify. *Son, sa,* and *ses* may therefore mean "his," "her," or "its."

Jean parle à sa mère.	John is talking to his mother.
Marie parle à son père.	Mary is talking to her father.

3. Possessive adjectives are repeated before each noun they modify:

mon père et ma mère	my father and mother
leurs livres et leurs stylos	their books and pens

4. Before a feminine word beginning with a vowel or "mute" *h*, the forms *mon, ton, son* are used instead of *ma, ta, sa:*

son histoire	his story, his history
son école	his (or her) school

5. In speaking of parts of the body, the definite article is usually used instead of the possessive adjective (except where it might be ambiguous):

J'ai mal à la tête.	I have a headache.

19. POSSESSIVE PRONOUNS

MASCULINE		FEMININE		
SINGULAR	PLURAL	SINGULAR	PLURAL	
le mien	*les miens*	*la mienne*	*les miennes*	mine
le tien	*les tiens*	*la tienne*	*les tiennes*	your (*fam.*)
le sien	*les siens*	*la sienne*	*les siennes*	his, hers, its
le nôtre	*les nôtres*	*la nôtre*	*les nôtres*	ours
le vôtre	*les vôtres*	*la vôtre*	*les vôtres*	yours
le leur	*les leurs*	*la leur*	*les leurs*	theirs

Examples:

Voici le mien.	Here's mine.
Laquelle est la vôtre?	Which is yours? (*fem. sing.*)
Apportez les vôtres; j'apporterai les miens.	Bring yours; I'll bring mine.

20. DEMONSTRATIVE ADJECTIVES

MASCULINE SINGULAR

ce (before a consonant)	*ce livre*	this (that) book
cet (before a vowel or "mute" *h*)	*cet arbre* *cet homme*	this (that) tree this (that) man

FEMININE SINGULAR

cette	*cette femme*	this (that) woman

PLURAL

ces	*ces hommes* *ces femmes*	these (those) men these (those) women

1. The demonstrative adjectives agree with the nouns they modify in gender and number. They must be repeated before each noun:

cet homme et cette femme	this man and this woman

2. The demonstrative adjective in French stands for both "this" and "that" (plural "these" and "those"). When it is necessary to distinguish between "this" and "that," -*ci* and -*là* are added to the noun.

Donnez-moi ce livre-ci.	Give me this book.
Voulez-vous cette robe-là?	Do you want that dress (over there)?
J'aime ce livre-ci mais je n'aime pas ce livre-là.	I like this book but I don't like that book.

21. DEMONSTRATIVE PRONOUNS

Masculine Singular	*celui*	this one, that one, the one
Feminine Singular	*celle*	this one, that one, the one
Masculine Plural	*ceux*	these, those, the ones
Feminine Plural	*celles*	these, those, the ones

Examples:

J'aime celui-ci.	I like this one.
Donne-moi celle de ton frère.	Give me your brother's (calculator (*la calculatrice*), for example).

22. Personal Pronouns

The forms of the pronouns will depend on how they are used in a sentence.

1. As the subject of a verb:

je	I
tu	you (*fam.*)
il	he, it
elle	she, it
on	we, one, people
nous	we
vous	you
ils	they
elles	they

    a. *Vous* is the pronoun normally used in talking to one person or several people. *Tu* is the familiar form used only when addressing people you know very well (a member of one's family or a close friend; also children, pets, etc.).

    b. *Il, elle, ils,* and *elles* are used as pronouns referring to things as well as to persons. They have the same number and gender as the nouns to which they refer. *Ils* is used to refer to nouns of different genders:

Où est le livre?	Where's the book?
Il est sur la table.	It's on the table.
Où est la lettre?	Where's the letter?
Elle est sur la table.	It's on the table.

| *Où sont les livres et les lettres?* | Where are the books and letters? |
| *Ils sont sur la table.* | They're on the table. |

2. As the direct object of a verb:

me	me
te	you (*fam.*)
le	him, it
la	her, it
nous	us
vous	you
les	them
en	some, any

3. As the indirect object of a verb:

me	to me
te	to you (*fam.*)
lui	to him, to her
nous	to us
vous	to you
leur	to them
y	to it, there

4. As the object of a preposition; disjunctive pronouns:

moi	I, me
toi	you (*fam.*)
soi	himself, herself, oneself, itself
lui	he, him
elle	she, her

nous	we, us
vous	you
eux	they, them (*masc.*)
elles	they, them (*fem.*)

5. As a reflexive pronoun:

me	myself
te	yourself (*fam.*)
se	himself, herself, itself, oneself
nous	ourselves
vous	yourself, yourselves
se	themselves

6. In affirmative requests and commands:

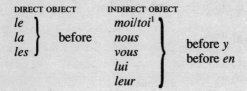

DIRECT OBJECT   INDIRECT OBJECT
le ⎫   *moi/toi*[1] ⎫
la ⎬ before   *nous*   ⎪
les ⎭   *vous*   ⎬ before *y*
                       lui   ⎪ before *en*
                       leur   ⎭

23. POSITION OF PRONOUNS

The direct and indirect pronoun objects generally precede the verb except in affirmative commands and requests.

---

[1] When *moi* or *toi* are used with *en*, they become *m'* and *t'* and precede *en*.

Examples: Donnez-*le-moi*.   BUT: Donnez-*m'en*.
          Lève-*toi*.   BUT: Va-t'en.

1. Position before a verb:

$$
\left.\begin{array}{l} me \\ te \\ se \\ nous \\ vous \end{array}\right\} \text{come before} \left.\begin{array}{l} le \\ la \\ les \end{array}\right\} \text{before} \left.\begin{array}{l} lui \\ leur \end{array}\right\} \begin{array}{l} \text{before } y \\ \text{before } en \end{array}
$$

Examples:

Il me le donne.	He gives it to me.
Il le lui donne.	He gives it to him (to her, to it).
Je l'y ai vu.	I saw him there.
Je leur en parlerai.	I'll speak to them about it.

2. Position after a verb:

$$
\left.\begin{array}{l} le \\ la \\ les \end{array}\right\} \text{come before} \left.\begin{array}{l} me\ (moi) \\ te\ (toi) \\ lui \\ \\ vous \\ leur \end{array}\right\} \text{before } y \text{ before } en
$$

Examples:

Donnez-le-lui.	Give it to him.
Donnez-leur-en.	Give them some.
Allez-vous-en.	Go away. Get out of here.

3. In affirmative commands, both the direct and indirect object pronoun follow the verb, the direct preceding the indirect:

Donnez-moi le livre.	Give me the book.
Donnez-le-moi.	Give it to me.
Montrez-moi les pommes.	Show me the apples.
Montrez-m'en.	Show me some.
Écrivez-lui une lettre.	Write him a letter.
Écrivez-la-lui.	Write it to him.

4. The pronoun objects precede *voici* and *voilà:*

Où est le livre?	Where's the book?
Le voici.	Here it is.
Les voilà.	Here they are.

24. Relative Pronouns

1. As the subject of a verb:

qui	who, which, that
ce qui	what, that which

Examples:

L'homme qui est là . . .	The man who is there . . .
Ce qui est bon . . .	What's good . . .

2. As the object of a verb:

que	whom, which, that
ce que	what, that which

Examples:

L'homme que tu vois . . .	The man who(m) you see . . .
Ce que je dis . . .	What I'm saying . . .

   3. As the object of a preposition:

qui (for a person)	whom
lequel (for a thing)	which

     Note: *dont* means whose, of whom, of which:

le problème dont je connais la solution . . .	The problem whose solution I know . . .
Le professeur dont je vous ai parlé . . .	The teacher about whom I talked to you . . .

25. INDEFINITE PRONOUNS

quelque chose	something
quelqu'un	someone
chacun	each (one)
on	one, people, they, etc.
ne . . . rien	nothing
ne . . . personne	no one

26. NOUNS USED AS INDIRECT OBJECTS

A noun used as an indirect object is always preceded by the preposition *à:*

Je donne un livre à la   I'm giving the girl a
   jeune fille.   book.

27. REPETITION OF PREPOSITIONS

The prepositions *à* and *de* must be repeated before
each of their objects:

Je parle au deputé et à   I'm speaking to the
   son secrétaire.   deputy and his
                    secretary.

Voici les cahiers de   Here are John's and
   Jean et ceux de   Mary's notebooks.
   Marie.

28. THE PARTITIVE

1. When a noun is used in such a way as to express
   or imply quantity, it is preceded by the article
   with *de*. This construction very often translates
   the English "some" or "a few."

J'ai de l'argent.   I have some money.
Il a des amis.   He has a few friends.

   In many cases, however, the article is used where
   we don't use "some" or "a few" in English:

A-t-il des amis ici?   Does he have friends
                     here?

2. The article is omitted:

   a. When an expression of quantity is used:

J'ai beaucoup d'ar-   I have a lot of money.
   gent.

Combien de livres   How many books do
  avez-vous?   you have?

    Exceptions: *bien* much, many, and *la plupart*
most, the majority:

bien des hommes   many men
la plupart des hommes   most men

    b. When the noun is preceded by an adjective:

J'ai acheté de belles   I bought some nice
  cravates.   ties.

    c. When the sentence is negative:

Il n'a pas d'amis.   He has no friends.
Mon ami n'a pas d'ar- My friend hasn't any
  gent.   money.

29. Negation

A sentence is made negative by placing *ne* before the
verb and *pas* after it:

Je sais.   I know.
Je ne sais pas.   I don't know.
Je ne l'ai pas vu.   I haven't seen it.

Other negative expressions:

ne . . . guère   hardly
ne . . . point   not (at all) (literary)
ne . . . rien   nothing
ne . . . nul, nulle   no one, no

ne . . . jamais	never
ne . . . personne	nobody
ne . . . plus	no longer
ne . . . ni . . . ni	neither . . . nor
ne . . . que	only
ne . . . aucun, aucune	no one

30. WORD ORDER IN QUESTIONS

1. Questions with pronoun subjects:
   There are two ways of asking a question with a pronoun subject:

   a. Place the pronoun after the verb:

Parlez-vous français?	Do you speak French?

   b. Place *est-ce que* ("is it that") before the sentence:

Est-ce que je parle trop vite?	Am I talking too fast?
Est-ce que vous parlez français?	Do you speak French?

2. Questions with noun subjects:
   When a question begins with a noun, the pronoun is repeated after the verb:

Votre frère parle-t-il français?	Does your brother speak French?
Votre sœur a-t-elle quitté la maison?	Has your sister left the house?

3. Questions introduced by interrogative words:
   In questions which begin with an interrogative
   word (*quand, comment, où, pourquoi*), the order
   is usually interrogative word—noun subject—
   verb—personal pronoun:

Pourquoi votre ami   Why did your friend
   a-t-il quitté Paris?   leave Paris?

31. ADVERBS

1. Most adverbs are formed from the adjectives by
   adding *-ment* to the feminine form:

froid	cold	*froidement*	coldly
certain	certain	*certainement*	certainly
naturel	natural	*naturellement*	naturally
facile	easy	*facilement*	easily

2. There are many irregular adverbs which must be
   learned separately:

vite	quickly	*mal*	badly

3. Adverbs are compared like adjectives (see pages
   328–329):

POSITIVE	COMPARATIVE	SUPERLATIVE
loin far	*plus loin* farther	*le plus loin* the farthest
bien well	*mieux* better	*le mieux* the best
mal poorly	*pire* more poorly, worse	*le pire* the worst

4. Some common adverbs of place:

ici	here
là	there
à côté	at the side
de côté	aside
devant	before, in front of
derrière	behind
dessus	on top
dessous	underneath
dedans	inside
dehors	outside
partout	everywhere
nulle part	nowhere
loin	far
près	near
où	where
y	there
ailleurs	elsewhere
là-haut	up there
là-bas	over there

5. Some common adverbs of time:

aujourd' hui	today
demain	tomorrow
hier	yesterday
avant-hier	the day before yesterday
après-demain	the day after tomorrow
maintenant	now
alors	then
avant	before
autrefois	once, formerly
tôt	early
bientôt	soon
tard	late

souvent	often
ne . . . jamais	never
toujours	always, ever
longtemps	long, for a long time
encore	still, yet
ne . . . plus	no longer, no more
à nouveau	again

6. Adverbs of manner:

bien	well
mal	ill, badly
ainsi	thus, so
de même	similarly
autrement	otherwise
ensemble	together
fort	much, very
volontiers	willingly
surtout	above all, especially
exprès	on purpose, expressly

7. Adverbs of quantity or degree:

beaucoup	much, many
assez	enough
ne . . . guère	not much, scarcely
peu	little
plus	more
ne . . . plus	no more
moins	less
encore	more
bien	much, many
trop	too, too much, too many
tellement	so much, so many

32. THE INFINITIVE

The most common endings of the infinitive are:

I	*-er parler*	to speak	(The First Conjugation)
II	*-ir finir*	to finish	(The Second Conjugation)
III	*-re vendre*	to sell	(The Third Conjugation)

33. THE PAST PARTICIPLE

1. Forms:

	INFINITIVE	PAST PARTICIPLE
I	*parler*	*parl-é*
II	*finir*	*fin-i*
III	*perdre*	*perd-u*

2. Agreement:

a. When a verb is conjugated with *avoir,* the past participle agrees in gender and number with the preceding direct object:

La pièce que j'ai vue hier était mauvaise.	The play I saw yesterday was bad.
Avez-vous vu le livre qu'il a acheté?	Have you seen the book he bought?
Avez-vous donné la chemise à Charles?	Did you give the shirt to Charles?
Non, je l'ai donnée à Claire.	No, I gave it to Claire.

b. In the case of reflexive verbs the past participle agrees with the reflexive direct object:

Ils se sont levés.	They got up.
Elle s' est lavée.	She washed herself.

c. In the case of intransitive verbs conjugated with *être*, the past participle agrees with the subject:

Marie est arrivée hier.	Mary arrived yesterday.
Jean et Pierre se sont levés.	John and Peter got up.
Ils sont arrivés.	They arrived.
Nous sommes rentrés très tard.	We came back very late.

34. THE INDICATIVE

SIMPLE TENSES

1. The present tense of *-er* verbs is formed by the verb stem plus the endings *-e, -es, -e, -ons, -ez, -ent.* The endings of *-ir* verbs are *-is, -is, -it, -issons, -issez,* and *-issent. -Re* verbs take *-s, -s, -, -ons, -ez,* and *-ent.* This tense has several English translations:

je parle	I speak, I am speaking, I do speak
ils finissent	They finish, they are finishing, they do finish
je me lève	I get up, I'm getting up

2. The imperfect tense is formed by dropping the *-ont* of the present *nous* form and adding *-ais, -ais, -ait, -ions, -iez, -aient.* It expresses a continued or habitual action in the past. It also indicates an action that was happening when something else happened:

Je me levais à sept heures.	I used to get up at seven o'clock.
Il dormait quand Jean est entré.	He was sleeping when John entered.
Il parlait souvent de cela.	He often spoke about that.

3. The future tense is formed by adding to the infinitive or future stem the endings *-ai, -as, -a, -ons, -ez, -ont.* It indicates a future action:

Je me lèverai tôt.	I'll get up early.
Il arrivera demain.	He'll arrive tomorrow.
Je le vendrai demain.	I'll sell it tomorrow.

4. The simple past tense (used only in formal written French) is formed by adding to the root the endings *-ai, -as, -a, -âmes, -âtes, -èrent* for *-er* verbs; the endings *-is, -is, -it, -îmes, -îtes, -irent* for *-ir* verbs; and for all other verbs either these last or *-us, -us, -ut, -ûmes, -ûtes, -urent.* It expresses an action begun and ended in the past.

Le roi fut tué.	The king was killed.
Les soldats entrèrent dans la ville.	The soldiers entered the city.

5. The past tense or *passé composé* is formed by adding the past participle to the present indicative of *avoir* or, in a few cases, *être*. It is used to indicate a past action which has been completed.

Je me suis levé tôt.	I got up early.
Il ne m'a rien dit.	He didn't tell me anything.
J'ai fini mon travail.	I finished my work. I have finished my work.
L'avez-vous vu?	Have you seen him? Did you see him?
Ils sont arrivés.	They arrived.

6. The pluperfect or past perfect tense is formed by adding the past participle to the imperfect of *avoir* or, in a few cases, *être*. It translates the English past perfect:

Il l'avait fait.	He had done it.
Lorsque je suis revenu, il était parti.	When I came back, he had gone.

7. The past anterior tense is formed by adding the past participle to the simple past of *avoir* or, in a few cases, *être*. It is used for an event that happened just before another event. It is used mostly in literary style.

Après qu'il eut dîné, il sortit.	As soon as he had eaten, he went out.
Quand il eut fini il se leva.	When he had finished, he got up.

8. The future perfect tense is formed by adding the past participle to the future of *avoir* or, in a few cases, *être*. It translates the English future perfect:

Il aura bientôt fini.	He will soon have finished.

Sometimes it indicates probability:

Il le lui aura sans doute dit.	No doubt he must have told him.
Il aura été malade.	He probably was sick.
Je me serai trompé.	I must have been mistaken.

9. The most common intransitive verbs that are conjugated with the verb *être* in the compound tenses are the following:
   aller, arriver, descendre, devenir, entrer, monter, mourir, naître, partir, rentrer, rester, retourner, revenir, sortir, tomber, venir.
   Examples:

Je suis venu.	I have come.
Il est arrivé.	He has arrived.
Nous sommes partis.	We have left.

10. Reflexive verbs are conjugated with the auxiliary *être* in the compound tenses:

Je me suis lavé les mains.	I have washed my hands.
Je me suis levé à sept heures ce matin.	I got up at seven o'clock this morning.
Elle s'est levée.	She got up.

CONDITIONAL

1. The conditional is formed by adding to the infinitive the endings *-ais, -ais, -ait, -ions, -iez, -aient*. It translates English "would" or "should":

Je le prendrais si j'étais à votre place.	I would take it if I were you.
Je ne ferais jamais une chose pareille.	I would never do such a thing.

2. The conditional perfect is formed by adding the past participle to the conditional of *avoir* or *être*. It translates the English "if I had" or "if I would have," etc.:

Si j'avais su, je n'y serais jamais allé.	If I had known, I would never have gone there.
Si j'avais eu assez d'argent je l'aurais acheté.	If I had had the money, I would have bought it.

35. The Imperative

1. The imperative of most verbs is generally formed from the present indicative tense. In the verbs of the first conjugation, however, the second person singular loses the final *s*:

donner	to give	*finir*	to finish
donne (*fam.*)	give	finis (*fam.*)	finish

donnez	give	*finissez*	finish
donnons	let us give	*finissons*	let us finish
vendre	to sell	*vendez*	sell
vends (*fam.*)	sell	*vendons*	let us sell

2. Imperatives of *être* and *avoir:*

être	to be	*avoir*	to have
sois (*fam.*)	be	*aie* (*fam.*)	have
soyez	be	*ayez*	have
soyons	let us be	*ayons*	let us have

36. Verbs Followed by the Infinitive

1. Some verbs are followed by the infinitive without a preceding preposition:

Je vais parler à Jean.	I am going to talk to John.
J'aime parler français.	I like to speak French.
Je ne sais pas danser.	I don't know how to dance.

2. Some verbs are followed by *à* plus the infinitive:

J'apprends à parler français.	I am learning to speak French.
Je l'aiderai à le faire.	I'll help him do it.

3. Some verbs are followed by *de* plus the infinitive:

Il leur a demandé de fermer la porte.	He asked them to shut the door.

37. THE SUBJUNCTIVE

The indicative makes a simple statement; the subjunctive indicates a certain attitude toward the statement—uncertainty, desire, emotion, etc. The subjunctive is used in subordinate clauses when the statement is unreal, doubtful, indefinite, subject to some condition, or is affected by will or emotion.

FORMS

1. Present Subjunctive:

   Drop the *-ent* of the third person plural present indicative and add *-e, -es, -e, -ions, -iez, -ient.* See the forms of the regular subjunctive in the Regular Verb Charts.
   The irregular verbs *avoir* and *être:*

que j'aie	*que je sois*
que tu aies	*que tu sois*
qu'il ait	*qu'il soit*
que nous ayons	*que nous soyons*
que vous ayez	*que vous soyez*
qu'ils aient	*qu'ils soient*

2. Imperfect Subjunctive:[1]

   Drop the ending of the first person singular of the past definite and add *-sse, -sses, -t, -ssions, -ssiez, -ssent,* putting a circumflex over the last vowel of the third person singular:

---

[1] The imperfect and the pluperfect subjunctive are not used today in conversational French. They do, however, appear in literature.

(THAT) I GAVE, MIGHT GIVE

que je donnasse
que tu donnasses
qu'il donnât
que nous donnassions
que vous donnassiez
qu'ils donnassent

(THAT) I FINISHED, MIGHT FINISH

que je finisse
que tu finisses
qu'il finît
que nous finissions
que vous finissiez
qu'ils finissent

(THAT) I SOLD, MIGHT SELL

que je vendisse
que tu vendisses
qu'il vendît
que nous vendissions
que vous vendissiez
qu'ils vendissent

3. Perfect Subjunctive:

Add the past participle to the present subjunctive of *avoir* (or, in a few cases, *être*):
avoir: que j'aie donné, que tu aies donné, etc.
être: que je sois allé, que tu sois allé, etc.

4. Pluperfect Subjunctive:[1]

Add the past participle to the imperfect subjunctive of *avoir* (or, in a few cases, *être*):

avoir: j'eusse donné, etc.
être: je fusse allé, etc.

---

[1] The imperfect and the pluperfect subjunctive are not used today in conversational French. They do, however, appear in literature.

USES

1. After verbs of command, request, permission, etc.:

Je tiens à ce que vous   I insist on your going
y alliez.   there.

2. After expressions of approval and disapproval, necessity, etc.:

Il n'est que juste que   It's only fair that you
vous le lui disiez.   tell him that.
Il faut que vous fassiez   You have to do that.
cela.

3. After verbs of emotion (desire, regret, fear, joy, etc.):

Je voudrais bien que   I'd like you to come
vous veniez avec   with us.
nous.
Je regrette que vous ne   I'm sorry you can't
puissiez pas venir.   come.

4. After expressions of doubt, uncertainty, denial:

Je doute que j'y aille.   I doubt that I'll go there.
Il est possible qu'il ne   It's possible that he may
puisse pas venir.   not be able to come.

5. In relative clauses with an indefinite antecedent:

Il me faut quelqu'un qui   I need someone to do
fasse cela.   that.

6. In adverbial clauses after certain conjunctions
denoting purpose, time, concessions, etc.:

Je viendrai à moins   I'll come unless it rains.
  qu'il ne pleuve.
Asseyez-vous en atten-   Sit down until it's
  dant que ce soit prêt.   ready.

7. In utterances expressing a wish or command:

Qu'ils s'en aillent!   Let them go away!
Dieu vous bénisse!   God bless you!
Vive la France!   Long live France!

VERB CHARTS

I. FORMS OF THE REGULAR VERBS

A. CLASSES I, II, III

Infinitive	Pres. & Past Participles	Present Indicative	Present Subjunctive[†]	Conversational Past	Past Subjunctive	Imperfect Indicative
-er ending parler to speak	parlant parlé	parl + e es e ons ez ent	parl + e es e ions iez ent	j'ai + parlé tu as il a nous avons vous avez ils ont	que j'aie + parlé que tu aies qu'il ait que nous ayons que vous ayez qu'ils aient	parl + ais ais ait ions iez aient
-ir ending finir to finish	finissant fini	fin + is is it issons issez issent	finiss + e es e ions iez ent	j'ai + fini tu as il a nous avons vous avez ils ont	que j'aie + fini que tu aies qu'il ait que nous ayons que vous ayez qu'ils aient	finiss + ais ais ait ions iez aient

Infinitive	Pres. & Past Participles	Present Indicative	Present Subjunctive†	Conversational Past	Past Subjunctive	Imperfect Indicative
-re ending	vendant	vend + s	vend + e	j'ai + vendu	que j'aie + vendu	vend + ais
vendre	vendu	s	es	tu as	que tu aies	ais
to sell		—	e	il a	qu'il ait	ait
		ons	ions	nous avons	que nous ayons	ions
		ez	iez	vous avez	que vous ayez	iez
		ent	ent	ils ont	qu'ils aient	aient

† Like the past subjunctive, the present subjunctive verb is always preceded by *que* or *qu'* + the appropriate pronoun, as in *"Il faut que je parte"* and *"Je veux qu'il quitte la maison."*

Past Perfect	Future	Future Perfect	Conditional	Conditional Perfect	Imperative
j'avais + parlé	parler + ai	j'aurai + parlé	parler + ais	j'aurais + parlé	
tu avais	as	tu auras	ais	tu aurais	parle
il avait	a	il aura	ait	il aurait	
nous avions	ons	nous aurons	ions	nous aurions	parlons
vous aviez	ez	vous aurez	iez	vous auriez	parlez
ils avaient	ont	ils auront	aient	ils auraient	
j'avais + fini	finir + ai	j'aurai + fini	finir + ais	j'aurais + fini	
tu avais	as	tu auras	ais	tu aurais	finis
il avait	a	il aura	ait	il aurait	
nous avions	ons	nous aurons	ions	nous aurions	finissons
vous aviez	ez	vous aurez	iez	vous auriez	finissez
ils avaient	ont	ils auront	aient	ils auraient	
j'avais + vendu	vendr + ai	j'aurai + vendu	vendr + ais	j'aurais + vendu	
tu avais	as	tu auras	ais	tu aurais	vends
il avait	a	il aura	ait	il aurait	
nous avions	ons	nous aurons	ions	nous aurions	vendons
vous aviez	ez	vous aurez	iez	vous auriez	vendez
ils avaient	ont	ils auront	aient	ils auraient	

B. Verbs Ending in *-CER* AND *-GER*

Infinitive[1]	Pres. & Past Participles	Present Indicative	Present Subjunctive[†]	Conversational Past	Past Subjunctive	Imperfect Indicative
placer[1] to place	*plaçant*[3] placé	place places place *plaçons* placez placent	place places place placions placiez placent	j'ai + placé tu as il a nous avons vous avez ils ont	que j'aie + placé que tu aies qu'il ait que nous ayons que vous ayez qu'ils aient	*plaçais* *plaçais* *plaçait* placions placiez *plaçaient*
manger[2] to eat	*mangeant* mangé	mange manges mange *mangeons* mangez mangent	mange manges mange mangions mangiez mangent	j'ai + mangé tu as il a nous avons vous avez ils ont	que j'aie + mangé que tu aies qu'il ait que nous ayons que vous ayez qu'ils aient	*mangeais* *mangeais* *mangeait* mangions mangiez *mangeaient*

[1] Similarly conjugated: *commencer, lancer, etc.*

[2] Similarly conjugated: *plonger, ranger, arranger, etc.*

[3] All spelling changes in verb forms will be italicized in this section.

360

Past Perfect	Future	Future Perfect	Conditional	Conditional Perfect	Imperative
j'avais + placé	placer + ai	j'aurai + placé	placer + ais	j'aurais + placé	
tu avais	as	tu auras	ais	tu aurais	place
il avait	a	il aura	ait	il aurait	
nous avions	ons	nous aurons	ions	nous aurions	*plaçons*
vous aviez	ez	vous aurez	iez	vous auriez	placez
ils avaient	ont	ils auront	aient	ils auraient	
j'avais + mangé	manger + ai	j'aurai + mangé	manger + ais	j'aurais + mangé	
tu avais	as	tu auras	ais	tu aurais	mange
il avait	a	il aura	ait	il aurait	
nous avions	ons	nous aurons	ions	nous aurions	*mangeons*
vous aviez	ez	vous aurez	iez	vous auriez	mangez
ils avaient	ont	ils auront	aient	ils auraient	

C. VERBS ENDING IN -ER WITH CHANGES IN THE STEM

Infinitive	Pres. & Past Participles	Present Indicative	Present Subjunctive[†]	Conversational Past	Past Subjunctive	Imperfect Indicative
acheter[1] to buy	achetant acheté	achète achètes achète achetons achetez achètent	achète achètes achète achetions achetiez achètent	j'ai + acheté tu as il a nous avons vous avez ils ont	que j'aie + acheté que tu aies qu'il ait que nous ayons que vous ayez qu'ils aient	achet + ais ais ait ions iez aient
appeler[2] to call	appelant appelé	appelle appelles appelle appelons appelez appellent	appelle appelles appelle appelions appeliez appellent	j'ai + appelé tu as il a nous avons vous avez ils ont	que j'aie + appelé que tu aies qu'il ait que nous ayons que vous ayez qu'ils aient	appel + ais ais ait ions iez aient

	Participles	Present	(j'ai + payé)	(que j'aie + payé)	(pay + endings)
payer[3] to pay	payant payé	paie paies paie payons payez paient	j'ai tu as il a nous avons vous avez ils ont (+ payé)	que j'aie que tu aies qu'il ait que nous ayons que vous ayez qu'ils aient (+ payé)	pay + ais ais ait ions iez aient
préférer[4] to prefer	préférant préféré	préfère‡ préfères préfère préférons préférez préfèrent	j'ai tu as il a nous avons vous avez ils ont (+ préféré)	que j'aie que tu aies qu'il ait que nous ayons que vous ayez qu'ils aient (+ préféré)	préfér + ais ais ait ions iez aient

[1] Verbs like *acheter*: *mener, amener, emmener, se promener, lever, se lever, élever*

[2] Verbs like *appeler*: *se rappeler, jeter*

[3] Verbs like *payer*: *essayer, employer, ennuyer, essuyer, nettoyer* (See note below.)

[4] Verbs like *préférer*: *espérer, répéter, célébrer, considérer, suggérer, protéger*

† Verbs ending in *-oyer, -uyer* may use *i* or *y* in the present (except for *nous* and *vous* forms), the future, and the conditional, as in *payer, essayer*. Verbs ending in *-oyer, -uyer* change *y* to *i* (as in *essuyer, ennuyer, employer, nettoyer*). These changes are indicated by the use of italics.

‡ Note the change from *é* to *è* in the *je, tu, il/elle/on,* and *ils* forms of verbs like *préférer*.

Past Perfect	Future	Future Perfect	Conditional	Conditional Perfect	Imperative
j'avais + acheté	*achèter* + ai	j'aurai + acheté	*achèter* + ais	j'aurais + acheté	
tu avais	as	tu auras	ais	tu aurais	*achète*
il avait	a	il aura	ait	il aurait	
nous avions	ons	nous aurons	ions	nous aurions	achetons
vous aviez	ez	vous aurez	iez	vous auriez	achetez
ils avaient	ont	ils auront	aient	ils auraient	
j'avais + appelé	*appeller* + ai	j'aurai + appelé	*appeller* + ais	j'aurais + appelé	
tu avais	as	tu auras	ais	tu aurais	*appelle*
il avait	a	il aura	ait	il aurait	
nous avions	ons	nous aurons	ions	nous aurions	appelons
vous aviez	ez	vous aurez	iez	vous auriez	appelez
ils avaient	ont	ils auront	aient	ils auraient	

j'avais + payé	*paier* or *payer*	+ ai	j'aurai + payé	*paier* or *payer*	+ ais	j'aurais + payé	*paie*
tu avais		as	tu auras		ais	tu aurais	
il avait		a	il aura		ait	il aurait	
nous avions		ons	nous aurons		ions	nous aurions	payons
vous aviez		ez	vous aurez		iez	vous auriez	payez
ils avaient		ont	ils auront		aient	ils auraient	
j'avais + préféré	préférer	+ ai	j'aurai + préféré	préfér	+ ais	j'aurais + préféré	*préfère*
tu avais		as	tu auras		ais	tu aurais	
il avait		a	il aura		ait	il aurait	
nous avions		ons	nous aurons		ions	nous aurions	préférons
vous aviez		ez	vous aurez		iez	vous auriez	préférez
ils avaient		ont	ils auront		aient	ils auraient	

D. Verbs Ending In -*OIR*

Infinitive	Pres. & Past Participles	Present Indicative	Present Subjunctive†	Conversational Past	Past Subjunctive	Imperfect Indicative	Imperative
recevoir[1] to receive	recevant reçu	reçois reçois reçoit recevons recevez reçoivent	reçoive reçoives reçoive recevions receviez reçoivent	j'ai + reçu tu as il a nous avons vous avez ils ont	que j'aie + reçu que tu aies qu'il ait que nous ayons que vous ayez qu'ils aient	recev + ais ais ait ions iez aient	reçois recevons recevez

Past Perfect	Future	Future Perfect	Conditional	Conditional Perfect	Imperative
j'avais + reçu tu avais il avait nous avions vous aviez ils avaient	recevr + ai as a ons ez ont	j'aurai + reçu tu auras il aura nous aurons vous aurez ils auront	recevr + ais ais ait ions iez aient	j'aurais + reçu tu aurais il aurait nous aurions vous auriez ils auraient	

[1] Verbs like *recevoir*: *devoir (dois, doive, dû)*.

E. Verbs Ending in *-NDRE*

Infinitive	Pres. & Past Participles	Present Indicative	Present Subjunctive	Conversational Past	Past Subjunctive	Imperfect Indicative
craindre[1] to fear	craignant craint	crains crains craint craignons craignez craignent	craigne craignes craigne craignions craigniez craignent	j'ai + craint tu as il a nous avons vous avez ils ont	que j'aie + craint que tu aies qu'il ait que nous ayons que vous ayez qu'ils aient	craign + ais ais ait ions iez aient
éteindre[2] to extinguish	éteignant éteint	éteins éteins éteint éteignons éteignez éteignent	éteigne éteignes éteigne éteignions éteigniez éteignent	j'ai + éteint tu as il a nous avons vous avez ils ont	que j'aie + éteint que tu aies qu'il ait que nous ayons que vous ayez qu'ils aient	éteign + ais ais ait ions iez aient

[1] Verbs like *craindre*: *plaindre*, to pity. The reflexive form, *se plaindre*, means "to complain," and in the compound tenses is conjugated with *être*.

[2] Verbs like *éteindre*: *peindre*, to paint; *teindre*, to dye.

Past Perfect	Future	Future Perfect	Conditional	Conditional Perfect	Imperative
j'avais + *craint*	craindr + ai	j'aurai + *craint*	craindr + ais	j'aurais + *craint*	
tu avais	as	tu auras	ais	tu aurais	*crains*
il avait	a	il aura	ait	il aurait	
nous avions	ons	nous aurons	ions	nous aurions	*craignons*
vous aviez	ez	vous aurez	iez	vous auriez	*craignez*
ils avaient	ont	ils auront	aient	ils auraient	
j'avais + *éteint*	éteindr + ai	j'aurai + *éteint*	éteindr + ais	j'aurais + *éteint*	
tu avais	as	tu auras	ais	tu aurais	*éteins*
il avait	a	il aura	ait	il aurait	
nous avions	ons	nous aurons	ions	nous aurions	*éteignons*
vous aviez	ez	vous aurez	iez	vous auriez	*éteignez*
ils avaient	ont	ils auront	aient	ils auraient	

F. Compound Tenses of Verbs Conjugated with *Être*

Conversational Past	Past Subjunctive	Past Perfect	Future Perfect	Conditional Perfect
je suis allé(e)	que je sois allé(e)	j'étais allé(e)	je serai allé(e)	je serais allé(e)
tu es allé(e)	que tu sois allé(e)	tu étais allé(e)	tu seras allé(e)	tu serais allé(e)
il est allé	qu'il soit allé	il était allé	il sera allé	il serait allé
elle est allée	qu'elle soit allée	elle était allée	elle sera allée	elle serait allée
nous sommes allé(e)s	que nous soyons allé(e)s	nous étions allé(e)s	nous serons allé(e)s	nous serions allé(e)s
vous êtes allé(e)(s)	que vous soyez allé(e)(s)	vous étiez allé(e)(s)	vous serez allé(e)(s)	vous seriez allé(e)(s)
ils sont allés	qu'ils soient allés	ils étaient allés	ils seront allés	ils seraient allés
elles sont allées	qu'elles soient allées	elles étaient allées	elles seront allées	elles seraient allées

G. Compound Tenses of Reflexive Verbs (All Reflexive Verbs Are Conjugated With *être*)

Conversational Past	Past Subjunctive	Past Perfect	Future Perfect	Conditional Perfect
je me suis levé(e)	que je me sois levé(e)	je m'étais levé(e)	je me serai levé(e)	je me serais levé(e)
tu t'es levé(e)	que tu te sois levé(e)	tu t'étais levé(e)	tu te seras levé(e)	tu te serais levé(e)
il s'est levé	qu'il se soit levé	il s'était levé	il se sera levé	il se serait levé
elle s'est levée	qu'elle se soit levée	elle s'était levée	elle se sera levée	elle se serait levée
nous nous sommes levé(e)s	que nous nous soyons levé(e)s	nous nous étions levé(e)s	nous nous serons levé(e)s	nous nous serions levé(e)s
vous vous êtes levé(e)(s)	que vous vous soyez levé(e)(s)	vous vous étiez levé(e)s	vous vous serez levé(e)(s)	vous vous seriez levé(e)(s)
ils se sont levés	qu'ils se soient levés	ils s'étaient levés	ils se seront levés	ils se seraient levés
elles se sont levées	qu'elles se soient levées	elles s'étaient levées	elles se seront levées	elles se seraient levées

H. Infrequently Used and "Literary" Tenses (Classes I, II, III)

Past Definite[1][†]			Past Anterior[2]			Imperfect Subjunctive[3]		
parlai	finis	perdis	eus parlé	eus fini	eus perdu	parlasse	finisse	perdisse
parlas	finis	perdis	eus parlé	eus fini	eus perdu	parlasses	finisses	perdisses
parla	finit	perdit	eut parlé	eut fini	eut perdu	parlât	finît	perdît
parlâmes	finîmes	perdîmes	eûmes parlé	eûmes fini	eûmes perdu	parlassions	finissions	perdissions
parlâtes	finîtes	perdîtes	eûtes parlé	eûtes fini	eûtes perdu	parlassiez	finissiez	perdissiez
parlèrent	finirent	perdirent	eurent parlé	eurent fini	eurent perdu	parlassent	finissent	perdissent

[1] Used in formal narrative only. In informal conversation and writing, use the conversational past (*j'ai parlé*, etc.)

[2] Used in literary style only, after *quand, lorsque, après que, dès que* for an event that happened just before another event. Example: *Après qu'il eut dîné, il sortit.* As soon as he had eaten, he went out.

[3] "That I spoke," "that I might speak," etc. This tense is infrequently found in ordinary conversation, but is used fairly often in literary works.

[†] All other regular verbs use either the *-er, -ir, -re* endings, depending upon the conjugation to which they belong. The past definite forms of irregular verbs must be memorized.

371

Past Perfect Subjunctive[4]

que j'eusse parlé	que j'eusse fini	que j'eusse perdu
que tu eusses parlé	que tu eusses fini	que tu eusses perdu
qu'il eût parlé	qu'il eût fini	qu'il eût perdu
que nous eussions parlé	que nous eussions fini	que nous eussions perdu
que vous eussiez parlé	que vous eussiez fini	que vous eussiez perdu
qu'ils eussent parlé	qu'ils eussent fini	qu'ils eussent perdu

[4] "That I had spoken," "that I might have spoken," etc. A predominantly literary tense.

372

II. FREQUENTLY USED IRREGULAR VERBS

The correct auxiliary verb is indicated in parentheses below each verb.
For compound tenses, use the appropriate form of the auxiliary verb + past participle.

Infinitive	Pres. & Past Participles	Present Indicative	Present Subjunctive	Imperfect Indicative	Future	Conditional	Imperative
acquérir to acquire (*avoir*)	acquérant acquis	acquiers acquiers acquiert acquérons acquérez acquièrent	acquière acquières acquière acquérions acquériez acquièrent	acquér + ais ais ait ions iez aient	acquerr + ai as a ons ez ont	acquerr + ais ais ait ions iez aient	acquiers acquérons acquérez
aller to go (*être*)	allant allé(e)(s)	vais vas va allons allez vont	aille ailles aille allions alliez aillent	all + ais ais ait ions iez aient	ir + ai as a ons ez ont	ir + ais ais ait ions iez aient	va allons allez

373

Infinitive	Pres. & Past Participles	Present Indicative	Present Subjunctive	Imperfect Indicative	Future	Conditional	Imperative
(s')asseoir[†] to sit (down) (être)	asseyant assis(e)(s)	assieds assieds assied asseyons asseyez asseyent	asseye asseyes asseye asseyions asseyiez asseyent	assey + ais ais ait ions iez aient	asseyer or assiér or assoir + ai as a ons ez ont	asseyer + ais or ais assiér + ait or ions assoir + iez aient	 assieds-toi asseyons-nous asseyez-vous
avoir to have (avoir)	ayant eu	ai as a avons avez ont	aie aies ait ayons ayez aient	av + ais ais ait ions iez aient	aur + ai as a ons ez ont	aur + ais ais ait ions iez aient	 aie ayons ayez
battre to beat (avoir)	battant battu	bats bats bat battons battez battent	batte battes batte battions battiez battent	batt + ais ais ait ions iez aient	battr + ai as a ons ez ont	battr + ais ais ait ions iez aient	 bats battons battez

[†] There is a variant form of the conjugation of *s'asseoir* based on the present participle *assoyant* and first person singular *assois*, but this is rather archaic and is rarely used. There are also two variant forms for the future stem: *assiér-* and *assoir-*. *Assiér-* is frequently used.

boire to drink (*avoir*)	buvant bu	bois bois boit buvons buvez boivent	boive boives boive buvions buviez boivent	buv + ais ais ait ions iez aient	boir + ai as a ons ez ont	boir + ais ais ait ions iez aient	bois buvons buvez
conclure to conclude (*avoir*)	concluant conclu	conclus conclus conclut concluons concluez concluent	conclue conclues conclue concluions concluiez concluent	conclu + ais ais ait ions iez aient	conclur + ai as a ons ez ont	conclur + ais ais ait ions iez aient	conclus concluons concluez

Infinitive	Pres. & Past Participles	Present Indicative	Present Subjunctive	Imperfect Indicative		Future		Conditional		Imperative
conduire to drive to lead (*avoir*)	conduisant conduit	conduis conduis conduit conduisons conduisez conduisent	conduise conduises conduise conduisions conduisiez conduisent	conduis +	ais ais ait ions iez aient	conduir +	ai as a ons ez ont	conduir +	ais ais ait ions iez aient	conduis conduisons conduisez
connaître to know (*avoir*)	connaissant connu	connais connais connaît connaissons connaissez connaissent	connaisse connaisses connaisse connaissions connaissiez connaissent	connaiss +	ais ais ait ions iez aient	connaîtr +	ai as a ons ez ont	connaîtr +	ais ais ait ions iez aient	connais connaissons connaissez
courir to run (*avoir*)	courant couru	cours cours court courons courez courent	coure coures coure courions couriez courent	cour +	ais ais ait ions iez aient	courr +	ai as a ons ez ont	courr +	ais ais ait ions iez aient	cours courons courez

Infinitive	Participles	Present	Subjunctive	Imperfect	Future	Conditional	Imperative
croire to believe (*avoir*)	croyant cru	crois crois croit croyons croyez croient	croie croies croie croyions croyiez croient	croy + ais ais ait ions iez aient	croir + ai as a ons ez ont	croir + ais ais ait ions iez aient	crois croyons croyez
cueillir to gather to pick (*avoir*)	cueillant cueilli	cueille cueilles cueille cueillons cueillez cueillent	cueille cueilles cueille cueillions cueilliez cueillent	cueill + ais ais ait ions iez aient	cueiller + ai as a ons ez ont	cueiller + ais ais ait ions iez aient	cueille cueillons cueillez
devoir to owe to ought (*avoir*)	devant dû	dois dois doit devons devez doivent	doive doives doive devions deviez doivent	dev + ais ais ait ions iez aient	devr + ai as a ons ez ont	devr + ais ais ait ions iez aient	*not used*
dire to say to tell (*avoir*)	disant dit	dis dis dit disons dites disent	dise dises dise disions disiez disent	dis + ais ais ait ions iez aient	dir + ai as a ons ez ont	dir + ais ais ait ions iez aient	dis disons dites

Infinitive	Pres. & Past Participles	Present Indicative	Present Subjunctive	Imperfect Indicative	Future	Conditional	Imperative
dormir to sleep (*avoir*)	dormant dormi	dors dors dort dormons dormez dorment	dorme dormes dorme dormions dormiez dorment	dorm + ais ais ait ions iez aient	dormir + ai as a ons ez ont	dormir + ais ais ait ions iez aient	dors dormons dormez
écrire to write (*avoir*)	écrivant écrit	écris écris écrit écrivons écrivez écrivent	écrive écrives écrive écrivions écriviez écrivent	écriv + ais ais ait ions iez aient	écrir + ai as a ons ez ont	écrir + ais ais ait ions iez aient	écris écrivons écrivez
envoyer to send (*avoir*)	envoyant envoyé	envoie envoies envoie envoyons envoyez envoient	envoie envoies envoie envoyions envoyiez envoient	envoy + ais ais ait ions iez aient	enverr + ai as a ons ez ont	enverr + ais ais ait ions iez aient	envoie envoyons envoyez
être to be (*avoir*)	étant été	suis es est sommes êtes sont	sois sois soit soyons soyez soient	ét + ais ais ait ions iez aient	ser + ai as a ons ez ont	ser + ais ais ait ions iez aient	sois soyons soyez

378

Infinitive	Participles	Present	Present subj.	Imperfect	Future	Conditional	Imperative
faillir† to fail (*avoir*)	faillant failli	*not used*	*not used*	*not used*	faillir + ai as a ons ez ont	faillir + ais ais ait ions iez aient	*not used*
faire to do to make (*avoir*)	faisant fait	fais fais fait faisons faites font	fasse fasses fasse fassions fassiez fassent	fais + ais ais ait ions iez aient	fer	fer	fais faisons faites
falloir to be necessary, must (used only with *il*) (*avoir*)	*no pres. part.* fallu	il faut	il faille	il fallait	il faudra	il faudrait	
fuir to flee (*avoir*)	fuyant fui	fuis fuis fuit fuyons fuyez fuient	fuie fuies fuie fuyions fuyiez fuient	fuy + ais ais ait ions iez aient	fuir + ai as a ons ez ont	fuir + ais ais ait ions iez aient	fuis fuyons fuyez

379

† Used in expressions such as *Il a failli tomber*. He nearly fell (lit., he failed to fall).

Infinitive	Pres. & Past Participles	Present Indicative	Present Subjunctive	Imperfect Indicative		Future		Conditional		Imperative
haïr to hate (*avoir*)	haïssant haï	hais hais hait haïssons haïssez haïssent	haïsse haïsses haïsse haïssions haïssiez haïssent	haïss	+ ais ais ait ions iez aient	haïr	+ ai as a ons ez ont	haïr	+ ais ais ait ions iez aient	haïs haïssons haïssez
lire to read (*avoir*)	lisant lu	lis lis lit lisons lisez lisent	lise lises lise lisions lisiez lisent	lis	+ ais ais ait ions iez aient	lir	+ ai as a ons ez ont	lir	+ ais ais ait ions iez aient	lis lisons lisez
mettre to put to place (*avoir*)	mettant mis	mets mets met mettons mettez mettent	mette mettes mette mettions mettiez mettent	mett	+ ais ais ait ions iez aient	mettr	+ ai as a ons ez ont	mettr	+ ais ais ait ions iez aient	mets mettons mettez
mourir to die (*être*)	mourant mort(e)(s)	meurs meurs meurt mourons mourez meurent	meure meures meure mourions mouriez meurent	mour	+ ais ais ait ions iez aient	mourr	+ ai as a ons ez ont	mourr	+ ais ais ait ions iez aient	meurs mourons mourez

	Participles	Present	Present Subj.	Imperfect	Future	Conditional	Imperative
mouvoir[†] to move (*avoir*)	mouvant mû	meus meus meut mouvons mouvez meuvent	meuve meuves meuve mouvions mouviez meuvent	mouv +ais ais ait ions iez aient	mouvr +ai as a ons ez ont	mouvr +ais ais ait ions iez aient	meus mouvons mouvez
naître to be born (*être*)	naissant né(e)(s)	nais nais naît naissons naissez naissent	naisse naisses naisse naissions naissiez naissent	naiss +ais ais ait ions iez aient	naîtr +ai as a ons ez ont	naîtr +ais ais ait ions iez aient	nais naissons naissez
ouvrir to open (*avoir*)	ouvrant ouvert	ouvre ouvres ouvre ouvrons ouvrez ouvrent	ouvre ouvres ouvre ouvrions ouvriez ouvrent	ouvr +ais ais ait ions iez aient	ouvrir +ai as a ons ez ont	ouvrir +ais ais ait ions iez aient	ouvre ouvrons ouvrez

[†] *Mouvoir* is seldom used except in compounds like *émouvoir,* to move (emotionally).

Infinitive	Pres. & Past Participles	Present Indicative	Present Subjunctive	Imperfect Indicative	Future	Conditional	Imperative
partir to leave to depart (*être*)	partant parti(e)(s)	pars pars part partons partez partent	parte partes parte partions partiez partent	part + ais ais ait ions iez aient	partir + ai as a ons ez ont	partir + ais ais ait ions iez aient	pars partons partez
plaire to please (to be pleasing to) (*avoir*)	plaisant plu	plais plais plaît plaisons plaisez plaisent	plaise plaises plaise plaisions plaisiez plaisent	plais + ais ais ait ions iez aient	plair + ai as a ons ez ont	plair + ais ais ait ions iez aient	plais plaisons plaisez
pleuvoir to rain (used only with *il*) (*avoir*)	pleuvant plu	il pleut	il pleuve	il pleuvait	il pleuvra	il pleuvrait	*not used*

382

Infinitive	Participles	Present Indicative	Present Subjunctive	Imperfect	Future	Conditional	Imperative
pouvoir[†] to be able, can (*avoir*)	pouvant pu	peux (puis)[†] peux peut pouvons pouvez peuvent	puisse puisses puisse puissions puissiez puissent	pouv + ais ais ait ions iez aient	pourr + ai as a ons ez ont	pourr + ais ais ait ions iez aient	*not used*
prendre to take (*avoir*)	prenant pris	prends prends prend prenons prenez prennent	prenne prennes prenne prenions preniez prennent	pren + ais ais ait ions iez aient	prendr + ai as a ons ez ont	prendr + ais ais ait ions iez aient	prends prenons prenez
résoudre to resolve (*avoir*)	résolvant résolu	résous résous résout résolvons résolvez résolvent	résolve résolves résolve résolvions résolviez résolvent	résolv + ais ais ait ions iez aient	résoudr + ai as a ons ez ont	résoudr + ais ais ait ions iez aient	résous résolvons résolvez

[†] The interrogative of *pouvoir* in the first person singular is always *Puis-je?*

Infinitive	Pres. & Past Participles	Present Indicative	Present Subjunctive	Imperfect Indicative	Future	Conditional	Imperative
rire to laugh (*avoir*)	riant ri	ris ris rit rions riez rient	rie ries rie riions riiez rient	ri + ais ais ait ions iez aient	rir + ai as a ons ez ont	rir + ais ais ait ions iez aient	ris rions riez
savoir to know (*avoir*)	sachant su	sais sais sait savons savez savent	sache saches sache sachions sachiez sachent	sav + ais ais ait ions iez aient	saur + ai as a ons ez ont	saur + ais ais ait ions iez aient	sache sachons sachez
suffire to be enough, to suffice (*avoir*)	suffisant suffi	suffis suffis suffit suffisons suffisez suffisent	suffise suffises suffise suffisions suffisiez suffisent	suffis + ais ais ait ions iez aient	suffir + ai as a ons ez ont	suffir + ais ais ait ions iez aient	suffis suffisons suffisez

	Participle	Present	Pres. subjunctive	Imperfect	Future	Conditional	Imperative
suivre to follow (*avoir*)	suivant	suis	suive	suiv + ais	suivr + ai	suivr + ais	suis
	suivi	suis	suives	ais	as	ais	
		suit	suive	ait	a	ait	
		suivons	suivions	ions	ons	ions	suivons
		suivez	suiviez	iez	ez	iez	suivez
		suivent	suivent	aient	ont	aient	
(se)taire to be quiet, to say nothing (*être*)	taisant	tais	taise	tais + ais	tair + ai	tair + ais	tais-toi
	tu(e)(s)	tais	taises	ais	as	ais	
		tait	taise	ait	a	ait	
		taisons	taisions	ions	ons	ions	taisons-nous
		taisez	taisiez	iez	ez	iez	taisez-vous
		taisent	taisent	aient	ont	aient	
tenir to hold, to keep (*avoir*)	tenant	tiens	tienne	ten + ais	tiendr + ai	tiendr + ais	tiens
	tenu	tiens	tiennes	ais	as	ais	
		tient	tienne	ait	a	ait	
		tenons	tenions	ions	ons	ions	tenons
		tenez	teniez	iez	ez	iez	tenez
		tiennent	tiennent	aient	ont	aient	
vaincre to conquer (*avoir*)	vainquant	vaincs	vainque	vainqu + ais	vaincr + ai	vaincr + ais	vaincs
	vaincu	vaincs	vainques	ais	as	ais	
		vainc	vainque	ait	a	ait	
		vainquons	vainquions	ions	ons	ions	vainquons
		vainquez	vainquiez	iez	ez	iez	vainquez
		vainquent	vainquent	aient	ont	aient	

Infinitive	Pres. & Past Participles	Present Indicative	Present Subjunctive	Imperfect Indicative	Future	Conditional	Imperative†
valoir to be worth (*avoir*)	valant valu	vaux vaux vaut valons valez valent	vaille vailles vaille valions valiez vaillent	val + ais ais ait ions iez aient	vaudr + ai as a ons ez ont	vaudr + ais ais ait ions iez aient	vaux† valons valez
venir to come (*être*)	venant venu(e)(s)	viens viens vient venons venez viennent	vienne viennes vienne venions veniez viennent	ven + ais ais ait ions iez aient	viendr + ai as a ons ez ont	viendr + ais ais ait ions iez aient	viens venons venez
vivre to live (*avoir*)	vivant vécu	vis vis vit vivons vivez vivent	vive vives vive vivions viviez vivent	viv + ais ais ait ions iez aient	vivr + ai as a ons ez ont	vivr + ais ais ait ions iez aient	vis vivons vivez
voir to see (*avoir*)	voyant vu	vois vois voit voyons voyez voient	voie voies voie voyions voyiez voient	voy + ais ais ait ions iez aient	verr + ai as a ons ez ont	verr + ais ais ait ions iez aient	vois voyons voyez

† The imperative of *valoir* is not often used.

LETTER WRITING

1. FORMAL INVITATIONS AND ACCEPTANCES

FORMAL INVITATIONS

Monsieur et madame de Montour vous prient de leur faire l'honneur d'assister à un cocktail, donné en l'honneur de leur fille Marie-José, le dimanche huit avril à neuf heures du soir.

M et Mme de Montour
35 avenue Hoche
Paris xvi ème.

R.S.V.P.

Mr. and Mrs. de Montour request the pleasure of your presence at a cocktail reception given in honor of their daughter, Marie-José, on Sunday evening, April eighth, at nine o'clock.

Mr. and Mrs. de Montour
35 avenue Hoche
Paris xvi ème.

R.S.V.P.

R.S.V.P. stands for *Répondez s'il vous plaît*. Please answer.

NOTE OF ACCEPTANCE

Monsieur et madame du Panier vous remercient de votre aimable invitation à laquelle ils se feront un plaisir de se rendre.

Mr. and Mrs. du Panier thank you for your kind invitation and will be delighted to come.

2. FORMAL THANK-YOU NOTES

le 14 mars 2005

Chère Madame,

Je tiens à vous remercier de l'aimable attention que vous avez eue en m'envoyant le charmant présent que j'ai reçu. Ce tableau me fait d'autant plus plaisir qu'il est ravissant dans le cadre de mon studio.

Je vous prie de croire à l'expression de mes sentiments de sincère amitié.

Renée Beaujoly

March 14, 2005

Dear Mrs. Duparc,

I should like to thank you for the delightful present you sent me. The picture was all the more welcome because it fits in so beautifully with the other things in my studio.

Thank you ever so much.

Sincerely yours,
Renée Beaujoly

3. BUSINESS LETTERS

M Roger Beaumont
2 rue Chalgrin
Paris

> *le 6 novembre 2005*
> *M le rédacteur en chef*
> *"Vu"*
> *3 Blvd. des Capucines*
> *Paris*

Monsieur,
   Je vous envoie ci-inclus un chèque de €110, montant de ma souscription pour un abonnement d'un an à votre publication.
   Veuillez agréer, Monsieur, mes salutations distinguées.

> *Roger Beaumont*

ci-inclus un chèque

> 2 Chalgrin Street
> Paris
> November 6, 2005

Editor-in-Chief
"Vu"
3 Blvd. des Capucines
Paris

Gentlemen:
   Enclosed please find a check for 110 euros to cover a year's subscription to your magazine.

> Sincerely yours,
> Roger Beaumont

Enc.

Dupuis Aîné
3 rue du Quatre-Septembre
Paris

le 30 septembre 2005
Vermont et Cie.
2 rue Marat
Bordeaux
Gironde

Monsieur,
   En réponse à votre lettre du dix courant, je tiens à vous confirmer que la marchandise en question vous a été expédiée le treize août par colis postal.
   Veuillez agréer, Monsieur, mes salutations distinguées,

Henri Tournaire
db/ht

3 Quatre-September St.
Paris
September 30, 2005

Vermont and Co.
2 Marat Street
Bordeaux
Gironde

Gentlemen:

   In reply to your letter of the tenth of this month, I wish to confirm that the merchandise was mailed to you parcel post on August 13.

Sincerely yours,
Henri Tournaire
db/ht

4. INFORMAL LETTERS

le 5 mars 2002

Mon cher Jacques,

Ta dernière lettre m'a fait grand plaisir.

Tout d'abord laisse-moi t'annoncer une bonne nouvelle : je compte venir passer une quinzaine de jours à Paris en début avril et je me réjouis à l'avance à l'idée de te revoir ainsi que les tiens qui je l'espère, se portent bien.

Colette vient avec moi et se fait une grande joie à l'idée de connaître enfin ta femme. Les affaires marchent bien en ce moment, espérons que ça continuera. Tâche de ne pas avoir trop de malades au mois d'avril, enfin il est vrai que ces choses-là ne se commandent pas.

Toute ma famille se porte bien, heureusement.

J'ai pris l'apéritif avec Dumont l'autre jour, qui m'a demandé de tes nouvelles. Son affaire marche très bien.

J'allais presque oublier le plus important, peux-tu me réserver une chambre au Grand Hôtel pour le cinq avril, je t'en saurais fort gré.

J'espère avoir le plaisir de te lire très bientôt.

Mes meilleurs respects à ta femme.

En toute amitié,
André

March 5, 2002

Dear Jack,

I was very happy to receive your last letter.

First of all, I've some good news for you. I expect to spend two weeks in Paris at the beginning of April and I'm looking forward to the prospect of seeing you and your family, all of whom I hope are well.

Colette's coming with me; she's delighted to be able at last to meet your wife. Business is pretty good right now. Let's hope it will keep up. Try not to get too many patients during the month of April, though I suppose that's a little difficult to arrange.

Fortunately, my family is doing well.

I had cocktails with Dumont the other day and he asked about you. His business is going well.

I almost forgot the most important thing. Can you reserve a room for me at the Grand Hotel for April the fifth? You'll be doing me a great favor.

I hope to hear from you soon. My best regards to your wife.

Your friend,
Andrew

Paris, le 3 avril 2005

Ma Chérie,

J'ai bien reçu ta lettre du trente et je suis heureuse de savoir que ta fille est tout à fait remise.

Rien de bien nouveau ici, sauf que Pierre me donne beaucoup de mal, enfin toi aussi tu as un fils de cet âge-là, et tu sais ce que je veux dire!

L'autre jour, j'ai rencontré Mme Michaud dans la rue, Dieu qu'elle a vieilli! Elle est méconnaissable!

Nous avons vu ton mari l'autre soir, il est venu dîner à la maison; il se porte bien et il lui tarde de te voir de retour.

Tu as bien de la veine d'être à la montagne pour encore un mois. Que fais-tu de beau toute la journée à Chamonix? Y a-t-il encore beaucoup de monde là-bas? Il paraît que les de Villenèque sont là. A Paris tout le monde parle des prochaines fiançailles de leur fille.

Nous sommes allés à une soirée l'autre soir chez les Clergeaud, cette femme ne sait pas recevoir, je m'y suis ennuyée à mourir.

Voilà à peu près tous les derniers potins de Paris, tu vois que je te tiens bien au courant, tâche d'en faire autant.

Embrasse bien Françoise pour moi.

Meilleurs baisers de ton amie,
Monique

Paris, April 3, 2005

Darling,

I received your letter of the thirtieth and I'm happy to learn that your daughter has completely recovered.

Nothing new here, except that Peter is giving me a lot of trouble. You have a son of the same age, so you know what I mean.

The other day I ran into Mrs. Michaud in the street. My, how she's aged! She's unrecognizable!

We saw your husband the other night—he had dinner at our house. He's well and is looking forward to your coming home.

You're lucky to be staying in the mountains for another month! What do you do all day long in Chamonix? Is it still very crowded? It seems that the de Villenèques are there. In Paris, the future engagement of their daughter is the talk of the town.

The other evening we went to a party given by the Clergeauds. She doesn't know how to entertain and I was bored to death.

That's about all of the latest Paris gossip. You see how well I keep you posted—try to do the same.

Give my love to Frances.

Love,
Monique

5. FORMS OF SALUTATIONS AND COMPLIMENTARY CLOSINGS

SALUTATIONS

FORMAL

Monsieur l'Abbé,	Dear Reverend:
Monsieur le Député,	Dear Congressman:
Monsieur le Maire,	Dear Mayor (Smith):
Cher Professeur,	Dear Professor (Smith):
Cher Maître, (Mon cher Maître),	Dear Mr. (Smith): (Lawyers are addressed as "Maître" in France.)
Monsieur,	Dear Sir:
Madame,	Dear Madam:
Messieurs,	Gentlemen:
Cher Monsieur Varnoux,	My dear Mr. Varnoux:
Chère Madame Gignoux,	My dear Mrs. Gignoux:

INFORMAL

Mon cher Roger,	Dear Roger,
Ma chère Denise,	Dear Denise,
Chéri,	Darling (*m.*),
Chérie,	Darling (*f.*),
Mon Chéri,	My darling (*m.*),
Ma Chérie,	My darling (*f.*),

COMPLIMENTARY CLOSINGS

FORMAL

1. *Agréez, je vous prie, l'expression de mes salutations les plus distinguées.*

("Please accept the expression of my most distinguished greetings.") Very truly yours.

2. *Veuillez agréer l'expression de mes salutations distinguées.*
("Will you please accept the expression of my distinguished greetings.") Very truly yours.

3. *Veuillez agréer, Monsieur, mes salutations empressées.*
("Sir, please accept my eager greetings.") Yours truly.

4. *Veuillez agréer, Monsieur, mes sincères salutations.*
("Sir, please accept my sincere greetings.") Yours truly.

5. *Agréez, Monsieur, mes salutations distinguées.*
("Sir, accept my distinguished greetings.") Yours truly.

6. *Votre tout dévoué.*
("Your very devoted.") Yours truly.

INFORMAL

1. *Je vous prie de croire à l'expression de mes sentiments de sincère amitié.*
("Please believe in my feelings of sincere friendship.") Very sincerely.

2. *Meilleures amitiés.*
("Best regards.") Sincerely yours.

3. *Amicalement.*
("Kindly.") Sincerely yours.

4. *Mes pensées affectueuses* (or *amicales*).
("My affectionate *or* friendly thoughts.") Sincerely.

5. *En toute amitié.*
Your friend. ("In all friendship.")

6. *Je te serre la main.*
("I shake your hand.") Sincerely.

7. *Affectueusement.*
   Affectionately.
8. *Très affectueusement.*
   ("Very affectionately.") Affectionately yours.
9. *Je vous prie de bien vouloir transmettre mes respects à Madame votre mère.*
   Please give my regards to your mother.
10. *Transmets mes respects à ta famille.*
    Give my regards to your family.
11. *Rappelle-moi au bon souvenir de ta famille.*
    Remember me to your family.
12. *Embrasse tout le monde pour moi.*
    ("Kiss everybody for me.") Give my love to everybody.
13. *Je t'embrasse bien fort.*
    Millions de baisers. } Love.
14. *Cordialement.*
    Cordially.
15. *Bien à vous.*
    Yours truly.

6. FORM OF THE ENVELOPE

Vermont et Cie.
5, rue Daunou
75002 Paris

Maison Dupuis Aîné
2, cours de l'Intendance
41200 Romorantin

M Jean Alexandre
6, rue Voltaire
37270 Montlouis

M. Robert Marcatour
c/o de M.P. Lambert
2, rue du Ranelagh
75016 Paris

E-MAIL AND INTERNET RESOURCES

1. SAMPLE E-MAIL

à: *azizam@yahoo.com*
de: *elianep@livinglanguage.com*
objet: *Apprendre le français*
cc: *jenb@livinglanguage.com*

Salut Aziza:
Comme promis, je t' envoie les informations (en pièces jointes) concernant notre voyage.
N' hésite pas à les faire suivre aux parents.
J' espère que tu vas bien, ainsi que toute ta famille.
Bises,
Eliane
PS: J' ai reçu les photos que tu m' a envoyées la semaine dernière. Elles sont super! J' ai téléchargé la plus belle—ta fille—sur mon écran . . .

Hello Aziza:
As promised, I am sending you the info (in the attachment) about our trip.
Don't hesitate to forward them to your parents.
I hope you are well, and your family too.
Love,
Eliane
PS: I've received the pictures that you sent me last week. They're great! I've downloaded the most beautiful—your daughter—onto my screen . . .

2. IMPORTANT E-MAIL VOCABULARY AND EXPRESSIONS

address book	*le carnet d'adresses*
e-mail address	*l'adresse e-mail*
password	*le mot de passe*
account ID	*le compte*
to read a message	*lire un message*
mailbox	*la boîte aux lettres*
spell check	*orthographe*
to send	*envoyer*
to insert signature	*insérer la signature*
to read	*lire*
to write	*écrire*
to answer	*répondre*
keep/mark as new	*marquer comme non lu*
add to address book	*ajouter au carnet d'adresses*

3. INTERNET RESOURCES

The following are resources for students of French that are available on the internet.

http://www.french-linguistics.co.uk/dictionary/
A dictionary from French into English and from English into French.

http://www.francemonthly.com
A travel site (and more) that will give you great ideas about where to travel. Beautiful pictures, and lots of cultural material.

http://www.yahoo.fr
Yahoo France. A good way to increase your French vocabulary and learn about French life.

http://www.lemonde.fr
Le Monde. A serious daily newspaper covering international and national news, as well as culture, sports, science, and more.

http://www.monde-diplomatique.fr
A monthly version of the same.

http://www.courrierinternational.com
Le Courrier International. A weekly newspaper that collects material from international press sources and translates it in French. A good way to practice French while getting an international perspective on the news.

http://www.paroles.net
A site that provides the lyrics for most French songs. A great way to practice and learn French, especially if you get the CDs and sing along.